AMERICAN SLAVERY

1619-1877

BY

PETER KOLCHIN

Consulting Editor: Eric Foner

HILL AND **WANG** • NEW YORK
A division of Farrar, Straus and Giroux

LIBRARY OF CONGRESS CATALOGING-IN-PUBLICATION DATA
Kolchin, Peter.
American slavery, 1619–1877 / Peter Kolchin ; consulting editor,
Eric Foner.
p.   cm.
Includes bibliographical references and index.
1. Slavery—United States—History.   I. Title.
E441.K64   1993   306.3'62'0973—dc20   92-46358   CIP

For Michael and David

Contents

Preface

THE PAST QUARTER CENTURY has witnessed a huge outpouring of books and articles on American slavery. Scholars have probed it from a wide variety of angles, exploring new questions as well as old, in the process substantially revising our understanding of an institution that was a central feature of American history until 1865. One of the main foci of this research has been the slaves themselves—their day-to-day behavior, family lives, religious practices, community organization, resistance, and social values—but virtually no topic has escaped historical attention. Scholars have interpreted and reinterpreted the economics of slavery, slave demography, slave culture, slave treatment, and slave-owner ideology; they have paid new attention to slavery in colonial America; they have explored variations conditioned by time and space, comparing slavery in different regions and countries as well as in different eras; and they have examined the abolition of slavery, debating the impact and consequences of emancipation. All history is subject to continuous revision, but few areas of historical study have seen the kind of extensive reworking that has transformed our understanding of American slavery. Indeed, the sheer volume of historical work on slavery has become so vast that keeping up with it is a task of herculean proportions even for experts in the field. For everyone else, it is simply impossible.

Despite the proliferation of this scholarly research, we still lack a volume that pulls together what we have learned to present a coherent history of slavery in America. Perhaps in part because of the enormous quantity of publications and in part because of the rapidity with which they have reshaped our understanding of diverse questions, no one has yet produced an account that satisfactorily synthesizes and makes sense of recent historical research on slavery. I believe that it is time to step back and consider where we now stand—where historians agree and disagree, what we have learned and what remains to be learned—and on the basis of this consideration to present a short interpretive survey of American slavery. Hence this book, which I hope will be useful to a broad range of readers, from those who know virtually nothing about the history of slavery to those who know a great deal about it.

In writing this volume, I have had several goals in mind. First, I have sought to create an account of slavery that is at the same time substantive and historiographical. Because historical reinterpretation is a continuing process, any understanding of slavery requires coming to grips with the diverse and changing ways in which historians have treated the institution. I thus combine a primary focus on the evolution of slavery itself with frequent brief (and I hope unobtrusive) discussions of historical controversies over slavery. These controversies, some of which have been resolved while others remain active, provide a useful means of exploring both the nature of slavery and its meaning and significance to later generations of Americans. In dealing with historical controversies, I have tried to explain divergent positions fairly, but I have not shied away from offering my own reasoned judgments where they seem warranted. This is an interpretive history.

Second, I have aimed for a balanced approach that pays attention to the slaves, the slave owners, and the system that bound them together. For years, historians treated slaves primarily as objects of white action rather than as subjects in their own right, and largely ignored the behavior and beliefs of the slaves themselves. Reacting against this emphasis, many scholars have more recently focused on the slaves as actors, stressing the world they made for themselves rather than the constraints imposed by their owners. I believe that neither slaves nor slave owners can be understood in isolation from each other: a well-rounded study of slavery must come to grips with slaves as both subjects and objects and must consider slavery from the perspective of both the masters and the slaves while adopting the perspective of neither. This book is not a history of African-American culture or of black Americans in the era of slavery (although it touches on both); several good surveys on those subjects already exist, including John Boles's recent volume, *Black Southerners: 1619–1869*. This is, rather, a history of American *slavery*, and my focus centers on the master–slave relationship broadly conceived, and its impact on both white and black Americans.

Third, I have striven to show how slavery changed over time. This volume covers an unusually broad chronological stretch, beginning in the early colonial period and ranging through emancipation and Reconstruction. By encompassing the entire span of American slavery, I believe that I am better able to come to grips with what many recent critics have seen as a major problem in interpreting slavery—how to deal with its evolutionary nature—than are historians who confine their attention to a particular era or fraction of one. Occasionally, in order to avoid needless repetition, I have found it desirable to consolidate topics into particular chapters; thus, I treat the transformation of Africans into African-Americans in chapter 2, the growth of the free black population in chapter 3, and slave resistance in chapter 5, even though such treatment stretches the limits of strict chronology. The book's basic structure, however, is simple and broadly chronological. The first three chapters cover the colonial and Revolutionary eras, the next three chapters examine the antebellum period, and the final chapter deals with emancipation and its aftermath.

Finally, although this is a study of *American* slavery, I have placed that slavery within a broad comparative context. During recent years, historians have become aware that slavery, although frequently termed the "peculiar institution," was hardly peculiar if by that term one means unique or unusual; indeed, throughout most of human history, slavery and other forms of coerced labor were ubiquitous. In the modern era, American slavery was part of a larger system of New World slavery that reached its height of development in the Caribbean and Brazil and emerged contemporaneously with the widespread use of forced labor in Eastern Europe, the most notable example of which was provided by Russian serfdom. The comparative approach to slavery has yielded important insights, enabling scholars both to note common patterns and to probe the ways in which geographically varied historical conditions shaped differing social relations. These insights have begun to reshape the interpretation of American slavery, but too often historians have maintained a parochial approach to that slavery, as if it developed largely in a vacuum. Because I believe that a comparative perspective helps to clarify the particular nature of American slavery, I frequently examine that slavery in the light of unfree labor elsewhere in the modern Western world, especially Caribbean slavery but also Brazilian slavery and Russian serfdom.

Writing a short, interpretive survey that synthesizes recent research, traces the evolution of American slavery over time, and places American slavery within a broad comparative context is a perilous undertaking that inevitably must produce casualties. One of these is detail. There is a good deal of information in this volume, but I have been more concerned with developing thematic clarity than with piling up as many facts as possible, and I make no pretense to producing an encyclopedic study that will tell the reader everything he or she ever wanted to know about American slavery; indeed, I hope that this book will serve as both an impetus and a guide to the further study of slavery. A second casualty is nuance. Put simply, in a book of this sort it is necessary to paint with broad strokes. Although I have tried to suggest the extraordinary variety of conditions and relationships that existed under American slavery, this variety may at times be lost in the effort to see the "big picture." I trust that readers will bear in mind that exceptions can be found to almost every generalization about slavery; the prudent analyst must be aware of these exceptions but at the same time avoid being incapacitated by them.

Let me turn to some technical matters, beginning with my use of several widely used terms. I use the words "America" and "American" in their restrictive meanings, to apply to the United States (or the colonies that later became the United States) and its residents; their common usage in this sense, although sometimes deplored in Canada and Latin America, is dictated by the lack of suitable synonyms. To refer more generally to territory or people throughout the Western Hemisphere, I use the terms "New World" and "the Americas" (as in "New World slavery" or "slavery in the Americas"). The term "black" has become widely accepted within the United States to refer to people of African or partial African origin (replacing "Negro," which prevailed until the late 1960s). I have adopted this American terminology, which must be distinguished from the tendency in many other areas (for example, Latin America) to use "black" only when referring to persons of unmixed or overwhelming African ancestry, while using other terms—"colored," "mulatto," "mestizo," and so on—for non-whites of lighter color. (I generally avoid use of "black" when such terminology would be confusing or awkward, however, as in discussion of color gradations among slaves and free blacks; the term "light black" leaves much to be desired.) I also use "African-American" (which has now largely replaced "Afro-American"), sometimes as a synonym for "black" American but often with a cultural connotation (as in "African-American family structure" or "African-American culture").

Like "black" and "American," the word "planter" has diverse connotations. Sometimes it has been applied to any landowning farmer, but to historians of the antebellum South it has usually meant a landowning farmer of substantial means; in the most restrictive usage, the term is reserved for those owning twenty or more slaves. Slaveholders themselves were usually much less rigid in their definition of "planter," frequently referring to someone with ten or twelve slaves as a "small planter." Because the condition and worldview of a slave owner with twelve slaves were not likely to be fundamentally different from those of a slave owner with twenty, I have adopted this somewhat more relaxed criterion for entry into planter ranks, while maintaining the distinction between a "farmer" (with few or no slaves) and a "planter" (with many). Further distinctions among "small slave owners," "small planters," and "large planters" (or "wealthy planters") are useful, but these are imprecise terms that vary over time and place. Someone owning fifty slaves would have qualified as a very large planter in Virginia in the 1720s but not in Louisiana in the 1840s (let alone Jamaica in the 1810s).

Whatever my own use of terminology, I follow the standard historical practice of quoting language exactly as it is found in the original sources (except for minor adjustments of capitalization and punctuation for greater readability). At times, this language may be offensive to modern readers. I regret any offense caused, but trust they will understand that quotations are designed to illustrate historical perceptions and opinions that often differed sharply from our own. It goes without saying that statements are quoted for what they reveal about the past, not for their acceptability in the present.

I have debated in my mind for some time the proper method of documentation for this book. On one side is the historian's natural proclivity to cite sources whenever possible; on the other is the suspicion that any footnoting that would accurately document my reading over a period of more than two decades in the vast primary and secondary literature on slavery and emancipation would be likely to prove distracting rather than illuminating for most readers. In the end, I compromised between reliance on traditional scholarly apparatus and desire for greater readability and decided to include notes, but only for direct quotations. The works of scholars mentioned but not quoted can be found in the lengthy (but still necessarily selective) bibliographical essay that appears at the end of the book; I hope this essay will guide interested readers to the leading secondary sources, as well as to some of the more accessible primary ones. Documentation for much of the statistical information in this book can be found in the six tables located in the Appendix immediately following the text.

During the preparation of this book, I have built up a number of intellectual debts that it is now my pleasure to acknowledge. I tried out some of my ideas about American slavery in comparative perspective in talks at Kenyon College, the University of New Mexico, and the University of Texas at Austin, as well as in a lecture to the Perspectives in the Arts and Humanities Series at the University of Delaware; I am grateful for the opportunity that these talks provided me to refine my thinking, as well as for the many helpful comments they elicited. I also appreciate the support I have received from the University of Delaware, including a General University Research Grant that helped finance the writing of this volume.

Although I cannot cite them all by name, I would like to acknowledge collectively all the historians who have written on slavery; in a very real sense, they have made this book possible. A much smaller number of historians *must* be mentioned by name, because they have made this book *better*. Drew Gilpin Faust, Howard Johnson, and Howard N. Rabinowitz, specialists in Southern and African-American history, read the penultimate version of this manuscript and gave me the benefit of their expertise. I am grateful for their valuable suggestions, which have improved this book in many ways; it goes without saying, of course, that I alone am responsible for whatever deficiencies remain. Eric Foner, consulting editor at Hill and Wang as well as an expert in Civil War–Reconstruction history, read two drafts of this manuscript and offered insightful comments that helped me strengthen my presentation, especially in chapters 2, 3, and 5; having long known of his brilliance as a scholar, I was delighted to learn of his skill and helpfulness as an editor.

My wife Anne M. Boylan, also a professional historian although not an expert on slavery, Southern history, or the Civil War and Reconstruction, read three (for some chapters four) drafts of the manuscript and has had to live with this project almost as closely as I have. She not only offered numerous specific suggestions for improvement but also helped me grapple with how to conceptualize *American Slavery* and served as a sounding board for ideas that panned out as well as those that did not, all the while maintaining her usual good sense and good cheer. She deserves much of the credit for whatever improvements the final version of this book shows over its predecessors.

Finally, Arthur W. Wang, although not a historian, deserves a special word of thanks. He has proven to be an ideal publisher, skillfully balancing the competing tasks of prodding an author not to fall too far behind schedule, providing support and encouragement, and offering helpful advice on how to streamline prose. It has been a pleasure to work with him.

AMERICAN
SLAVERY
1619-1877

1

Origins and Consolidation

I

ALTHOUGH AMERICANS LIKE to think that the United States was "conceived in liberty," the reality is somewhat different. Almost from the beginning, America was heavily dependent on coerced labor, and by the early eighteenth century slavery, legal in all of British America, was the dominant labor system of the Southern colonies. Most of the Founding Fathers were large-scale slave owners, including George Washington, "father of his country," Patrick Henry, author of the stirring cry "Give me liberty or give me death," and Thomas Jefferson, who proclaimed in the Declaration of Independence that "all men are created equal." Indeed, eight of the United States's first twelve Presidents, in office for forty-nine of the new nation's first sixty-one years, were slaveholders. When, beginning about 1830, a small band of abolitionists boldly proclaimed that slavery was a dreadful sin, the majority of Americans, North as well as South, regarded them as fanatics whose provocative rantings threatened the well-being of the Republic.

During the century and a half between the arrival of twenty blacks in Jamestown in 1619 and the outbreak of the American Revolution in 1776, slavery—nonexistent in England itself—spread through all the English colonies that would soon become the United States (as well as through those that would not). It grew like a cancer, at first slowly, almost imperceptibly, then inexorably, as colonists eager for material gain imported hundreds of thousands of Africans to toil in their fields. During the eighteenth century, slavery became entrenched as a pervasive—and in many colonies central—component of the social order, the dark underside of the American dream.

II

IN ORDER TO UNDERSTAND the unfree origins of the United States, it is useful to put American developments in a broader world context, for until the nineteenth century unfree status of one type or another—slavery, serfdom, peonage—was the lot of much of humankind. Scholars have documented a staggering variety of "slaveries" that served a multitude of diverse purposes. To those accustomed to thinking of slaves as agricultural laborers and house servants, it may be startling to learn that slaves have also served as warriors, government officials, wives, concubines, tutors, eunuchs, and victims of ritual sacrifice. In many pre-modern societies there were high-status slaves who exercised considerable authority; such elite slaves ranged from stewards who managed vast agricultural estates in China and early-modern Russia to high government officials in Rome and the Ottoman Empire. Throughout much of Asia, Africa, and Latin America, slaves served in the armed forces, at times—especially in the Islamic world—achieving high rank and wielding considerable power.

Slavery has also varied widely in terms of gender and ethnicity. If throughout the Western Hemisphere demand was greatest for young men to serve as physical laborers, in most of Africa and the Near East female slaves were more highly prized than male, both because of their widespread use as wives and concubines and because in many societies women traditionally served as the main agricultural producers. In ancient times, military victors frequently killed some or all of the vanquished adult males but enslaved the women and children.

Often slaves have differed physically from their masters, and racial contrast proved highly useful to American masters in legitimizing their position, but such distinction has by no means been universal. Somehow masters had to create a "we–they" dichotomy necessary to distinguish those who might legitimately be enslaved from those who could not, but in the absence of racial contrast, other attributes, such as religion and nationality, could serve the same purpose: both Muslims and Christians traditionally believed that only heathens (non-Muslims and non-Christians, respectively) could be enslaved, and numerous groups enslaved those from other countries, tribes, or nationalities while sparing members of their own communities. But even ethnic distinction was not essential to slavery; sociologist Orlando Patterson has found that in about one-quarter of fifty-seven slaveholding societies he studied, at least some masters and slaves shared the same ethnic identity.

Although slavery has exhibited such extraordinary diversity over time and space that it might seem virtually impossible to generalize about its nature, a particular type of slavery, which exhibited certain common features, emerged in the Western (that is, European-derived) world in the sixteenth and seventeenth centuries. Most prevalent in the New World (the Americas), although it also existed in other areas of European colonization (such as South Africa), this modern Western slavery was a product of European expansion and was preeminently a system of labor. It emerged to meet the pervasive labor shortage that developed wherever landholders tried to grow staple crops—sugar, coffee, tobacco, rice, and later cotton—for market in areas of population scarcity. Spreading slowly at first, it assumed enormous proportions in the seventeenth and eighteenth centuries and helped propel the economic transformation of the leading colonial powers, especially Great Britain.

This new system of bonded labor was distinguished by both its scope and its ethnic composition. It was closely associated with the spread of the plantation as a productive unit ideally suited for the regimentation of agricultural labor and hence the large-scale cultivation of staple crops; although slaves in the Americas served in diverse capacities, New World slavery was preeminently geared to such commercial agriculture. The Southern United States represented the northernmost outpost of this plantation system, which reached its apogee of organizational development on the large sugar estates of Jamaica, Saint Domingue (later called Haiti), Cuba, and other Caribbean colonies. Equally important was the new ethnic composition of modern Western slavery: despite some exceptions —a small although by no means negligible number of Indian slaves, a smaller number of Indian and black slave owners—most slaves were Africans and their descendants, whereas most masters were Europeans and their descendants. This ethnic contrast did not totally define the character of New World slavery, for diverse conditions and traditions fostered major variations among slave societies in both slavery and race relations; the very understanding of the terms "white" and "black," for example, differed in Brazil, Jamaica, Louisiana, and Virginia. Nevertheless, at both the global and the individual level, the racial character of New World slavery was significant: that slavery was predicated on new, unequal relationships between Europe and Africa and between white and black.

Whatever the variations among New World slave societies, their orientation around commercial agriculture gave them an essential unity and made them part of an economic order. Slaves were brought to the Americas for their ability to work; slavery there constituted, first and foremost, a system of labor. As such, it had more in common with the serfdom that was emerging in Russia and some other parts of Eastern Europe than with many of the pre-modern slaveries mentioned above. It is within the context of this modern Western slavery that the development of American slavery is best understood.

III

COLONIAL AMERICA WAS overwhelmingly agricultural. Although some early migrants hoped to become fabulously wealthy without having to work, by finding gold or discovering the fabled Northwest Passage to the Pacific, it soon became clear to settlers that survival depended on working the land. Colonial Americans, like other people of their time, expended much of their energy feeding themselves, but they also found the land well suited to growing a variety of crops greatly in demand abroad, and it was these crops—the most important of which were tobacco in the upper South and rice in the lower South—that provided the basis for much of their wealth. (Sugar, a still more valued commodity, became the staple crop of the Caribbean islands.) Cultivating these crops, however, required labor; in an environment where land was plentiful and people few, the amount of tobacco or rice one could grow depended on the number of laborers one could command. The desire to develop commercial agriculture under conditions of population scarcity gave rise in North America—as it did in the Caribbean and in South America—to forced labor.

This development was not so wrenching for the settlers as one might expect, for they were used to a highly stratified world in which the rich and powerful savagely exploited the poor and powerless. "Gentlemen" not only expected to receive the deference of their social inferiors but were willing to expend considerable force to ensure it. Historian Lawrence Stone has aptly noted the pervasive use of physical punishment to maintain order and authority in early-seventeenth-century England: "Whips and stocks were used by the Crown upon its lesser subjects, by the nobleman upon his servants, by the village worthies upon the poor, by the dons upon the undergraduates, by the City Companies upon the apprentices."[1] The contemporary equivalent of a shoplifter might be whipped, branded with the letter "T" (for "thief"), pilloried in the stocks, or transported to America. In many ways the world from which early colonists came was a world of pre-modern values, one that lacked the concepts of "cruel and unusual punishment," equal rights, and exploitation; it was a world that instead took for granted natural human *in*equality and the routine use of force necessary to maintain it. In short, it was a world with few ideological constraints against the use of forced labor.

The precise form that this forced labor took in colonial America, however, was by no means predetermined. The initial demand for labor was precisely that—for labor—and was largely color-blind. In addition to paying freely hired workers wages that were unusually high by European standards, the seventeenth-century colonists experimented with two other sources of unfree labor—Indians and Europeans—before their widespread importation of Africans.

English attitudes toward the native inhabitants of America were complex. Idealization of "noble savages," far less prevalent than it was among the French in Quebec, coexisted with interest in Christianizing "pagans" and the dominant goal of repressing, expelling, or killing "beasts" viewed as threats to civilization. Indians also served as slaves, at first usually victims of military defeat or kidnapping but subsequently also bought and sold on the open market. Such slaves were most numerous in South Carolina, where the governor estimated in 1708 that there were 1,400 Indian slaves in a population of 12,580, but they could be found in all the English colonies. Small numbers of Indian slaves persisted into the nineteenth century; others intermarried with Africans, and their descendants blended into the black population.

For a variety of reasons, however, Indian slavery never reached very substantial proportions on the British-controlled American mainland. Colonists complained that Indians were "haughty" and refused to work properly. Behind such complaints lay the very real refusal of many Indian men to perform agricultural labor, traditionally seen by them as women's work, and to engage in disciplined, supervised labor, to which they were unaccustomed. Equally important, the Indians used their familiarity with the terrain to escape and conspire against their captors. Because it has historically been difficult to enslave people on their home turf, the English found it convenient to export Indians captured in battle rather than hold them locally; in 1676, for example, after Massachusetts settlers crushed the bloody Indian uprising they termed King Philip's War, the head of the rebel leader Metacom was exhibited on a pole as an example to other would-be insurrectionists, but many of his followers (including his wife and son) were sold as slaves to the West Indies. Finally, there were simply not enough Indians in the colonies to fill the settlers' labor needs. Many—in some areas most—died in massive epidemics that swept through a population without immunity to such European diseases as smallpox and measles, while others perished in battle. Ultimately, the policy of killing the Indians or driving them away from white settlements proved incompatible with their widespread employment as slaves.

Far more common—indeed, the basis of the seventeenth-century work force in the southern two-thirds of the English mainland colonies—were European laborers. Most came as indentured servants. Indenturing (or apprenticing) children, youths, and less often adults to "masters" was widely practiced in seventeenth-century England and served a variety of functions from poor relief to job training and labor procurement. In the colonies, however, indentured servitude was transformed into an institution whereby Europeans desiring to come to America but unable to afford passage sold themselves into temporary slavery in exchange for free transatlantic transportation; especially in the South, where it served to provide large quantities of cheap labor to eager landowners, it lost much of its protective and educative function and assumed a harsher, more rapacious character. Terms of indenture varied considerably: most servants came voluntarily, but some arrived in America after being kidnapped or sentenced for criminal behavior; most adults served four or five years, but children often served seven years or more; and both adults and children found their servitude extended for criminal behavior (including disobedience, flight, and childbearing). During their indenture, servants were essentially slaves, under the complete authority of their masters; masters could (and readily did) apply corporal punishment to servants, forbid them to marry, and sell them (for the duration of their terms) to others.

Indentured servitude flourished because it simultaneously met the needs of labor-hungry colonial landowners and those of would-be European migrants. Landowners saw servitude as a gold mine. It not only offered a solution to their labor problem but also enabled them to increase their landholdings further, for most early colonies provided those who paid for people's transatlantic passage with a "headright" or land allotment—often fifty acres—for each person (including oneself) transported. When John Carter imported eighty indentured servants in 1665 to work for him in Virginia, he received a headright of four thousand acres. In short, indentured servitude provided the emerging colonial gentry relatively cheap labor, more land, and the honor that accrued to those with authority over other humans.

To laborers, servitude held out an equally alluring attraction: the chance to escape hardship—poverty, hunger, unemployment, over-population, prison, or political turmoil—and to start anew in a distant, wonderful land. Although in the eighteenth century servant ranks were swelled by emigrants from Ireland and Germany, as well as by convicts transported in lieu of lengthy prison terms or death, most early servants were English, and came voluntarily. Severe economic dislocations in England in the first half of the seventeenth century—combined with the political disruption of the 1640s and 1650s that saw civil war culminate in the beheading of King Charles I, the dictatorship of Oliver Cromwell, and the restoration of the monarchy in 1660 under Charles II—produced an abundant supply of would-be servants. They were overwhelmingly composed of young men (male servants outnumbered female by more than three to one) from the bottom half of the social order; although they came from diverse backgrounds, only a shared sense of desperation born of absent opportunity can explain their willingness to leave everything they had ever known for years of uncertain servitude in America.

Once in the colonies, indentured servants had diverse experiences. Some, especially in New England, engaged in (or were taught) skilled trades such as blacksmithing and carpentry; well into the nineteenth century, apprenticing children to artisans remained a way of providing for their education. Others worked as domestics. Most seventeenth-century servants, however, wound up as agricultural laborers, especially in the tobacco fields of Virginia and Maryland. They lived hard lives under the authority of men anxious to get as much work out of them as possible before their terms of service were up. Many ran away, an offense that—if they were apprehended—brought its perpetrators whippings, brandings, bodily mutilations, and extended terms of servitude. Many others succumbed to the new environment; recent evidence suggests that in the mid-seventeenth-century Chesapeake colonies almost half of all servants died while still under indenture. Some of those who survived eventually became independent craftsmen or landowners, but more still never achieved independence: unable to find wives because of the paucity of women, they remained single, continued to work for their better-established neighbors, and often lived in those neighbors' households as well. (Women servants who survived their indentures generally faced a brighter future than men; the surplus of males enabled most women to marry and many to improve their status by marrying "up.") Not all indentured servants were recent immigrants: within the colonies men and women were bound out for indebtedness and crime, and a small floating underclass of laborers lived perpetually in the margins of servitude, serving multiple terms of indenture.

IV

THROUGHOUT MOST of the seventeenth century, indentured servants filled the bulk of the colonies' labor needs. Although a Dutch captain sold twenty Africans in Virginia in 1619, and small numbers of blacks trickled into the mainland colonies over the following decades, until the 1680s the non-Indian population of the British mainland colonies remained overwhelmingly white. So long as a ready supply of indentured labor continued to exist, colonists saw little reason to go to the expense and bother of importing large numbers of Africans, who, unlike English laborers, had to undergo prolonged adjustment to alien conditions—strange masters had unusual customs and spoke an unintelligible language—before becoming productive members of the work force. Equally important, because the Portuguese and Dutch dominated the African slave trade until the British triumph in the Anglo-Dutch war of 1664–67, the English colonists found slaves expensive and hard to obtain.

Beginning in the 1680s, however, the mainland colonies underwent a massive shift from indentured to slave labor. Some simple statistics drive home the point. Between 1680 and 1750, the estimated proportion of blacks in the population increased from 7 percent to 44 percent in Virginia and from 17 percent to 61 percent in South Carolina (see table 1). "They import so many Negros hither," wrote Virginia planter William Byrd II in 1736, "that I fear this Colony will some time or other be confirmed by the Name of New Guinea."[2]

This shift, which has been documented most carefully for the Chesapeake colonies, was the product of a fundamental change in the relative supply of indentured servants and slaves, in the face of escalating colonial demand for labor. Because servants were held only temporarily and then freed, a rapidly growing colonial population required an equally rapid growth in the number of indentured immigrants for servants to remain a constant proportion of the population. Between 1650 and 1700, the population of Virginia more than tripled; if indentured servants were to continue providing the bulk of the agricultural labor force, servant immigration would have had to triple, or come close to tripling, too.

In fact, at the same time that colonial demand for labor was surging, a sharp *decrease* occurred in the number of English migrants arriving in America under indenture. White immigration into the Chesapeake colonies—most of it indentured—peaked between 1650 and 1680 and then declined sharply. In some areas the decline was dramatic. In York County, Virginia, for example, the ratio of servants to slaves plummeted from 1.9 in 1680–84 to 0.27 in 1685–89 and 0.07 in 1690–94; within a decade, indentured servants had almost totally disappeared from the county. The flow of servants did not entirely end: during the first half of the eighteenth century, transportation of convicts to Maryland increased substantially, Pennsylvania attracted a huge wave of indentured Germans, and some English servants continued to come voluntarily. By the end of the seventeenth century, however, it was clear that indentured Europeans could no longer fill the labor needs of the Southern colonies.

Changing conditions on both sides of the Atlantic were responsible for this development. In England, the restoration of the monarchy in 1660 was followed by both political stabilization and an economic upturn. Wages rose, employment opportunities improved, agricultural productivity increased, and the population—which began to grow somewhat more slowly than it had earlier—no longer appeared excessive, as it had to many English observers in the first half of the century. In the colonies, opportunities for unskilled immigrants declined in the late seventeenth century, as land became more densely settled and hence less readily available. (In part for this reason, indentured servants who came to America from England in the eighteenth century tended to be substantially more literate and more skilled than those in the seventeenth.) A downturn in tobacco prices beginning in the early 1680s may also have discouraged merchants from importing servants into the Chesapeake. In short, for a variety of reasons, selling themselves into indentured servitude in America no longer seemed like a very attractive proposition to many English subjects.

In the face of this rather sudden decline in the supply of European servants, labor-hungry Chesapeake landowners looked elsewhere for replacements. Fortunately for them, the late seventeenth century witnessed not only a decline in the availability of European laborers but also an increase in the availability of African. British naval superiority brought with it dominance of the African slave trade, a dominance symbolized by establishment of the slave-trading Royal African Company in 1672 and receipt of the royal *Asiento* (or right to supply the Spanish colonies with slaves) in 1713. Although most British-traded slaves continued to go to the sugar islands in the Caribbean, where demand for them was greatest, mainland colonists found their supply of Africans eased as well. Historian Russell Menard has calculated that between 1674 and 1691, the ratio of slave prices to servant prices (measured in constant British pounds) fell steadily, from 2.88 to 1.83. Under these conditions, colonists who could no longer secure an adequate supply of white indentured servants were quite willing to use black slaves in their place.

With large-scale importation of Africans under way, landowners had additional, if subsidiary, reasons for preferring slaves to servants. Slaves were held permanently rather than for a few years, and female slaves passed their status on to their children. Thus, although they cost more to purchase than servants, as the ratio of slave prices to servant prices declined slaves increasingly seemed like a better long-term investment, especially to the wealthiest planters, who could most easily afford their initial cost and who therefore led the switch from indentured to slave labor. Basic demographic changes among the black population (discussed more fully in chapter 2, section III) reinforced this preference. Early African residents of the Chesapeake colonies had relatively few children in America and suffered from exceedingly high mortality rates that made them risky investments. A modest decline in those rates by the late seventeenth century was followed by a sharp increase in fertility rates in the early eighteenth; as a result, whereas in the seventeenth century the slave population failed to reproduce itself and had to be replenished in much the same way the servant population did, in the eighteenth century it became a self-perpetuating labor force. An initial investment in slaves bought a lifetime (and more) of labor.

Slaves also offered masters a reduced level of successful flight, an important consideration everywhere but especially in Virginia, where, in the wake of the abortive rebellion led by Nathaniel Bacon in 1676, planters were increasingly concerned about controlling unruly laborers. Both slaves and servants ran away and, when caught, received for their efforts a wide range of nasty punishments, including whippings, bodily mutilations, and—for servants—lengthened servitude. Eighteenth-century colonial newspapers (there were none in the seventeenth century) were filled with advertisements for fugitives, both white and black; a typical notice from the *Pennsylvania Journal* of September 26, 1751, advertised for return of "an Irish Servant Man, Named Christopher Cooney, of Short Stature, pale Complexion, short brown Hair"; the listing noted that he "has a Scarr on his left Cheek, near his Nose, has lost one of his under fore Teeth, has had his Right Leg broke, and walks with his Toes turning outwards."[3] But because of their color, slaves found it much more difficult than servants to escape. Despite brandings and mutilations designed to mark them as bound, once beyond the immediate vicinity of their servitude servants were often able to establish themselves as free; because blacks were presumed to be slaves unless they could show otherwise, they found unauthorized movement more difficult. Racial distinction, in short, facilitated enslavement.

V

THE EARLY RELATIONSHIP between slavery and race has prompted considerable historical debate. Some scholars have stressed the existence of racial prejudice among the English before their resort to African slavery, and have argued that it was this prejudice that led to the enslavement of Africans in America. Others have seen racism largely as a function of slavery, maintaining that people held as slaves came to be seen as slavish by nature. Although in their baldest form these two positions—enunciated most starkly in the 1950s by Carl N. Degler on the one hand and Oscar and Mary F. Handlin on the other—seem to be mutually exclusive, there is considerable evidence to support modified versions of both, and when properly reformulated they are not so incompatible as they first appear; perhaps for this reason, the debate has gradually lost much of its acrimony. Indeed, what we now know suggests that the most appropriate question is not whether slavery caused prejudice or prejudice caused slavery (a false choice, since the evidence sustains neither of these two conjectures) but rather how slavery and prejudice interacted to create the particular set of social relationships that existed in the English mainland colonies.

The initial demand for labor that eventually led to slavery was, as we have seen, color-blind. The colonists came from a hierarchical society that lacked the modern world's clear demarcation between free and unfree status. They saw nothing particularly noteworthy about some people working—even under constraint—for the well-being of others, and they experimented with forced labor of Indians and Europeans before resorting to that of Africans. The turn to Africans came not because of any ideological concerns but because the flow of indentured white labor seemed to be drying up.

Research by scholars such as Winthrop D. Jordan has clearly demonstrated that well before the shift from indentured to slave labor the English already harbored three stereotypes about Africans that facilitated their enslavement by setting them off as different (and hence liable to different treatment). First, they were "black," or so they seemed; it is highly significant that the English saw Africans as black and themselves as white—in both cases inaccurately—for associated with the former term were numerous pejorative meanings ranging from dirty to immoral, whereas the latter carried equally positive connotations of purity, virtue, and godliness. Second, they were "savage" or "uncivilized"; that is, their culture was very different from that of Europeans and appeared to the English to be manifestly outlandish and inferior. Third, they were "heathens," an attribute that may have been the most important of all, for in an era when being the wrong kind of Christian put one in mortal danger in most of Christendom (including most of the English colonies), being a non-Christian automatically put one beyond the pale.

Clearly, the English were struck by differences between themselves and Africans, and negative stereotypes of Africans helped shape race relations in America during the early years of slavery. The significance of those stereotypes for the introduction and maintenance of slavery must not be exaggerated, however, for none of them proved essential; indeed, it soon became clear that diminution and even removal of the three perceived differences that set Africans apart from Europeans provided little basis for questioning slave status. Thus, the emergence through interracial sexual contact of light-colored slaves who lacked the stigma of blackness did not necessitate their manumission, any more than did the emergence of "acculturated" slaves who lacked the African's "savagery." At first it appeared that religious convergence might prove more of a stumbling block, and some planters withheld Christian instruction from Africans in the belief that their conversion might require their emancipation. Such fears were put to rest during the last third of the seventeenth century, however, when one colony after another passed laws making it clear that "the conferring of baptisme doth not alter the condition of the person as to his bondage or ffreedome"; in other words, Christians could be held as slaves.[4]

Furthermore, if Africans appeared to be fundamentally different, throughout much of the seventeenth century they received treatment only marginally different from that afforded other members of the "lower ranks." Brutal repression of "rowdy" elements in Britain as well as savage colonization of Ireland preceded the English assault on Native Americans and enslavement of Africans, and demonstrate the insufficiency of race as an explanation of policy toward blacks. If the English regarded Africans as inferior by nature, members of the English gentry regarded their own lower classes—and the Irish—in much the same way: they were ignorant and "brutish" and required physical repression to keep them in line. The Irish were widely perceived as wild, degraded, and of questionable Christianity, "more uncivill, more uncleanly, more barbarous and more brutish in their customs and demeanures, then in any other part of the world that is known."[5]

Within the colonies, there was often little clear demarcation between blacks and lower-class whites during the first decades of settlement. Indentured servants were subject to many of the same constraints as slaves, and the two groups often lived together, worked together, played together, and sometimes slept together and ran away together. Landowning Virginians feared the "giddy multitude" (or rabble), but this was a rather heterogeneous lower-class group of servants and slaves, whites and blacks that seemed to threaten the social order. Until the very end of the seventeenth century, blacks remained too few in number to constitute a distinct threat of their own.

In all the mainland colonies, seventeenth-century race relations showed a flexibility that would later seem astonishing. This flexibility was evident in Massachusetts, where slaves never formed more than a tiny fraction of the population and most blacks were house servants or skilled workers, but it also existed in the mainland colony with the highest proportion of slaves, South Carolina, where blacks served as trappers, hunters, guides, and fishermen, and, as historian Peter Wood put it, "servants and masters shared the crude and egalitarian intimacies inevitable on a frontier."[6] Historians T. H. Breen and Stephen Innes have demonstrated that "in seventeenth-century Northampton County, Virginia . . . Englishmen and Africans could interact with one another on terms of relative equality for two generations." Between 1664 and 1677, at least 13 (out of 101) blacks became free landowners, most through self-purchase; in 1668, some 29 percent of blacks in the county were free.[7] In short, there was not yet an impenetrable barrier separating the races. Although almost all blacks came to the colonies as slaves, most whites came as unfree laborers, too, and there was much that united them.

Even in these early years, however, the treatment of black laborers differed from that of white in important respects. They required more "breaking in"—in terms of language, customs, work habits, and simple obedience—especially by the late seventeenth century, when most came directly from Africa without undergoing "seasoning" in the West Indies, as had previously been common. Although some Africans seem to have served, like whites, as temporary indentured servants during the first half century of English settlement in America, most, unlike whites, already served for life. But most important, whereas the great majority of European migrants came to America voluntarily, none of the Africans did.

More than anything else, it was the involuntary nature of blacks' migration to America that dictated their growing separation from the white labor force. As historian Edmund S. Morgan pointed out, desire to attract continued white immigration imposed limits on the severity of treatment of indentured servants, especially with the slackening of European arrivals after the 1670s, and prevented those servants from being reduced to the ranks of slaves. Gradually, the status and treatment of European migrants improved. An increasing proportion were literate and possessed skills that enabled them to take advantage of opportunities offered by the burgeoning colonial economies; in the eighteenth century, unlike the seventeenth, few white servants in the South (and virtually no women) engaged in agricultural labor. That was now the lot of blacks, who as involuntary migrants did not have to be lured to America by attractive conditions.

As the status of white migrants gradually improved, that of blacks in America became more clearly defined as well. Whereas the legal status of the few blacks who resided in the colonies remained uncertain prior to the 1660s, a spate of legislation passed during the subsequent century regulated the condition of the growing population of black slaves and set them off from white settlers. These acts established that slaves—and the children of slave women—would serve for life; limited the rights of slaves and even of free blacks (they could not vote, testify in court against whites, or marry whites); prohibited slaves from carrying arms or leaving home without written permission; discouraged masters from freeing slaves by a variety of provisions including requiring legislative approval for each act of manumission and requiring manumitted slaves to leave their home colony within six months; and mandated severe corporal punishment for those who dared challenge white authority. Because slavery was absent in England, the slave law that developed in her overseas possessions was (unlike that of the Spanish empire) entirely a product of colonial legislation, with each colony passing its own slave laws. The timing and substance of these laws consequently varied somewhat. Virginia's first major slave code, enacted in 1680, was strengthened in 1705; South Carolina's perfunctory code of 1690 was superseded by that of 1696 and then overhauled in more comprehensive legislation of 1712, which in turn was substantially revised in 1740. Both colonies, like others, continued to enact new legislation on a piecemeal basis. By the middle of the eighteenth century, however, slavery was solidly entrenched, both in fact and in law, as the labor system of the Southern colonies and was legally established in the Northern colonies as well.

Ironically, racial lines hardened despite a growing convergence between white and black. Over the generations, interaction between Africans and their descendants on the one hand and Europeans and their descendants on the other sharply reduced the cultural—and sometimes the physical—gap between the races (see chapter 2). But even as this process occurred, most white Americans came to assume that blacks were so different from whites that slavery was their natural state. (Such sentiment would receive far more detailed expression in the nineteenth century when the abolitionist onslaught provoked an elaborate justification of slavery.) As Virginia planter Landon Carter put it in 1770, "Kindness to a Negroe by way of reward for having done well is the surest way to spoil him although according to the general observation of the world most men are spurred on to diligence by rewards."[8] Whereas a century earlier, freedom was a vague concept and the lot of most laborers, white and black, was to one extent or another unfree, now the assumption among whites was practically universal that blacks were slave and whites free.

VI

IN FULL SWING by the late seventeenth century, the British-operated slave trade was a big business in the eighteenth. Many of the foremost families in England (and New England) grew rich off it. Leaving a home port such as Liverpool or Boston with a cargo of weapons, manufactured goods, and rum, a slaving ship would proceed to the west coast of Africa, where these items were exchanged for slaves to be sold in the mainland or island colonies (or elsewhere; in the eighteenth century, the British provided slaves to much of the New World). Successful voyages brought large profits, but the risks were also great: sea travel was hazardous under the best of circumstances, and on most ships between 5 and 20 percent of the slaves (and crew) died in transit. (Mortality rates gradually declined over the course of the eighteenth century.) Exceptional circumstances—attack by pirates, bad weather—could jeopardize an entire cargo. Even insurance, which during the eighteenth century covered an increasing proportion of traders against unforeseen losses, provided uncertain protection; in 1781, running short on water, the captain of the *Zong* ordered 132 Africans thrown overboard, because his insurance covered death from drowning but not from starvation.

Most American slaves came from the coastal region of West Africa. European and American traders dubbed this region "Guinea" and assigned various portions of it descriptive designations such as Ivory Coast, Gold Coast, and Slave Coast that suggested the nature of their appeal. A much smaller number of American slaves—although perhaps as many as 40 percent of those brought to South Carolina —came from the Congo/Angola region farther south. Enslaved Africans belonged to a multiplicity of nationalities with diverse languages, customs, and political structures, although the bulk of slaves came from three distinct geographic zones—upper Guinea, lower Guinea, and Congo/Angola—each of which was marked by loose cultural and linguistic commonality. As historian Daniel C. Littlefield has shown, both the slave traders and their American customers were (unlike their nineteenth-century descendants) conscious of the slaves' diverse ethnic origins, and showed marked preferences— based in part on perceived physical distinctions and in part on ethnic stereotyping that could vary from place to place—for certain nationalities. Among South Carolina slave owners, for example, big, strong, dark slaves from Gambia and the Gold Coast were most in demand; "Coromantes and Whydahs, because of their greater hardiness, were supposed to be especially desirable as field hands, whereas Ibos, Congos, and Angolas, allegedly weaker, were said to be more effective as house servants."[9]

More mundane considerations, however, of which the most important was simple availability, determined the geographic origins and ethnic composition of slaves shipped across the Atlantic. Seeking to avoid contact with the inhospitable African environment, European traders operated from a series of "factories" or forts along the coast, each headed by a "factor." They received, especially in the early years of the slave trade, considerable cooperation from African rulers and merchants; although ultimately traffic in slaves was based on force, and the transatlantic trade led to increasing disruption of African societies, Africans—no strangers themselves to slavery— joined Europeans in buying and selling human property. The African

slave trade involved considerable partnership, albeit of an increasingly unequal nature, between white and black traders. Over time,
as the growing demand for slaves put increasing strains on established sources of supply, the trade's center shifted southward and
reached deeper into the African interior.

Africans became slaves in a variety of ways, all of which had
existed before European contact but became more prevalent under
the stimulus of the transatlantic trade. Some were sentenced into
slavery for criminal activity or indebtedness. Others were kidnapped, either by whites or more often by Africans who sold them
to whites. The largest number, however, were prisoners of war,
victims of military conflicts among African nations and, increasingly,
objects of such conflicts, which approached at the crudest level pure
slave-raiding ventures. Whatever their route to slavery, however,
slaves sold to Europeans faced a different future from those held by
Africans. Although it is important not to romanticize African slavery
or gloss over the suffering it imposed on its victims, slaves sent to
America faced particular hardships. Slaves in Africa served in diverse
roles from wives and concubines to household servants, agricultural
laborers, and victims of ritual sacrifice, but plantation slavery was
rare in seventeenth- and eighteenth-century West Africa. Slaves
there usually lived within the immediate households of their owners
in an environment that was not altogether foreign to them; they—
and especially their children—could hope gradually to lose their
marginal status and be absorbed into the families and society of their
masters. Slaves destined for America, by contrast, lost everything
they knew—possessions, home, loved ones—and embarked on a
strange new life in an alien world.

The transit to this new world was a frightful experience. Marched
in chains to points of embarkation, sold to strange-looking men who
spoke an incomprehensible language, branded, dragged struggling
into long canoes that took them to ships waiting offshore, Africans
began their voyage to America in despondency and often in panic.
Some had never before seen giant ships, the ocean, or white men;
"I was now persuaded that I had gotten into a world of bad spirits
and that they were going to kill me," recalled Olaudah Equiano,
one of the very few victims of the slave trade later able to describe
their experiences in writing.[10] Like many other captives, Equiano,
anticipating the worst he could imagine, feared he was about to be
eaten. (Europeans, too, often imagined Africans as cannibals.)

Next came the transatlantic voyage, or "Middle Passage." Men were usually kept in chains, in holds; women and children, fewer in number, were sometimes allowed greater freedom of movement. In ships run by "tight packers," who deplored the waste of space provided by holds five feet high and who consequently installed middle shelves, creating two levels of two and a half feet, slaves were often crammed together so closely they could barely move. If the weather was good, slaves would be taken on deck daily and "danced," a painful exercise for those in chains thought to combat scurvy (caused, unbeknownst to anyone at the time, by a deficiency of vitamin C).

Conditions on slaving ships reached their worst when poor weather prolonged travel and forced slaves to remain belowdecks for extended periods. A particularly graphic account of such conditions is provided in a book published in 1788 by Alexander Falconbridge, a doctor on numerous slaving voyages:

> Some wet and blowing weather having occasioned the port-holes to be shut and the grating to be covered, fluxes and fevers among the negroes ensued. While they were in this situation, I frequently went down among them till at length their rooms became so extremely hot as to be only bearable for a very short time . . . The floor of their rooms, was so covered with the blood and mucus which had proceeded from them in consequence of the flux, that it resembled a slaughterhouse . . . Numbers of the slaves having fainted they were carried upon deck where several of them died and the rest with great difficulty were restored.[11]

Traders noted that the African captives were especially prone to a disease they labeled "fixed melancholy," whose sufferers became morose, moody, and unresponsive, staring into space, refusing food, and in extreme cases committing suicide, usually by jumping overboard.

Arrival in America brought an end to the Middle Passage, but also brought its own terror: sale. Whether subjected to a "scramble," whereby prospective purchasers rushed on board seeking the likeliest slaves at a fixed price, or to a public auction, the Africans found themselves examined, poked, and prodded by eager customers. Once again, anger, humiliation, and fear of impending doom gripped them.

It is almost with relief that one turns from gruesome descriptions to cold statistics of the slave trade. Scholars have long debated the number of Africans brought to the New World. The first scholarly "census," by Philip Curtin in 1969, yielded a preliminary estimate of 9.5 million, a figure that has since gradually inched upward as researchers have continued to discover new evidence. Although precise figures must remain elusive, according to the best current estimates a total of 10 to 11 million living slaves crossed the Atlantic Ocean from the sixteenth through the nineteenth century. (Since others died in wars and in transit, Africa's total population loss was much greater.) As David Eltis has shown, the forced migration of slaves to the Americas significantly exceeded the voluntary immigration there of free persons until the 1830s, and the cumulative total of African migrants exceeded that of Europeans until the 1880s.

America absorbed relatively few of these Africans. The great bulk—more than 85 percent of the total—went to Brazil and the various Caribbean colonies of the British, French, Spanish, and Dutch. Others went to the Spanish mainland. The United States, or more accurately for most of the slave-trade years the colonies that would later become the United States, imported only 600,000 to 650,000 Africans, some 6 percent of all the slaves brought from Africa to the New World.

From this small beginning, however, emerged by far the largest slave population in the Western Hemisphere. The key to this apparent paradox lies in the self-reproducing nature of the slave population in the United States, where well before the importation of slaves was legally ended in 1808 an excess of births over deaths produced what demographers refer to as "natural population growth." Virtually everywhere else in the Americas—Brazil, Jamaica, Cuba, Saint Domingue—slavery was dependent on continued importation of Africans; once that importation ended, the slave population declined. Thus, in 1810, the 1.1 million slaves in the United States constituted almost twice the total number it had imported from Africa during the preceding two centuries; during the next fifty years, the slave population more than tripled again, to almost 4 million in 1860. By contrast, Brazil and the Caribbean were graveyards for Africans and their descendants; Jamaica, for example, imported a total of more than three-quarters of a million Africans, but at the time of emancipation in 1834, its slave population stood at only 311,000. In short, in the United States, the slave population at emancipation was more than six times as large as the number of slaves it had imported; in Jamaica, the slave population was less than half as large as the number it had imported.

Scholars do not fully agree on the reasons for the unusual natural growth of the American slave population. Some stress factors largely extraneous to slavery, such as America's self-sufficiency in food, which made it possible for masters to provide slaves with a comparatively healthy diet, and the absence of many tropical diseases that proved deadly to large numbers of slaves in the Caribbean and Brazil. Other scholars point to variations in crops, noting that most slaves in America raised tobacco and cotton rather than sugar, which typically imposed exceptionally harsh conditions and an exhausting pace of labor on its cultivators. (The slave population in the Bahamas did grow naturally; significantly, those islands both enjoyed a temperate climate and lacked substantial sugar cultivation.) Still others emphasize the unusually high fertility of American slaves. Not only did women form a higher proportion of the slave population in America than in the Caribbean and Brazil (which continued to import large number of Africans) but a higher proportion of American slave women bore children and those who did so bore on the average more children.

Although historians continue to debate the factors responsible for the atypical growth of the American slave population, their disagreements are less over the existence of these factors than over their relative importance. It is clear that for a variety of reasons American slaves had both higher birth rates and lower mortality rates than those elsewhere in the Americas. Among most New World slaves, deaths consistently exceeded births; in America, as we shall see in chapter 2, births came to exceed deaths during the eighteenth century. During the first half of the nineteenth century, the slave population grew naturally at an annual rate of about 2 percent.

The consequences of this demographic contrast are highly significant and will receive attention throughout this volume. Elsewhere in the New World, absence of natural population growth meant that the majority of adult slaves were African-born and—since traders imported almost twice as many men as women—male. In the United States, however, American-born (or creole) slaves came to outnumber Africans well before the War for Independence, and during the following decades the proportion of Africans became tiny. The largely creole character of the slave population profoundly shaped the nature of American slavery, especially during its last century, affecting both relations between masters and slaves and those among the slaves themselves.

VII

ALTHOUGH THE CENTURY preceding the American Revolution saw slavery spread throughout all of the colonies that would soon constitute the United States, significant variations emerged, based on differing regional economies. Wherever there was widespread agricultural production for market, slavery became entrenched as the basis of the labor system. Elsewhere, it existed more as a "luxury" than as the fundamental underpinning of the economy. (For statistics documenting this section, see table 1.)

Slavery on the North American mainland emerged first in the tidewater region of the Chesapeake colonies—Virginia, Maryland, and the northeast corner of North Carolina. Here rich land, a moderate climate, and, most important of all, abundant waterways (necessary for transportation) provided the perfect conditions for tobacco cultivation. Annual exports of tobacco (almost all from the Chesapeake colonies) surged from 20,000 pounds in 1619 to 38 million pounds in 1700, as growers sought to take advantage of the seemingly insatiable European demand, and then stabilized at a fluctuating level of 25 to 60 million pounds in the eighteenth century.

Tobacco provided the basis for a highly commercial, increasingly prosperous, and almost totally rural society in the upper South. Throughout the colonial period, Virginia was the most populous of Britain's mainland colonies; more important, Virginia and Maryland not only led all other mainland colonies in the value of their exports to Britain but together provided more than half the value of those exports. The upper South was a society of people on the make: market-oriented farmers (both large and small), traders, and land speculators. It was also a society with an intense demand for labor, which was met by European indentured servants until the 1680s and by African slaves thereafter. Demand for new slaves remained strong through the first half of the eighteenth century but weakened markedly after that as soil exhaustion and overproduction turned tobacco boom into tobacco crisis; in the second half of the century, planters cut back their tobacco acreage, increased their cultivation of wheat, and sharply curtailed their purchase of Africans. Slavery, however, remained firmly entrenched. On the eve of the American Revolution, slaves constituted about one-third the population in Maryland and North Carolina and two-fifths in Virginia, but these figures mask significant intra-colonial variation: in the backcountry, largely self-sufficient farming precluded the use of many slaves, but in most of the tobacco-producing areas along the Chesapeake, at least half the inhabitants were slaves.

A second regional slave economy emerged along the coast of the lower South, in South Carolina, Georgia, and the southeastern portion of North Carolina. First settled by the English half a century later than the Chesapeake, South Carolina had a small, struggling population until rice was introduced as a staple crop in the 1690s. Rice soon became as central to the economy of the lower South as tobacco was to that of the upper South; rice exports (almost all from South Carolina and, after the mid-eighteenth century, Georgia) soared from 12,000 pounds in 1698 to 18 million pounds in 1730 and 83 million in 1770. From the middle of the eighteenth century, Carolinians also began producing indigo (unlike rice, grown on dry land) for export, but rice remained the lower South's most important and profitable crop, and the economy, as in the Chesapeake colonies, remained oriented almost exclusively to commercial farming. (Unlike Virginia, however, South Carolina had an urban center, Charleston, whose 1770 population of 12,000 placed it fourth—after Philadelphia, New York, and Boston—in Britain's mainland colonies; many wealthy planters kept city homes where they lived in the "sickly" summer months to avoid the malarial rice swamps.)

Two satellite settlements bordered South Carolina. To the south lay Georgia, originally founded by James Oglethorpe in 1733 as a refuge for debtors; by mid-century, this philanthropic purpose lay abandoned as landowners rushed to emulate their Carolina neighbors and grow rice. To the north was the lower Cape Fear River valley in southeastern North Carolina, where migrants from South Carolina appropriated the choicest land in the 1720s and 1730s; the area quickly became a prime source of naval stores—tar, pitch, turpentine, and lumber.

Commercial agriculture produced in the lower South an economy even more heavily dependent on slave labor than was that of the upper South. Because a number of South Carolina's founders resettled from the West Indies and brought their slaves with them, the colony had from an early date a higher proportion of slaves in its population than any other British colony on the American mainland. This lead persisted, for unlike the colonies to its north, South Carolina did not experience a reduction in demand for (or delivery of) slaves in the third quarter of the eighteenth century. Throughout the pre-Revolutionary period, slaves constituted a majority of the colony's population—a large majority in the coastal rice-producing parishes. In Georgia, too, the allure of profits proved impossible to resist. Although the idealistic founders of the colony originally banned slavery altogether, indignant planters forced the abandonment of this policy in 1750; within a few years, slaves constituted close to half the colony's population.

Still a third slave society emerged in a part of the South not under British control: Louisiana. First settled by the French at the end of the seventeenth century, ceded to Spain in 1763, and briefly reacquired by Napoleon in 1800 before being sold to the United States in 1803, colonial Louisiana lacked the overwhelming staple-crop domination of Britain's plantation colonies. Settlers grew tobacco, indigo, and rice, but sugar did not become a major crop until the very end of the eighteenth century, and Louisiana's rulers valued the colony more for strategic than for economic reasons. Most of the small population in French Louisiana arrived involuntarily, as soldiers, criminals sent to garrison France's American empire, and slaves (who engaged in a wide range of occupations, from agricultural labor to skilled crafts and domestic service); a census taken in 1766, shortly after Louisiana came under Spanish control, revealed that slaves slightly outnumbered free whites.

Louisiana never prospered under the French, and although conditions improved somewhat during Spanish rule—cultivation of sugar spread rapidly in the 1790s, and the trading city of New Orleans numbered some 8,000 inhabitants at the turn of the century—the territory remained a sparsely populated land of vast untapped potential when purchased by the United States. During the next half century, it would become a leading producer of sugar and cotton, the heart of the new Southwest—and site of the largest slave market in the United States. Its acquisition also introduced into the United States a significant population, both white and black, under French cultural influence; that influence would continue to lend a distinctive quality to race relations in southern Louisiana.

A final regional pattern is evident in the Northern colonies, where slavery, although legal everywhere, assumed much smaller proportions than in the South. In most of the North, lack of substantial commercial agriculture precluded a demand for large-scale forced labor; slaves served in a variety of capacities, from house service to skilled crafts and day labor, but slavery did not serve as the basis for the economy. In a few areas—often where water transportation provided ready access to market—commercial agriculture flourished, although on a much smaller scale than in the South, and created a demand for more widespread use of slave labor. In New York, for example, slaves cultivated wheat on farms along the Hudson River and on Long Island; and in the Narragansett country of Rhode Island, they helped raise dairy cows and racehorses. In such areas, slaves could exceed 20 percent of the population, although the colony-wide proportion of slaves in New York and Rhode Island was much smaller.

Nowhere in the Northern colonies, however, did the concentration of slaves approach that in the South. What is more, after the middle of the eighteenth century Northern demand for slaves slackened, and on the eve of the Revolution slaves constituted a declining proportion of the population. As a consequence, despite regional variations within the South, the division that became most essential was between the South, where slavery was solidly entrenched as a system of labor, and the North, where it was not. The peripheral nature of Northern slavery meant that when it came under attack —as it would during the last third of the eighteenth century—it would be relatively easy to abolish. The result would be very different in the South, where slavery stood at the heart of the economic and social system. In the antebellum period, the line would be clearly drawn between the slave South and the free North; although not so clear as it would later become, that line was already evident on the eve of the Revolution.

2

The Colonial Era

I

THROUGHOUT ITS HISTORY, American slavery evolved and changed. Although the process of evolution was continuous, it is convenient for analytical purposes to divide that history into two broad chronological periods, colonial (lasting until about 1770) and antebellum (beginning about 1800), separated by the era of the American Revolution. Although colonial slavery lasted more than twice as long as antebellum, the latter has received substantially more attention from historians, in part because the sources available for studying it are more abundant and in part because in the middle of the nineteenth century slavery became the central issue in a national political debate that led to a bloody civil war. Recently, however, scholars have begun to subject colonial slavery to more intense scrutiny, in the process making clearer how slavery changed over time.

The colonial era saw the emergence in America of a true slave society, the transformation of a society in which some people (relatively few, at first) were slaves into one in which slave labor formed the basis of the economy and social order. At first, novelty and experimentation characterized social relations: first- and second-generation slaves confronted first- and second-generation masters, most of whom were new not only to slavery but also to one another and indeed to America. Gradually, social patterns hardened: as masters and slaves were born into slave relations, behavior that had once been tentative and experimental became established and routine. At the same time, despite the persistence of pronounced regional variations, American slavery as a whole acquired some common features that distinguished it in significant ways from slavery elsewhere.

I I

AMERICAN SLAVERY developed within a particular environment, conditioned by particular demographic patterns. Imported and held for their ability to work the land, slaves lived under varied conditions, shaped by the demands of cultivating a diversity of staple crops. Nevertheless, the basic population mix—the ratios of blacks to whites and of slaves to non-slaves, the size of slaveholdings—provided a rough commonality to the slaveholding environment of colonial America that belied specific regional differences. Because that environment was distinctive, American slavery differed in important respects from the slavery that existed elsewhere in the New World.

As the eighteenth century progressed, American slavery developed a mainstream with a distinctive demographic configuration. Rooted in the South, this slavery was characterized by the prevalence of small to medium-sized plantations and by the presence of large numbers of both slaves and free whites. Unlike the North, where slavery was increasingly marginal, the South developed as a true slave society, in which slavery served as the bedrock of the economy and of the social order. Unlike much of the Caribbean, however, the South emerged as a slaveholding society in which whites constituted a significant proportion of the population—the majority in the South as a whole—and non-slaveholders made up a majority of the white population.

The contrast between the South and the Caribbean is instructive. In much of the Caribbean, where sugar was the dominant cash crop, blacks outnumbered whites by up to ten to one and slaves were typically held in very large units. Because sugar cultivation required substantial investments in expensive refining machinery as well as in land and labor, sugar plantations were usually very large-scale operations; on the eve of emancipation in Jamaica, more than three-quarters of all slaves lived on holdings of over 50 slaves and about half lived on holdings of over 150.

In the American South, where tobacco (and later cotton) was the most important staple crop, the situation was very different. Because there were few economies of scale in growing tobacco, small holdings were common, and even on larger plantations the actual cultivation of tobacco was frequently organized in smaller units. Blacks constituted a minority of the population (about 35 percent in 1790), and even in the lower South formed only about half the population (see tables 1 and 3). The only colony (and state) to have a substantial black majority was South Carolina, and even there the majority never approached the overwhelming ten-to-one ratio present in Jamaica, Antigua, and Saint Domingue; at the peak of black predominance in the 1720s and 1730s, blacks outnumbered whites in South Carolina by about two to one. The great majority of American slaves lived on holdings of under fifty. To be sure, there were other slave societies in which small holdings prevailed; in much of Brazil the ratio of slaves to masters was quite similar to that in the South. Nevertheless, by international standards American slaves lived on small holdings, dispersed among many whites with whom they came into frequent contact.

Of course, significant regional variations marked the conditions under which slaves lived and worked; at opposite extremes, there were exceptions to the prevalent pattern of numerous slaves living on modest-sized holdings. In the North, slaves were few and slave-holdings were typically tiny. Despite the existence of large slave-based estates in New York and Rhode Island, most Northern slaves were held in very small groups—usually no more than three or four slaves per owner—and worked as farmhands, servants, craftsmen, and general laborers. Consider New York, which throughout the eighteenth century had far more slaves than any other Northern colony. The 33 slaves residing in Orange County in 1702 were owned by 15 families; the 29 slaves in Dutchess County in 1714 had 13 different owners. As late as 1790, about one white household in five in New York City owned slaves, but three-quarters of these slave-holding households contained only one or two slaves each. Under such circumstances, most slaves lived and worked in close proximity to whites, and their labor required little organization or regimentation.

At the opposite extreme was the low country of South Carolina (and, after the middle of the eighteenth century, Georgia), the area of the American mainland where slaveholding patterns most closely approached (without, however, reaching) those of the Caribbean. Because rice planters had to invest in complex irrigation systems needed alternately to flood and drain the land, rice, like sugar, was most efficiently cultivated on a large scale. Spurred by cultivation of rice—and, at the end of the eighteenth century, Sea Island cotton—slavery was more pervasive and slaveholdings were on the average much larger in the low country than anywhere else in America. As early as 1726, only a generation after the beginning of substantial rice cultivation, slaves made up more than 70 percent of the population in South Carolina's St. George Parish, and two-thirds of those slaves lived on holdings of more than 25. By the end of the eighteenth century, slaveholding was much more concentrated, with slaves composing about 84 percent of the low country's rural population and holdings with hundreds of slaves common; in 1790, the 11 parishes that made up the Charleston District contained 79 holdings with 100 or more slaves. Absenteeism was common among wealthy planters, many of whom preferred to spend their time in increasingly elegant Charleston rather than among "brutish" Africans on their isolated estates.

These conditions gave rise to widespread use of the "task" system, under which each slave was assigned a job in the morning and was free to stop work upon its completion. Unable or unwilling to engage in minute supervision of agricultural operations, absentee planters often allowed their low-country slaves an unusual degree of self-management, with estates left in the hands of trusted black "drivers" who were in effect overseers, and who operated under the loose control of white "stewards," each of whom supervised several estates.

The task system, which emerged over the course of the eighteenth century and reached its full fruition in the antebellum period, was significant both for the autonomy that it provided low-country slaves and for its atypicality. Along the coast of South Carolina and Georgia, more than anywhere else on the mainland, slaves developed their own "internal economy" based on flexible work schedules and the ability to accumulate and dispose of their "own" property on their "own" time; as historian Philip D. Morgan, who has pioneered in exploring this internal economy, noted, "on a much reduced scale, there were lowcountry slaves who resembled the protopeasants found among Caribbean slaves."[1] But although its proponents argued that the task system provided slaves with powerful incentive to hard work, most Southern slave owners viewed the self-management and economic independence that it fostered among slaves as subversive of the discipline, order, and dependence essential to slave labor. For this reason, although planters elsewhere in the South occasionally experimented with the task system, and many masters introduced limited task features while maintaining gang labor—for example, assigning daily tasks to gangs—the task system as a whole never became widespread outside the South Carolina and Georgia low country.

Indeed, it is important to keep in mind the unusual nature of low-country slave conditions when considering the South as a whole. Even in the colonial period, the low country contained only a small fraction of America's slaves; in 1750, South Carolina and Georgia together counted about 40,000 slaves, or about 17 percent of those in the American colonies. (Most of these 40,000 lived in the low country, but a small number resided in the South Carolina backcountry, where the population was overwhelmingly white and slaveholdings were typically small.) By contrast, 144,872 slaves, or about 61 percent of the American slaves, lived in Virginia and Maryland. As slavery expanded westward in the antebellum years, low-country conditions became far more atypical, significant primarily for representing an extreme variant in the range of American slave relations.

Much more representative of normal American slaveholding patterns were conditions in the upper South, where most slaves lived on small and medium-sized units. Many of these slaves had masters of relatively modest means; more than half the Chesapeake slave owners in the early eighteenth century owned fewer than five slaves. Of course, to say that a majority of slave owners were small slave owners does not imply that a majority of slaves had such owners; from the *slave's* perspective, owners with ten or more slaves were more typical than owners with one to five. (For more detailed information on the distribution of slaveholding, see chapter 4, section III). But relatively few slaves experienced life on very large plantations, because even those slaves owned by the wealthy planters who increasingly dominated society in Virginia (and to a lesser extent Maryland and North Carolina) were frequently *held* in smaller groups.

During the first half of the eighteenth century, planters with numerous slaves typically divided their holdings between a home plantation staffed by abundant supplies of servants and artisans and up-country "quarters" where, under the supervision of overseers, groups of perhaps eight to ten slaves cultivated tobacco (and later, increasingly, wheat). (These "quarters" must not be confused with the slave quarters that slaves inhabited on large plantations; in the antebellum period, the term "quarters" almost always referred to the slave quarters, not to the small up-country holdings that shared the term in the colonial Chesapeake.) At the time of his death in 1732, Robert "King" Carter was probably the wealthiest man in Virginia, with 390 slaves of working age; these slaves, however, were located on 48 different holdings, with only 23 residing on his home plantation. Newly imported Africans often received their training in the quarters, where overseers could resort to extreme measures to break the recalcitrance of those who resisted new ways, while planters filled their home plantations with "country-born" slaves or Africans who had learned to conform to what was expected of them. Multiple holdings remained widespread among the "gentry" in the second half of the eighteenth century, but with fewer Africans arriving in the Chesapeake, planters felt less compelled to keep their slaves divided into very small groups, and the size of holdings increased; in 1770, Robert Carter III (King Carter's grandson) kept about 100 slaves at his home estate of Nomini Hall and had some 250 more scattered among 12 plantations in 4 counties. In 1774, Thomas Jefferson held 45 slaves on his Monticello plantation and 142 others on 6 additional holdings; in 1786, George Washington kept 67 of his 216 slaves (the majority of whom were legally the property of his wife, Martha) at his Home House, with the remainder located on 5 other plantations.

If one important characteristic of American slavery was the presence of a substantial number of slaves living dispersed among many whites on relatively small holdings, a second was the high proportion of *non-slaveholding* whites. Although the South was a slaveholding society, substantial numbers of Southerners had no direct interest in or experience with slavery. Non-slaveholding whites were most numerous in the backcountry; in 1790, 77 percent of the backcountry households in South Carolina were without slaves, and slaveholding was even less prevalent in backcountry Virginia and North Carolina. Even in the plantation regions, however, large numbers of whites held no slaves; during the second half of the eighteenth century, between one half and two-thirds of the white households in the tidewater region of Virginia and Maryland owned slaves, with a gradual increase in the proportion of slave owners occurring in the years preceding the Revolution. In the South as a whole, slave owners always constituted a minority of the white population.

The substantial presence of white non-slaveholders in the slave-holding South had dual implications. On the one hand, it tempered the slave owners' dominance of society and introduced a source of potential political conflict among white Southerners, especially after the rise of republican (and, later, democratic) sensibilities beginning in the 1760s. Although slave owners managed—through a combination of political compromise and ideological broadside—to contain the threat of a major anti-slavery campaign by fellow Southerners, planters could never be totally sure of non-slaveholders' loyalty to the social order. On the other hand, the large number of non-slaveholding whites undercut the opportunity for slaves to engage in various skilled jobs—precluding the emergence of the kind of buffer class of free mulattoes that existed in an overwhelmingly black slave society such as that of Saint Domingue, a class that performed various support and managerial tasks and shielded planters from their African laborers—and hardened the racial line between white and black. Non-slaveholding whites could be intensely jealous of those they perceived as haughty aristocrats, but they also were highly susceptible to racist appeals to white solidarity: they may have been poor, but at least they were white.

III

TWO DEVELOPMENTS of signal importance combined with the demographic configuration outlined above to shape the evolution of slavery during the century preceding the American Revolution: the simultaneous emergence of an American-born master class and of an American-born (or creole) slave class. The former went hand in hand with the triumph of resident over absentee behavior among slave owners, while the latter accompanied a fundamental demographic transformation that in turn stipulated far-reaching changes in the lives of the slaves. Both developments contributed to the increasingly distinctive character of American slavery.

The resident orientation of American slave owners must be seen in the context of the widespread absenteeism that prevailed elsewhere—among slave owners in Jamaica, Saint Domingue, and much of Brazil, as well as among serf holders in Russia. Masters in those countries often looked upon their holdings primarily as investments to be milked, investments that needed little of their attention so long as they provided the requisite income. Often such slave owners lived far from their slave property—perhaps in a colonial city, or in the mother country of England or France—and visited their plantations only occasionally, receiving periodic reports on them from stewards. Other planters spent a number of years supervising their holdings in the colonies and then retired at a relatively young age to their estates in the mother country.

Whether or not they lived on their slaveholdings, however, such planters were likely to possess an absentee *mentality*; their hearts would be elsewhere, and they would show relatively little interest in the day-to-day chores of plantation administration. The huge numerical preponderance of unassimilated Africans rendered a West Indian plantation an inhospitable environment for most British planters; as historian Richard Dunn put it, "The West Indian slave masters could not expect to assimilate or acculturate such a huge alien population. If they wished to preserve their own identity, they had to segregate themselves socially and culturally from the blacks." A similar condition prevailed in Russia, where, as Daniel Field noted, the serf owner "was almost an outsider even on his ancestral estate."[2]

American masters were rarely outsiders on their estates. With some exceptions, they lived on their farms and plantations and involved themselves on a regular basis with the lives of their slaves. Of course, some masters found it necessary to be away from home for prolonged periods of time, and others chose to be. But such absenteeism, which was especially prevalent in the South Carolina and Georgia low country, was not typical of the South as a whole. Even more important, it did not vitiate the resident *mentality* of slave owners who considered their holdings home even when they were away, and took a lively interest in their management. Far more than the typical Jamaican, Cuban, Haitian, Russian, or even Brazilian master, the typical American was actively concerned with managing his slaves.

The emergence of this resident mentality constituted one of the most important developments of colonial society. From the beginning, English residents of Massachusetts and Virginia—unlike many of their French and Spanish neighbors—thought of themselves as permanent settlers; they brought their families when possible, established agricultural communities, and came to America to live. English migrants to the colonies usually remained English at heart, and even their children still identified strongly with the mother country; wealthy colonists, for example, frequently sent their sons back to England for a proper education. Without fully realizing it, however, these colonists were gradually becoming Americans. They looked to their colonial legislatures rather than Parliament or King to represent their interests; those legislatures set their taxes and passed their laws (including those regulating slavery). By the early eighteenth century, gentlemen in the mainland colonies formed what amounted to a self-governing elite, an elite that associated its interests with those of their colony. They took great interest in their government, community, and property—including slave property.

Determination to run their own affairs was widespread among both large and small slave owners. Small and medium-sized owners, who were much more numerically prevalent than in the Caribbean, almost always managed their own slaves. Large planters often used overseers, but they also often actively directed the work of those overseers and interfered in their management of slave life and labor. Because it inevitably involved at least some delegation of authority, employment of overseers presented a major dilemma to planters with a resident mentality.

Planters were rarely satisfied with the performance of their overseers. The task of inducing slaves to work efficiently required overseers to walk a nearly impossible line between allowing excessive leniency and resorting to draconian measures, maintaining at the same time a properly deferential attitude toward their employers. Diaries of planters who visited their quarters are full of entries such as that of William Byrd, who in 1709 "found that [overseer John] Blackman left everything in a sad condition for which reason I refused to pay him," or Landon Carter, who after a visit to his "Fork" quarter in 1757 noted that "the overseer there is but a Chattering fellow, promises much but does little, for which I have given him a piece of my mind. He protests he will mend."[3] Complaining of lazy, drunk, overbearing, insubordinate, and inefficient behavior, large slave owners sometimes dispensed with white overseers entirely, especially after the middle of the eighteenth century, when few new slaves were being imported and the labor force required less "breaking in"; two alternative methods of slave management included using a trusted slave in place of a white overseer or consolidating the small quarters into larger holdings and managing them oneself, perhaps with the help of a son or other relative.

Each of these alternatives, however, brought its own problems. Black overseers seemed to possess many of the same deficiencies as white; in 1766, Landon Carter, complaining that his trusted black assistant Jack Lubar was "too easy" with the laborers "and too deceitful and careless himself," concluded that "a negroe can't be honest" and determined to "get new overseers every where."[4] Managing slaves oneself was in many ways the least problematic solution to the task of estate management, for most masters were convinced that they alone knew how to handle affairs properly; for this reason, there was an increasing tendency for all but the wealthiest planters to serve as their own managers. Still, this undertaking required of slave owners an extraordinary commitment to engaging in the details of daily plantation life that was largely incompatible with their typical desire to reign as benevolent patriarchs who set overall policy but did not sully their hands with the mundane course of life's numerous petty squabbles.

Of course, dealing with overseers was a problem only for the wealthy few; the vast majority of slave owners in the American South were able to serve as their own managers. But the overseer problem, which remained a source of considerable anguish to substantial planters in the antebellum period as well, provides a graphic illustration of the difficulties those planters faced in reconciling what were essentially irreconcilable demands. They were strongly tempted at times to ignore their troublesome property and leave it entirely in the hands of overseers; convinced that they knew and loved their slaves far better than any hired subordinates, however, and that they knew far more about farming as well, most masters were unwilling to give up control. Their resident mentality was of utmost importance in shaping the nature of the slave regime.

Equally significant, and distinctive, was the increasingly creole character of the slave population. In New World countries as diverse as Jamaica, Trinidad, Saint Domingue, and Brazil, where the demands of sugar cultivation imposed particularly harsh working conditions, the number of slave deaths consistently exceeded the number of slave births; as a result, the slave population grew only as a result of massive imports from Africa, and until abolition of the slave trade most adult slaves were Africans. In the American colonies, by contrast, the proportion of Africans declined sharply; by the onset of the American Revolution, only about one-fifth of all slaves were African-born. After the abolition of the slave trade in 1808, the number of African slaves plunged, and at the time of emancipation in 1865, almost all Southern slaves—over 99 percent—were American-born. Whereas in much of the New World the majority of slaves were Africans (and the great majority were either Africans or the children of Africans), in the British mainland colonies (and then the United States) an increasingly creole slave population became more and more distanced from its ancestral roots.

The timing of this transformation from an African to a creole slave population varied by colony and depended in part on differing patterns of slave importation. In the North and in the upper South, the shift was well under way during the second quarter of the eighteenth century and was largely completed during the third quarter, when importation of Africans effectively came to an end. According to estimates by Allan Kulikoff, whereas in 1728 about half of black slave adults in the Chesapeake colonies had arrived during the previous ten years, by 1750 only 17 percent of slave adults in Virginia were composed of such recent arrivals; between the 1750s and the 1770s, the proportion of Africans in the black population of Maryland and Virginia dropped from one-third to one-tenth. In the lower South, by contrast, continued heavy importation of slaves until 1808 slowed the shift from Africans to creoles, although even there the proportion of creoles gradually rose; in South Carolina, according to estimates of Philip D. Morgan, American natives constituted 37.4 percent of adult slaves in 1730, 43.7 percent in 1750, and 55.6 percent in 1770. (Creoles formed a larger proportion of all slaves, because few children were imported from Africa.)

A crucial demographic transformation accompanied the emergence of a creole-based slavery. Slave populations that were predominantly African rarely experienced natural growth. A number of factors—the most important of which included an excess of males, limited opportunity for family formation, and prolonged breast feeding of babies—depressed birth rates among African-born slaves in America. At the same time, mortality rates were usually high among newly imported slaves, who lacked natural immunity to local diseases. As a result, the number of deaths exceeded the number of births, and the slave population grew only through continued importation of Africans.

During the eighteenth century, however, in a development unique among major New World slave societies, American slaves achieved natural population growth. Natural reproduction and a predominantly creole slave population emerged in close mutual interaction with each other: if American-born slaves had higher birth and lower death rates than Africans, natural population growth in turn produced an increasingly creole slave population. Gradually, the ratio of males to females fell while that of children to adults rose, and a slave body that had been dominated by young, African males was transformed into a balanced population of creoles—children and adults, men and women.

This process took place in all the Southern mainland colonies in the eighteenth century, but occurred first—and has been most closely studied—in the Chesapeake region. Some simple statistics reveal the depth of the demographic transformation that accompanied growth of a creole slave population there. In All Hallow's Parish, Maryland, the ratio of males to females fell steadily, if erratically, from 1.8 during the 1690s to 1.5 during the 1740s and 1.1 in 1776; during the same period, the ratio of adults to children tumbled from 2.9 to 1.3 and then to 0.99. In the tidewater region of Virginia and Maryland, the sex ratio among black adults declined from 1.5 in the 1720s and 1730s to 1.1 by the 1750s. African women in the Chesapeake region bore on the average three children, whereas creole women bore six. In Virginia, the black population experienced natural *decrease* (from excess of deaths over births) between 1680 and 1710, slight natural increase during the 1710s and 1720s, and rapid increase beginning in the 1730s; from the 1740s on, natural reproduction was a much greater cause of black population growth than was importation of slaves.

In the lower South, where Africans continued throughout the eighteenth century to constitute a much higher (although diminishing) proportion of the black population, the demographic transformation began somewhat later and progressed less rapidly; in South Carolina, unlike Virginia and Maryland, deaths exceeded births among slaves during the 1720s and 1730s. There, too, however, the ratio of males to females gradually decreased—from about 1.7 in the 1730s to 1.2 in the 1770s—women began bearing more children, and after the middle of the century the black population grew from natural increase as well as slave importation. Despite regional variations, by the outbreak of the War for Independence slaves throughout the United States were predominantly—in most states overwhelmingly—American-born, and were more than reproducing themselves.

By the end of the colonial era, a mature slave society with several noteworthy features had coalesced. These features included an American-born, largely resident master class; a creole, self-reproducing slave class; relatively small slaveholdings; and a large white population, a high proportion of which was composed of non-slaveholders. Together, these features set the contours for the evolution of American slavery and of master–slave relations. They also provided the particular setting within which Africans became Americans.

IV

MOST SLAVES in colonial America were either Africans or the children and grandchildren of Africans. Their enslavement by Europeans and the children and grandchildren of Europeans created a complex set of overlapping relationships: complementing the master–slave relationship was that between whites and blacks, Europeans and Africans, Christians and "pagans." Colonial slavery thus required of its participants—both masters and slaves but especially the latter—a major cultural adjustment.

This process has given rise to an important debate among scholars over the "Americanization" of Africans. Crudely put, the debate has pitted those who believe that in America slaves quickly abandoned most of their African ways and adopted the dominant culture of their new land against those who stress the continuing African cultural legacy among black Americans. The former view, which for many years prevailed among scholars, was most forcefully propounded by sociologist E. Franklin Frazier, who maintained that "probably never before in history has a people been so nearly completely stripped of its social heritage as the Negroes who were brought to America." The opposing position, vigorously espoused during the 1940s and 1950s by anthropologist Melville Herskovits, for many years found fewer academic adherents but has in the past two decades received support from black nationalists eager to celebrate African culture; the most sweeping recent case for the African character of black life in America was made by Sterling Stuckey, who insisted that down to the Civil War "the great bulk of the slaves were scarcely touched by Christianity" and slave culture was essentially African.[5]

Although this debate is likely to continue, for it is fueled by strong ideological passions, it is clear by now that the "Americanization" versus "African survival" dichotomy is misleading. The descendants of Africans brought to America were neither Africans nor cultural carbon copies of white Americans. They were influenced by—and in turn influenced—the behavior of their masters, but their customs, beliefs, and values were distinctive because so, too, was their history. On the basis of shared experiences as slaves, together with a common African background, they created a new, African-American, culture.

Africans brought involuntarily to America remained basically Africans at heart. They found their new environment—strange masters, language, customs—confusing, and longed for the homes and loved ones they had left behind. Many at first refused to accept the permanence of their new situation, showing their resistance in a variety of ways from flight to sullen noncompliance with orders, and often receiving for their efforts a range of harsh punishments designed to promote more cheerful obedience. Although most new slaves eventually adapted to the unwanted conditions in which they found themselves and came to recognize the inevitability of their slave status, they rarely accepted its legitimacy. Remembering his youth in South Carolina at the turn of the nineteenth century, Charles Ball, a fugitive slave who published his autobiography in 1837, sharply differentiated African from American-born slaves: Africans, he wrote, "feel indignant at the servitude that is imposed upon them, and only want power to inflict the most cruel retribution upon their oppressors . . . They are universally of opinion, and this opinion is founded in their religion, that after death they shall return to their own country, and rejoin their former companions and friends."[6]

African identity among blacks was, ironically, a product of their presence in America. Newly imported slaves came from diverse countries with a variety of languages and customs and at first lacked a sense of being Africans. In America, however, the contrast that was most striking was between black and white, African and European, and a generalized African identity came to assume greater salience than that of any particular African nationality.

One reason this was so was that despite specific differences in language and customs, on a broader level the slaves shared many elements of a common cultural background. They came from a premodern world that lacked the distinction between natural and supernatural, secular and sacred, a world in which the individual lived in close relationship with ancestors, spirits, and gods (often associated with various natural phenomena) and believed in the existence of a more remote High God who ruled over all. It was a world in which ancestor-spirits watched over their descendants and made sure they followed traditional customs (hence the importance of proper burial), and in which priests and witch doctors cured illness and injured enemies. It was a world that emphasized family and community, accepted polygynous marriage, was unfamiliar with private ownership of land, took for granted non-rational causality, placed great importance on taboos and ritual, and operated in conformity with a slow, cyclical sense of time in which patience was a virtue. The existence of this common cultural background—which shared some notable characteristics with the pre-modern background of the English settlers but in other respects was strikingly different—meant that even as specific ethnic attributes faded in America, a general African approach or style survived.

The American legacy of this common African heritage is evident in numerous elements of black culture, from music to magic. African communality persisted in the antiphonal, call-and-response pattern that pervaded the music of American slaves (and their descendants) as they sang of their work and religious faith or as they passed secret messages disguised as harmless song. The influence of African artistic traditions was evident in the folk art of black Americans, particularly in the colonial period, in creative expressions as diverse as textile designs, quilting patterns, and styles of wood carving and basket weaving. Folk medicine, charms, and love potions easily survived the passage from Africa to America, and every large plantation was likely to have its conjurer (whose authority was often considerable among whites as well as blacks). The ring shout, a combination of dance and song in which participants moved with increasing fervor in a counterclockwise circular direction, persisted in much of the South. And most of all, the slaves maintained their traditional religious sense of a world without sharp demarcation between the sacred and secular, a world of pervasive spiritual presence; this sense would find new expression in the Christianity that American blacks adopted and shaped to their own needs during the last century of their bondage.

Specific cultural practices of the newly imported slaves proved less enduring. Despite regional variations—the old ways were most resilient in isolated areas with an overwhelmingly black population—everywhere a basic discontinuity shaped the early history of blacks in America. This discontinuity was most immediately physical or geographic: Africans were ripped from everything they knew and deposited as unwilling inhabitants in a strange new world. It was also to a substantial degree cultural, for blacks found that it was impossible to continue as before under the changed conditions they faced in America. The descendants of Africans brought to America were not themselves Africans.

Africa grew increasingly remote to a black population that was more and more preponderantly creole. The children of Africans imported to America, like other second-generation Americans, rarely spoke more than a few words of their parents' native language. Similarly, as historian Albert J. Raboteau noted, "in the United States the gods of Africa died."[7] Blacks born in America did not think of themselves as Ibos or Angolas and often were unaware of their specific ethnic roots.

The descendants of Africans brought to America were Americans. They were not, however, the same as other Americans, for out of their African heritage and their distinctive history they fashioned a new, African-American culture. The process of creating this culture was by no means linear; the pace varied over both time and space in conformity with diverse conditions. (Periods of increased slave imports from Africa, for example, saw renewed African cultural influences as well.) Nor did the process occur in isolation from whites: African-Americans emerged as a people through intense interaction between black and white Americans, an interaction that saw significant cultural influences in both directions. If in some respects blacks and whites inhabited very different worlds in colonial America, those worlds were closely intertwined and bore more in common than was readily apparent to the inhabitants of either.

V

THE DISTINCTIVE ENVIRONMENT in which American slaves lived conditioned the creation of African-American culture. The increasingly creole nature of the slave population, the high ratio of whites to blacks, and the resident character of the slave owners sped the transition from African to African-American and rendered that transition more complete than in most other slave societies in the New World.

Four examples, involving such diverse topics as breast feeding, running away, naming children, and dancing, illustrate this process. In most of the Caribbean islands, where the huge preponderance of blacks over whites facilitated the perpetuation of African customs, slave women maintained the traditional African practice of nursing their babies until they reached about two years of age. Since lactating women are much less likely than others to conceive, this breast-feeding practice acted to depress the birth rate and hence contributed to the absence of natural growth among the slave population. Developments differed, however, on the British mainland. Although slave women imported from Africa followed the traditional breast-feeding practice, one reason for the relatively low birth rate among first-generation slaves, those born in America quickly adopted the local custom of nursing for only about a year. As a result, slave births were normally spaced about two years apart rather than the typical Caribbean pattern of more than three years. This shift is one important factor in explaining both the emergence of natural growth among the slave population of the mainland colonies and the contrast between the birth rate of slaves in those colonies and that of slaves elsewhere in the New World.

The evolution of slave flight reveals a similar erosion of traditional African behavior under radically new circumstances. Although both African and American-born slaves ran away for a wide variety of reasons (see chapter 5, sections VI and VII), they differed in important respects in the manner of their flight. Recent studies have established that in both the upper and lower South, newly enslaved Africans often fled in groups, striving somehow either to return to Africa or to establish African-style villages on the frontier. Creole fugitives, by contrast, showed less interest in replicating African communal culture than in avoiding detection, and therefore usually absconded alone (or less often in pairs). Flight continued to be a pervasive feature of slavery, but runaway slaves adjusted their tactics to local conditions so as to maximize their chances of success.

A more complex transformation is evident in the changing pattern of names slaves gave their children. (Although masters often assigned names to newly imported slaves and sometimes intervened in the naming of slave babies, American-born slaves were able to name the majority of their babies.) As one might expect, the number of African names decreased over time: in a study of slave naming in North Carolina and South Carolina, John C. Inscoe found that whereas prior to 1750, 14 percent of newborn slaves received names that were "pure African," the proportion declined to 9 percent by the early nineteenth century and 5 percent by the Civil War years. (Additional names may have represented Americanized versions of African names, such as "Joe" for "Cudjo.") As African names declined in frequency, biblical names became more common, increasing from 10 percent of the total before 1750 to 20 percent in the early nineteenth century and 28 percent on the eve of emancipation.

Equally noteworthy was the change in significance of those African names that continued to appear. Many of these names were day names ("Quash" for boys born on Sunday and "Cuffee" for those born on Friday, for example; "Quasheba" for girls born on Sunday and "Juba" for those born on Monday), or names indicating order of birth ("Sambo" meant second son). But among slaves born in America, these names quickly lost their original meanings; Cuffees were as likely to be born on another day as on Friday, and Sambos were first or third sons as well as second. (The same change occurred among translated names: slaves named "January" and "Easter" could be born in July.) African—and other—names were passed on from generation to generation, but those names had lost much of their original meaning.

The same process is evident in slaves' continuing use of pet names such as "Caesar," "Pompey," "Venus," and "Juno." These names were almost always originally provided—often with satiric or condescending intent—by slave owners, who frequently insisted on renaming Africans, whether with classical or with standard English names, in order to establish clearly their new status. Although at first Africans frequently resisted their new names (and thereby their new identity), they usually came eventually, however reluctantly, to accept them, and even sometimes to pass them on to their children. Classical names, which decreased from 21 percent of North

Carolina and South Carolina slave names before 1750 to 14 percent between 1800 and 1809 and 8 percent between 1860 and 1865, may continue to have been imposed at times by slave owners, especially on domestic servants, who seem to have been especially prone to possess such "cute" appellations. But they were also passed on by the slaves themselves. Third- and fourth-generation slaves may often have been as unaware of the original intent of classical names as they were of the original meaning of African names. Both continued to appear (albeit with decreasing frequency) because parents liked the way they sounded and because they served to link children with their ancestors who had also borne them.

If changing naming practices can serve as an index of slave acculturation—the increasing number of biblical names is clearly related to the growing influence of Christianity among the slave population—they also indicate the degree to which American slaves shaped their own distinctive culture. Not only did the slaves select the names for their own children, but they did so in ways that served their own purposes and differentiated themselves from whites around them. Continued use of African and classical names, as well as of names of uncertain origin that were rarely used by whites (for example, "Sukey"), was accompanied by the widespread practice of avoiding the first name of one's owner. Even as slaves had increasingly "American" names, therefore, their names continued to differ significantly from those of whites. Like whites, they used names to reinforce family ties, but they did so differently because the threat to those ties was so much greater. In naming their children, for example, slaves relied on a pool of names that had been established over generations and included, as we have seen, a wide variety of types; because males were much more likely than females to be forcibly separated from their families, however, boys received the names of immediate family members—fathers, grandparents, uncles—more often than girls. In short, although slave naming patterns indicate a rapid process of Americanization, the end result was by no means identical to that among white Americans.

A final example, that of slave dancing in New Orleans, confirms the persistence of African folkways among American slaves well into the nineteenth century, as well as the transformation of those folkways under new conditions. Nighttime carousing and dancing, prevalent among New Orleans's predominantly African-born black population during French and Spanish rule, continued unabated after the city came under American control in 1804. In 1817, reacting to complaints from white residents, New Orleans's mayor set aside a public square—officially named Place Publique and then Circus Square but informally known as Congo Square—for black revelry, and restricted it to Sunday afternoons. The weekly dancing on Congo Square quickly became institutionalized as a major black cultural manifestation, which enabled hundreds of slaves to congregate on their day off to dance, sing, and trade information, as well as to buy and sell food and other items. Many whites were attracted to watch the festive activities.

A heavy African component characterized the Congo Square gatherings. Dancers moved in rings, organized by nationality—each marked by distinctive tattoos—playing on African drums and stringed instruments; African languages crowded out French and English, and voodoo rituals (brought by refugees from Haiti) flourished. Architect Benjamin Latrobe, who witnessed one of the Sunday dances in 1819, was struck by what he considered the uncivilized nature of the event—"I have never seen any thing more brutally savage, and at the same time dull and stupid than this whole exhibition"—but noted that "there was not the least disorder among the croud, nor do I learn, on enquiry, that these weekly meetings of the negroes have ever produced any mischief."[8]

Nevertheless, the Sunday meetings were banned as a public nuisance in the late 1830s. Although they were permitted to resume in 1845 and continued until 1862, the resurrected festivities differed markedly from those of an earlier era. As New Orleans boomed in the antebellum period, the center of a huge domestic slave trade whereby hundreds of thousands of bondsmen and -women moved from the seaboard states to the rich cotton-producing region of the Southwest, its slave population became increasingly "Americanized" (although it never entirely lost its distinctive character). To slaves who were now overwhelmingly American-born, African customs grew increasingly remote and the Sunday afternoon dances at Congo Square represented more an opportunity to gather for a good time than to keep alive old traditions. No longer did participants exhibit filed teeth and tattoos or congregate by tribal groupings; violins, tambourines, and banjos replaced more exotic instruments; singing in English—"Hey, Jim Along"—replaced African song and music. Although Sunday dances at Congo Square persisted, they did so in radically altered form; what had begun as an African tradition had been transformed into an African-American one.

Of course, regional differences affected the growth of African-American culture and society. The small size and dispersed nature of the slave population in most of the North—as well as in much of the Southern backcountry—facilitated rapid acculturation and encouraged the emergence of considerable individual autonomy among blacks, whose freedom of movement appeared to pose little threat to the social order. At the same time, however, the paucity of blacks limited the ability of slaves to associate with one another, restricted community development, and often forced spouses to live apart from each other because they had separate owners.

At the opposite extreme, slaves in the South Carolina and Georgia low country lived in unusual isolation from whites and absorbed Euro-American ways much more slowly—and partially—than most American slaves. The overwhelming preponderance of blacks, continuing heavy infusion of Africans, geographic isolation, and owner absenteeism combined to limit contact between white and black and to permit the emergence of a new culture centered on a new language: Gullah. Both the language and the culture developed out of a complex interaction among two major groups of Africans (from Guinea and the Congo/Angola region), African-Americans, and white Americans and served to set low-country blacks off from others on the American mainland. Into the twentieth century, the language of the Gullah people, especially on the Sea Islands off South Carolina and Georgia, remained largely unintelligible to both whites and blacks unfamiliar with it.

Despite the existence of these contrasting regional patterns, slave life in colonial America was marked by a number of common developments that differed more in timing and intensity than in direction. The growth of African-American society went through three basic stages. If this trend was most clearly evident in the upper South, where the majority of slaves lived, it was present in the lower South (and to a considerable extent in the North) as well.

Until the end of the seventeenth century, there were few blacks in any of the colonies (and many of those had spent time in the West Indies before coming to the mainland). As a result, those blacks lived in an overwhelmingly white society (upon which they had relatively slight influence), had little opportunity to interact on a widespread basis with other blacks, and went through a rapid period of acculturation.

During the first half of the eighteenth century, heavy importation of Africans produced an agricultural laboring class that from Maryland south was increasingly made up of blacks. The increased number of blacks made possible an expanded social life among slaves; for the first time they could form widespread social ties—of marriage and friendship—with one another (although the excess of males over females among Africans precluded marriage for some men). At the same time, the surge in African imports slowed the rate of black acculturation and produced substantial anxiety among whites about the stability of the social order.

Gradually, as Africans had children of their own in America and new imports declined as a proportion of blacks in the colonies, a predominantly African laboring population became one of African-Americans. As we have seen, this basic transformation occurred at different times in different colonies, beginning earlier and proceeding faster in the upper South than in the lower. By the outbreak of the Revolution, about 80 percent of blacks in America and as many as 90 percent of those in the upper South and in the North were American-born; even in the lower South, creoles constituted a substantial majority of the population. Accompanying this demographic transformation was the formation of a new African-American society. Social stability increasingly replaced the turbulence associated with earlier boom times, slaves developed their own complex familial and social structures, and an African-American culture emerged under conditions that in most areas allowed both increased privileges for acculturated blacks and close interaction between black and white.

VI

THREE ESSENTIAL DEVELOPMENTS marked the transition from African to African-American and the growing complexity of slave society in America. The first was the growth of black families. The second was the growing occupational diversity and socioeconomic differentiation within the slave body. The third was the beginning of a long process whereby blacks in America were introduced to—and appropriated as their own major elements of—Protestant Christianity. Although none of these elements was totally absent among

Africans in America, all were facilitated by (and indices of) the emergence of a stable, American-born, and increasingly acculturated slave population.

The establishment of slavery in America entailed the destruction of families, as Africans—mostly young men—were torn from their loved ones at home and placed among strangers. Newly imported slaves rarely lived in families; indeed, they often lived in sex-segregated barracks. Although many Africans eventually found spouses and produced children of their own, their opportunities for family formation remained limited. Many lived on small holdings where there were few eligible mates, and African males outnumbered females by margins of two to one. Nor were most planters solicitous of the family rights of new slaves, for whom they had developed few ties of affection and in whom they were interested almost solely as instruments for the accumulation of wealth.

The emergence of a predominantly creole slave population changed all this. Many slave owners came to take greater interest in the lives (and general welfare) of American-born slaves—with whom they had sometimes grown up—than in those of newly purchased Africans who appeared strange and "savage" (see section VII, below). More important still, the growing number of blacks in America, the increased size of holdings, and the more equal sex ratios provided greater opportunities for finding spouses than had previously existed. During the half century before the War for Independence, second- and third-generation American slaves built a new system of family relations to replace that shattered by the slave trade; basic family patterns that would persist through the antebellum period became established, patterns that resembled in broad outline those found among white Americans but that differed from them in important specifics (see chapter 5, section III). Recent historians have properly stressed the degree to which the slaves themselves created, re-created, and defended their families, often against overwhelming odds. One reason they were able to do this, however, lies in the favorable demographic patterns they encountered (unlike slaves in, for example, Jamaica, Saint Domingue, or nineteenth-century Cuba).

Some occupational diversity among slaves existed from the very beginning. In the frontier conditions of early South Carolina, shortage of skilled personnel encouraged the use of slaves in a variety of positions—as guides, hunters, trappers, sailors, and lumberers—

many of which would later be seen as inappropriate. In the Northern colonies, where demand for agricultural labor was limited, many slaves worked in skilled crafts or domestic service; this was especially true in cities such as New York and Boston. And everywhere, small numbers of slaves—including especially high concentrations of children and of older slaves incapacitated for field work—served as domestics.

Africans were imported, however, for their physical labor, and throughout the South the vast majority cultivated crops on farms and plantations. The intense demand for agricultural labor resulting from the tobacco and rice booms, the absence (with the exception of Charleston) of a significant urban population, the relatively small size of holdings (especially in the upper South), and the perception among whites that Africans were uncivilized savages who needed training in the most rudimentary of skills combined to limit sharply opportunities for non-agricultural employment. Women as well as men labored in the fields; as early as 1722, in the revised version of his *History of Virginia*, Robert Beverley noted that "slaves of both sexes are employed together in tilling and manuring the ground," whereas "a white woman is rarely or never put to work in the ground."[9]

Gradually, as a higher proportion of slaves became acculturated to Euro-American ways and as creoles became the dominant element in the black population, occupational diversity among slaves increased. Emergence of larger slaveholding units made possible greater division of labor and prompted demand for more domestic servants by planters eager to attain—and show off—an aristocratic way of life. As the upper South's tobacco boom turned to tobacco crisis in the third quarter of the eighteenth century, demand for labor waned and opportunities for male slaves to engage in non-agricultural work increased. (This trend was accentuated during the Revolution; see chapter 3, section III.) In South Carolina, the growth of Charleston, the colonial South's only major urban center, created new demand for house servants and craftsmen, while the growing economic autonomy of slaves who worked on the task system led to limited but real slave property accumulation—and differentiation—in the low country.

Although the proportion of slaves engaged in specialized, non-field labor varied, depending on factors as diverse as region, size of holding, nature of local economy, and whim of owner, it increased throughout the South over the course of the eighteenth century. Whereas there were only 4 craftsmen among the 525 male slaves listed in estate inventories in four Maryland counties before 1710 (a minuscule 0.76 percent), there were 13 out of 213 (6.10 percent) in the 1720s, with carpenters most numerous. During the second half of the eighteenth century, skilled employment among slaves became far more common, especially on the "home" holdings of wealthy planters, who typically relied on their own slaves for virtually all their non-agricultural needs. In 1786, for example, the 41 adult slaves who resided at George Washington's Home House included 4 carpenters, 4 spinners, 3 drivers and stablers, 2 smiths, 2 seamstresses, a waggoner, a carter, a gardener, and many domestic servants.

The proportion of slaves engaged in skilled occupations was greater still in the South Carolina and Georgia low country, where the paucity of white labor dictated heavy reliance on blacks and large slaveholdings facilitated division of labor. One English observer in the 1770s, noting the slaves' "amazing aptness for learning trades," suggested that "many owners, from motives of profit and advantage, breed them to be coopers, carpenters, bricklayers, smiths, and other trades."[10] He was right, although "train" or "encourage" would have been more accurate than "breed." The growth of non-agricultural employment among slaves was especially marked in the second half of the eighteenth century; according to recent calculations by Philip D. Morgan, the proportion of "skilled" workers among adult male slaves inventoried in South Carolina grew from 15.5 percent in the 1750s to 28.6 percent in the 1790s. Most numerous among such skilled slaves were woodworkers, watermen, house servants, and drivers.

Women had far fewer occupational opportunities, and the vast majority of adult women continued to perform agricultural labor; the proportion of South Carolina's adult female slaves with skilled occupations rose from 2.7 percent in the 1750s to 8.5 percent in the 1790s, but even then reached a level less than one-third that of men. The principal alternative to field work for women was domestic service (a collection of jobs by no means limited to women). Especially on large estates, women served as cooks, washers, personal servants, and less often as nannies and wet nurses, and many slaveholders of even relatively modest means kept at least one servant. In the late eighteenth century, the decline of the upper South's tobacco economy freed larger numbers of plantation women to engage in domestic production, principally through spinning and weaving; as historian Carole Shammas has recently shown, it was in part for this reason that the proportion of working women engaged in house service on nine large Virginia plantations increased from less than 15 percent before 1760 to about 25 percent in the late eighteenth century and 33 percent in 1800.

It would be a mistake to overemphasize the social divisions between "skilled" slaves and those who worked in the field, or to see the former as a kind of slave "aristocracy." Most slaveholding units were much too small to permit the development of sharp stratification among slaves, and ties of kinship and friendship often bound field laborers to craftsmen and house servants. Furthermore, specialized occupations were often held only temporarily: children who were too young and the old and infirm who were too weak to perform heavy agricultural labor were routinely assigned to house service or gardening chores, while other jobs were doled out as rewards for good behavior or performance. The existence of this occupational mobility militated against the emergence of separate slave strata and acted to reinforce a powerful sense of oneness in oppression that slaves shared regardless of their immediate condition.

It is also important to realize that slaves with specialized occupations did not necessarily receive better treatment than their brothers and sisters in the fields. Although they usually enjoyed more privileges—often including exemption from backbreaking labor, a chance to nibble delicacies cast from the master's table, and the opportunity to travel away from home—they also faced unusual obstacles. Because they were more noticeable than most slaves, and more was expected of them, they were more likely to arouse the ire of their masters or other authorities. House servants were in a particularly vulnerable position, for there were innumerable opportunities to displease one's master, and planter diaries are filled with entries like William Byrd's from 1709: "I had another quarrel with my maid Anaka," or "I beat Anaka for letting the child piss in bed," or "Eugene was whipped for pissing in bed and Jenny for concealing it."[11] Anaka, Eugene, and Jenny must have yearned for the anonymity of ordinary slaves whose behavior did not receive such close scrutiny.

Of course, the very term "skilled" was something of a misnomer—non-agricultural jobs did not necessarily require the pos-

session of greater skills than field labor—that served to lump together categories of slave occupations with divergent tendencies.
House servants were often the most dependent of slaves, for their
work revolved around their need to please their masters, whereas
craftsmen could enjoy an unusual measure of independence from
immediate white supervision. "Skilled" slaves were by no means a
monolithic group.

The increase in occupational diversity that occurred over the
course of the eighteenth century was a general indication of the
maturing of both slavery and African-American society. If African
slaves were overwhelmingly young males imported for their labor
power, males whose opportunities for family and social life were
often severely limited and who almost always were consigned to toil
in the tobacco and rice fields, creole slaves represented a more stable
and balanced population. They lived in families, developed increasingly complex forms of social organization, and adjusted, albeit not
always easily, to the world in which they found themselves. At the
same time that they enjoyed greater opportunities for social life of
their own, they were also able to interact more with the whites
around them.

Exposure to the religion of their masters represented an important
part of that process. Perhaps in no respect did colonial and antebellum slavery differ so much as in that of slave religion. For much
of the colonial period, both blacks and whites resisted the efforts of
a few missionaries to convert "pagans," and the great majority of
slaves remained untouched by Christianity. A serious movement to
bring Christianity to the slaves, however, gathered force in the middle of the eighteenth century and grew in intensity for more than
a century, a movement embraced with fervor by growing numbers
of blacks. By the late antebellum period, Protestant Christianity lay
at the heart of the slave community.

Africans in America usually clung to their native religions. Slave
autobiographer Charles Ball recalled that his grandfather, a native
African brought to Calvert County, Maryland, about 1730, insisted
"that the religion of this country was altogether false, and indeed,
no religion at all"; when the younger Ball was sold to a South Carolina
planter in the early nineteenth century, he found his new home
populated by numerous Africans, some who prayed to good and evil
African gods and others "who must have been, from what I have

since learned, Mohamedans.'"[12] The preservation of traditional ways was easiest in areas of heavy African concentration, but virtually everywhere most newly imported slaves maintained the religious beliefs, if not always the practices, of their native lands.

One reason they were able to do so was that for many years white Americans showed little interest in proselytizing among blacks. At first many slave owners worried that they might have to free slaves converted to Christianity. Some masters—and other whites as well—were simply indifferent to the religion of their slaves, or indeed to religion in general; throughout much of the colonial period it was relatively easy in the South, unlike New England, to pay little attention to religion. But numerous slave owners were actively hostile to those who would preach to their slaves, fearing that the Christian message of the equality of all souls before God would produce unrest; as the ministers of the South Carolina Society for the Propagation of the Gospel lamented in 1713, "The Masters of Slaves are generally of Opinion that a Slave grows worse by being a Christian; and therefore instead of instructing them in the principles of Christianity which is undoubtedly their duty, they malign and traduce those that attempt it."[13]

Toward mid-century, this aversion of both white and black to slave conversion began to change. The Great Awakening of the late 1730s and early 1740s, the first of a series of religious revivals that swept across America, created new interest among whites both in religion and in converting slaves to Christianity; of even greater impact were the evangelical revivals of the 1770s and 1780s. Although some evangelicals—including at first George Whitefield—were critical of slavery, their main impact was not in fostering opposition to the institution but in persuading white Southerners of their "Christian duty" to instruct blacks in the "truths" of the Gospel and treat their slaves in a "Christian" manner. Evangelicals actively sought out black as well as white converts and accepted them as spiritual equals. This "mission to the slaves" aroused considerable opposition among many whites (as well as support from those who believed that "Christianity has a tendency to tame fierce and wild tempers") and did not reach full fruition until the period 1820–60; still, as historian John B. Boles noted, "the half-century following 1740 was the critical period during which some whites broke down their fears and inhibitions about sharing their religion with the slaves in their midst, and some blacks—only a few at first—came to find in Christianity a system of ideas and symbols that was genuinely attractive."[14]

Increasing numbers of slaves found the message of evangelical Protestantism appealing. Focus on the conversion experience rather than on formal theology heightened the accessibility of Christianity to slaves (and to poor whites as well). The message of the spiritual equality of all before God, and the willingness of Baptists and Methodists to welcome the humble and downtrodden, blacks as well as whites, as "brothers" and "sisters" in their churches, proved attractive to those more used to hearing the language of the lash than the word of God from whites. But equally important was the growth of a substantial group of creole slaves who lacked their parents' ties to (and memories of) Africa and whose greater fluency in English reduced linguistic barriers to conversion. American-born slaves were, unlike Africans, likely targets for conversion.

As early as 1710, Virginia planter William Byrd noted in his diary, "After church I invited nobody home [evidently it was usually his practice to entertain on Sundays] because I design to break that custom [so] that my people may go to church." Although such interest in exposing slaves to Christianity was rare in the early eighteenth century, it became common in the second half of the century, especially in the upper South. "I give leave to all to go to Church who are so inclined," recorded Landon Carter in 1775; his requirement that those "who are not so inclined" must stay home and work no doubt served as a catalyst to his slaves' religiosity. Carter's behavior at this time was relatively passive: he allowed his slaves to go to church but seemed unconcerned with their spiritual development and lamented in 1776 that his overseer had "turned a Baptist, and only wants to convert my People." Soon thereafter, however, Carter himself "turned a Baptist," and turned as well to the religious instruction of his "people."[15] On the eve of the American Revolution, the stage was set for the massive conversions that would take place in the interracial revival meetings that swept much of the South in the late eighteenth and early nineteenth centuries.

The Christianization of American blacks was an uneven process: it proceeded in fits and starts, was welcomed by some (whether slave or slave owner) more readily than others, and generally progressed least rapidly in areas of heavy black and African concentration, such as the South Carolina and Georgia low country. Still, over the course of the eighteenth century, an increasing proportion of slaves were exposed to—and embraced—the religion of their masters. In their hands, it did not remain entirely the same as the religion of the masters; as we shall see (in chapter 5, section IV), black Christianity came to differ from that of whites in a number of important ways and served to meet the needs of an oppressed people. But in the broad view, these differences were of nuance rather than essence (and resembled differences among various Christian denominations); from the vantage point of other religions, black and white Christians clearly shared the same basic faith—and usually (under slavery) shared the same religious services as well. Christianization represented a major guidepost in the slaves' journey from African to African-American.

VII

BORN IN VIOLENCE, slavery survived by the lash. Beginning with the initial slave trade that tore Africans away from everything they knew and sent them in chains to a distant land to toil for strangers, every stage of master–slave relations depended either directly or indirectly on physical coercion. The routine functioning of Southern farms and plantations rested on the authority of the owners and their representatives, supported by the state, to inflict pain on their human property. Plenty of pain was inflicted.

Slave owners directed especially repressive measures against Africans, for newly imported slaves offered pervasive resistance to the conditions under which they found themselves. They ignored the Anglicized names their owners awarded them; they refused to perform the new tasks they were assigned; they ran away; and they sometimes lashed out in anger at their oppressors, inflicting injury and even death. New slaves, in short, needed to be "broken in," made to accept their status, a goal that required close supervision, routine application of the lash, and willingness to take draconian measures against those who refused to toe the line.

Slaves who transgressed could look forward to a wide range of gruesome punishments—most imposed informally by owners and overseers but some officially meted out upon sentence by special slave courts that existed in all the Southern colonies—including branding; nose slitting; amputation of ears, toes, and fingers (and less often of hands and feet); castration; and burning at the stake. Although such punishments must be seen in the context of widespread use of corporal punishment in the seventeenth century against the "lower orders" of whites, the level of repression directed at slaves, especially Africans, was of a different magnitude from that experienced by white Americans, both because such repression was seen as necessary for the establishment and preservation of slavery and because slaves were powerless to stop it.

What is more, masters and judicial authorities continued to inflict barbarous punishments on slaves in the eighteenth century, when corporal punishment against free white adults became far less common than it previously had been. Even relatively enlightened planters resorted to harsh measures. William Byrd's diary is filled with accounts of beatings and whippings, and in 1710 he casually observed that "my wife against my will caused little Jenny to be burned with a hot iron, for which I quarreled with her." (One suspects that he was annoyed primarily because the girl was burned against his will, not because she was burned.) Methodist minister Charles Wesley was shocked, upon first visiting South Carolina in 1736, at the routine talk among slave owners of ingenious punishments designed to make slaves suffer; one "gentleman" recommended that one "first nail up a negro by the ears, then order him to be whipped in the severest manner, and then to have scalding water thrown over him, so that the poor creature could not stir for four months after," while others spoke of extracting teeth and performing bodily mutilations. "Good God! Are these Christians?" exclaimed New Jersey–born tutor Philip Fithian upon hearing of similar tortures during his year-long sojourn in Virginia in 1773–74. In Louisiana, a free Negro convicted of torturing and killing a white girl was sentenced in 1780 to have her right hand cut off before being hanged; the court ordered that after her death her head should be "stuck up upon a pole at her former place of residence" with "her right hand to be nailed to the same Post."[16]

As such examples indicate, slavery continued to be based on savage repression and instillation of fear. At the same time, there occurred over the course of the eighteenth century a gradual change in the way this repression and instillation of fear operated. Although whipping remained a routinely applied punishment, there was a significant decrease in the use of extreme physical abuse such as branding, castration, and other forms of bodily mutilation. They did not entirely disappear, but by the second half of the century they not only were far less common than they had been but also met with widespread public disapproval; it became unfashionable to boast of cruelty to one's slaves. Instead, many slave owners began to talk about how they cared for them.

Precisely how and why this change occurred remain to be fully explored, but at least three important developments appear to have interacted in bringing it about. Over the course of the eighteenth century, many people (on both sides of the Atlantic) became far more concerned with the way human beings treated one another. As we shall see (in chapter 3), whereas virtually no whites questioned the moral basis for slavery at the beginning of the century, such questioning was widespread by its end. More to the point here, there occurred a fundamental change in attitudes toward cruelty, rights, and fairness, with far-reaching results as varied as a sharp decline in the use of corporal punishment on free adults and the growth of the concept of "natural rights." This change also produced widespread sentiment favoring "humane" treatment of the less fortunate, including slaves.

Equally important were changes that occurred among both the slaves and the masters. It was easy to look upon Africans in an instrumental manner: they were "savages" imported to work, and few planters expressed much interest in their lives, except for a lively concern with training them in that work and securing their obedience. As a greater proportion of slaves became creoles, however, slave owners began to look upon them differently. American-born slaves required far less disciplining than Africans: they did not have to be trained in new tasks, taught to understand simple orders, or—most important—convinced that their slave status was inescapable. They did not, like Africans, have to be beaten into a sullen obedience. Many slave owners came to have real feelings of affection for slaves they knew from birth; a planter's attitude toward a slave he or she watched grow through childhood and into adulthood was bound to differ from that toward an African "savage" who defiantly rejected his new status.

Slave owners were changing, too: just as the slaves were becoming American-born, so, too, were the masters. The emerging resident status—and mentality—of most American slave owners inevitably brought with it a host of proprietary attitudes toward their surroundings. As Africans became African-Americans, many resident slave owners came to look on them as their "people"—the term "my people" was used pervasively by slave owners during the century before emancipation—who deserved care and support in exchange for loyalty and work. In short, slave owners began to develop the kind of paternalistic outlook that would reach fruition in the antebellum period (see chapter 4, section V).

As resident slave owners developed increased interest in the lives of their slaves, many masters began to think of themselves as benevolent patriarchs who looked after their slaves but also kept them in line, and to think of their "people" as inferior members of their own extended families. In fact, such masters interacted extensively with their slaves, showing concern not just for their work but also for their lives, including health, family relations, religion, and leisure-time activities. Planters' diaries are filled with entries such as William Byrd's "I talked with my people" (1740), or Landon Carter's "I gave my people a holiday this day, notwithstanding my work is so backward" (1772), or George Washington's "[I] allowed all my People to go to the races in Alexandria" (1786).[17]

The existence of such attitudes did not, of course, vitiate slavery's cruelty. Most benevolent masters resorted to the whip—some quite frequently—and behind all the talk of love and protection lurked the master's power to compel obedience, by whatever means were necessary. The application of that power, however, was less naked and less crude than it had been; needless violence was less frequently flaunted. Because the rules were more clearly understood by those on both sides, they did not have to be so rigidly enforced, and could be tempered by the awarding of petty privileges and expression of humane sentiment. Such interaction between white and black was especially noteworthy in the upper South, where the vast majority of slaves (as well as masters) were American-born by the 1760s, and where the approximately even numbers of whites and blacks made it unlikely that large numbers of either would live in isolation from the other. Indeed, historian Mechal Sobel has recently gone so far as to argue that by the end of the colonial period in Virginia, white and black cultures had essentially merged: "both blacks and whites held a mix of quasi-English and quasi-African values."[18]

This thesis of cultural homogenization takes a legitimate point too far: clearly, as Sobel suggests, the pre-modern values that blacks brought from Africa bore some resemblance to those that white settlers brought from Europe, and her suggestion that white Virginians became increasingly "Africanized" is intriguing. At the same time, although white and black Virginians (and Americans in general) developed an intense relationship with each other, and pervasively shaped each other's way of life, it is an exaggeration to speak of their cultures merging into one common whole. Despite physical proximity, the slaves lived in a very different world from the masters; because their historical experiences were different, so, too, were their evolving cultures. Furthermore, as we have seen (in chapter 1, section V), at the very time that whites and blacks in America were in many ways becoming more like each other, class and racial lines were actually hardening: whereas before the 1680s there were few blacks in the mainland colonies and their status often differed only marginally from that of white indentured servants, during the next half century, as slavery became established as the South's dominant labor system, the gap between black and white appeared appreciably greater and class lines came more and more to approximate racial lines. Whites were assumed to be free, blacks slaves.

Those lines continued to harden, even as the most gruesome brutalities were visited upon slaves less often and as slave owners came increasingly to think of themselves as benevolent guardians of a simple people. The coexistence of these two trends may appear paradoxical, but they were not incompatible, for a "softening" of slavery in no way implied a blurring of the lines separating black from white, slave from free; throughout the antebellum period, passage of laws imposing new restrictions on slaves—for example, making it a crime to teach them to read, and tightening their supervision by white "patrols"—coincided with increased attention to their material welfare. There was much interaction, and an increasingly intense relationship, between the two sides, but at the same time the masters and slaves lived in very different worlds; those worlds evolved in close conjunction with each other, but they remained separate as black Southerners built a distinctive African-American culture based on their shared experiences under slavery and white Southerners built their own distinctive society based on their shared experiences with slavery.

And yet the package was never as neat as it seemed, or was supposed to be. Conditions varied widely both among and within regions; laws were enforced sporadically at best; behavior was tolerated that in theory should not have existed. In 1771, a grand jury presentment in Georgia revealed that "Slaves are permitted to Rent houses in the lands and Invirons . . . of Savannah," and that "in said houses meetings of Slaves are very frequent, Spirits and other licquors are sold, and Stolen goods often Concealed."[19] This kind of lapse, repeated in numerous forms elsewhere, prevented slavery from ever approaching the theoretical order the laws defined and critics decried. Human variation belied the rigidity of the system.

3

The American Revolution

I

THE REVOLUTIONARY ERA witnessed the first major challenge to American slavery. Almost overnight, it seemed, an institution that had long been taken for granted came under intense scrutiny and debate: critics questioned its efficacy and morality, proponents rushed to its defense, and thousands of slaves took advantage of wartime turmoil to flee their bondage. Tangible results of this challenge included the abolition of slavery in the North, a sharp increase in the number of free blacks in the upper South, and the ending of the African slave trade. Despite these developments, however, slavery in the Southern states emerged from the agitation of the era largely unscathed. Indeed, for all the talk of natural rights, manumission, and abolishing imports from Africa, the slave population of the new nation in 1810 was more than twice what it had been in 1770.

II

UNTIL THE MIDDLE of the eighteenth century there was little questioning in the colonies—or anywhere else, for that matter—of slavery. For centuries, a wide range of social thinkers had seen the institution as fully compatible with human progress and felicity. Aristotle, Thomas Aquinas, and John Locke differed from one another in many ways, but the three, proponents respectively of reason, Christian theology, and liberty, agreed in finding slavery an acceptable part of the social order. In the seventeenth and early eighteenth centuries, only a handful of thinkers in the British colonies dared challenge this long-standing consensus; the most notable early criticism of slavery came from the pen of Massachusetts judge Samuel Sewall, whose cautious pamphlet *The Selling of Joseph* (1700) elicited an immediate and forceful rebuttal (*A Brief and Candid Answer*) from merchant-politician John Saffin. This was, however, an isolated exchange that made little impression upon contemporaries, few of whom bothered either to defend or to attack slavery. Largely taken for granted, the institution was simply not much of an issue for the white colonists.

Where slavery did compel attention, it was almost always over pragmatic considerations involving the utility of particular policies, not the morality of human bondage. The first substantial movement in defense of slavery occurred in newly settled Georgia, where for a variety of practical reasons—chief of which was concern that the Spanish in Florida would incite slave revolt among their neighbors to the north—an act of 1735 barred slaves from the colony; proponents of slavery, who stressed the necessity of black labor for the prosperity of the semitropical colony, carried the day by 1750, when the prohibition was lifted. Other colonists, however, worried about the threat to security posed by too many slaves. As planter William Byrd II noted in 1736, in praising Georgia's prohibition on slavery, too many slaves produced "the necessity of being severe," for "numbers make them insolent" and their "base Tempers require to be rid with a tort Reign, or they will be apt to throw their Rider." Lamenting that "this is terrible to a good naturd Man," Byrd opined that "the farther Importation of them in Our Colonys should be prohibited lest they prove as troublesome and dangerous everywhere, as they have been lately in Jamaica."[1] Precisely such fears —supplemented by the desire to raise money—prompted several colonies to pass import duties on slaves, beginning in the 1690s.

In the Revolutionary era, slavery for the first time became a serious social issue. Relatively few people called for its immediate abolition, but many, including some slave owners, expressed real concern over its morality as well as its utility. This questioning of slavery, even when it did not lead to clear-cut support for universal emancipation, represented a significant departure from the general neglect of the subject that had previously prevailed. The challenge to an established institution in turn elicited vigorous protests from those convinced that their interests, and the social fabric in general, were being recklessly threatened.

A variety of factors converged, beginning in the third quarter of the eighteenth century and accelerating during the Revolutionary War, to produce this development. Perhaps most basic was a fundamental shift that occurred in the middle decades of the eighteenth century, under the influence of the Enlightenment thought that flourished among Western European and American intellectuals, in attitudes toward cruelty, rights, fair play, and toleration of differences: in short, how human beings should treat one another. Because of this pervasive shift, these years must be regarded as a kind of watershed, separating the modern from the pre-modern eras. Seventeenth-century settlers in the colonies—and usually their children as well—lived in a world that took for granted stocks and tongue-borings, religious proscriptions, fear of witches, and savage repression of the lower orders. The Founding Fathers who led the American Revolution spoke instead of natural rights, political liberty, freedom of religion, and equality before the law. In this new intellectual climate, the treatment, and even the ownership, of slaves became a pertinent subject.

Especially significant were changing notions of what constituted legitimate treatment of those who were poor, weak, or different. A new concern for humane treatment—symbolized by the stricture in the Eighth Amendment to the United States Constitution against "cruel and unusual punishments"—led to a sharp decrease in the use of corporal punishment on free adults. Although this decrease did not extend to slaves (or children), heightened attention to the mistreatment of slaves was evident both among outsiders shocked by the barbarities they witnessed and among resident masters concerned with the lives of their people. This opposition to the physical mistreatment of slaves did not necessarily lead to opposition to slavery itself; indeed, in the antebellum years, accentuating the humane treatment of slaves became a prime concern of the peculiar institution's defenders, who believed that by softening slavery they would render it more secure. Still, attention to treatment was a necessary first step in the overall challenge to slavery, because it involved the questioning of established practices; once begun, it was not always clear where such questioning would stop.

Take South Carolina planter and merchant Henry Laurens, whose letters during the 1740s and 1750s were filled with straightforward business comments on the buying and selling of Africans; "please to observe that prime People turn to best Account here," he wrote his supplier in 1757, that "the Males [are] preferable to the Females & that Callabars are not at all liked with us when they are above the Age of 18, Gambias or Gold Coast are prefer'd to others, Windward Coast next to them." By 1763, however, expressing qualms that were increasingly prevalent among others of his generation, Laurens had decided that he "would rather not pursue the African Trade" (although he did not immediately cease participating in it). Later in the year he went further still, agreeing with a Moravian missionary who had written to him complaining that children whose parents owned slaves grew up lazy; Laurens responded that he "wished that our oeconomy & government differ'd from the present system but alas—since our constitution is as it is, what can individuals do?"[2] Within a few years, in action highly atypical of whites in labor-hungry South Carolina, Laurens had moved beyond this cautious disquiet over slavery and decided that individuals could, in fact, make a difference; in 1779, he and his son John, both active Patriots, promoted an unusual (and ultimately unsuccessful) scheme to enroll in the Revolutionary army three thousand slaves who would be freed at the end of the war.

Among intellectuals, a spreading belief in human malleability sparked questions about the grounds for enslaving Africans. In the seventeenth century, English thinkers (on both sides of the Atlantic) had been struck by what they considered the savagery of Africans, and in the first half of the eighteenth century, many white Americans had come to see blacks as innately depraved, fit only for slavery. In the second half of the eighteenth century, however, growing awareness of the cultural diversity of peoples, accompanied by intense interest in the question of human nature, spawned new thinking on the question of black "depravity." Perhaps it was their slave status that created slave-like behavior, rather than the behavior that justified the status; if so, blacks removed from slavery would no longer act like slaves. Because discovery of talented blacks could confirm this environmentalist hypothesis, poet Phillis Wheatley and mathematician Benjamin Banneker received considerable attention during the late eighteenth century; even Thomas Jefferson, who had more doubts than many of his contemporaries about the intellectual potential of blacks and who dismissed Wheatley as a mediocre poet, was impressed by Banneker. "I am happy to be able to inform you that we have now in the United States a negro . . . who is a very respectable Mathematician," the Virginian wrote the Marquis de Condorcet in 1791. "I shall be delighted to see these instances of moral eminence so multiplied as to prove that the want of talents observed in them is merely the effect of their degraded condition, and not proceeding from any difference in the structure of the parts on which intellect depends."[3]

The spread of capitalism, and the new "dismal science" of economics that it spawned, contributed significantly to the questioning of slavery. Slavery lacked a basic ingredient of capitalism: the free hire of labor through mutual agreement of consenting parties. Substituting the physical coercion of the lash for the economic coercion of the marketplace, slavery thus did violence to the central values implicit in capitalist relations. While most late-eighteenth-century merchants only dimly perceived (or did not perceive at all) the conflict between slavery and a capitalist worldview, the logic of belief in free trade and the freedom of the individual to succeed—or fail—on the basis of one's own efforts inexorably led to challenges to slavery's legitimacy. Early political economists—including Adam Smith, whose book *The Wealth of Nations* (1776) remained for decades the most influential justification of the principles underlying capitalism—believed that slavery, by preventing the free buying and selling of labor power and by eliminating the possibility of self-improvement that was the main incentive to productive labor, violated central economic laws; like government regulation of wages, prices, and interest rates, slavery constituted an artificial restraint of trade.

The view that slavery was immoral because it violated fundamental economic law—which eighteenth-century thinkers almost invariably elevated to either natural or divine law—was especially prevalent among the Quakers, who in both Britain and America took the lead first in opposing slavery and then in organizing abolitionist groups to combat it. A small sect dominated by hardworking businessmen "distinguished by their mercantile wealth and above all by their entrepreneurial leadership," Quakers rejected religious authority in favor of an "Inner Light" that would guide each individual to religion and morality; by the 1760s, most had come to view slavery as unethical. To Quakers, the slave represented the diametric opposite of the dependable, orderly, and industrious worker that they strove to create. As prominent Quaker abolitionist John Woolman put it, explaining his response in 1757 to a Virginian who insisted that blacks were too slothful to be free, "I replied, that free Men, whose Minds were properly on their Business, found a Satisfaction in improving, cultivating, and providing for their Families; but Negroes, labouring to support others who claim them as their Property, and expecting nothing but slavery during Life, had not the like Inducement to be industrious."[4] Among Quakers, more than among any other group, environmentalism combined with a capitalist worldview and religious sensibilities to produce principled opposition to slavery.

More widespread was the related view that slavery was inefficient and socially degrading to society at large. The germs of the "free labor" critique of slavery that would be fully developed in antebellum years were already present in diverse strains by the middle of the eighteenth century. Planters as different as William Byrd II and Thomas Jefferson joined outside observers in worrying that growing up with slaves made white Southerners lazy, haughty, and overbearing. Others feared that white children would absorb the "brutish" behavior of the blacks who surrounded them and become degraded themselves. But it was the harmful economic impact of slavery that seemed most obvious of all. Planters had long lamented what they considered the slovenly work habits of their slaves, who needed to be coaxed and chided, bribed and beaten to engage in their everyday labor, and in times of pique they had wondered aloud whether plantation management was worth the effort. During the second half of the eighteenth century, such concern was exacerbated in the upper South by the crisis in the tobacco economy.

Economic hardship proved especially conducive to questioning established relations, including slavery; indeed, many outside observers, and some Southerners as well, blamed slavery itself for the economic hardship. New Jersey–born minister-in-training Philip Fithian, who spent 1773–74 in Virginia tutoring the children on Robert Carter III's Nomini Hall plantation, was no abolitionist, but he was convinced that slavery degraded the manners, morals, and work habits of whites and blacks alike. When he broached the subject of

"Negroes in Virginia" with Carter's wife (whom he greatly admired), he was pleased to find that "she esteems their value at no higher rate than I do." They agreed that if the slaves were sold, the money loaned out, and the land allowed to lie uncultivated, "the bare Interest of the price of the Negroes would be a much greater yearly income than what is now received from their working the Lands." Fithian's conclusion was pointed: "How much greater then must be the value of an Estate here if these poor enslaved Africans were all in their native desired Country, & in their Room industrious Tenants, who being born in freedom, by a laudable care, would not only inrich their Landlords, but would raise a hardy Offspring to be the Strength & the honour of the Colony."[5]

New religious developments provided a final source of anti-slavery thought. It is not always easy to isolate religious from other motivation in the second half of the eighteenth century, because people so commonly phrased other sentiments in religious terms; a thin line, for example, frequently separated economic law from natural law or divine law in the rhetoric of the time. Nevertheless, it is clear that the religious revivals that began with the Great Awakening in the 1740s and spread through much of the South in the 1770s and 1780s had a major impact on thinking about slavery. Not only did evangelical Christians show a new interest in the souls of the slaves, but they also often displayed real anguish about slavery itself. Especially in the upper South, Methodists and Baptists, who stressed humility, submission, and the equality of all souls before God, seemed ready during the last quarter of the eighteenth century to follow the Quakers into anti-slavery agitation.

Before the outbreak of the Revolutionary War, then, slavery had emerged for the first time as a major issue. Although diverse strains of thought had converged to produce this development, they were in a broad sense related to each other. On both sides of the Atlantic, the third quarter of the eighteenth century saw a remarkable growth of intellectual activity among educated gentlemen—and a much smaller number of ladies—convinced that they represented the dawn of a bright new era. These gentlemen thought, wrote, and exchanged information about an extraordinary range of subjects, from the orbiting of planets and the taxonomy of animal species to human nature and ideal forms of government. Maintaining that the key to progress lay in reason, they questioned established beliefs, such as the divinity of Christ, and established institutions, such as monarchy and hereditary privilege. It is hardly surprising that these modern Renaissance thinkers also questioned slavery.

In America, these were also the men who led the movement for independence and have often been referred to as Founding Fathers. Usually members of the colonial elite, they included lawyers such as John Adams and self-educated artisan-intellectuals such as Benjamin Franklin and Thomas Paine. In the South, however, they were most often wealthy planters. An extraordinary generation of planter-politicians—historian Clement Eaton termed it the "great generation"—led the American states to independence, created a new government, and dominated that government during its early years. Although they ranged from Maryland to Georgia, they were most concentrated in Virginia; one thinks immediately of George Washington, Thomas Jefferson, James Madison, and Patrick Henry (all among the largest slave owners of their day) but could easily add others, such as George Mason and Edmund Randolph. Although these leaders were part of an international community of intellectual-statesmen that even before the outbreak of the American Revolution had come to challenge the legitimacy of slavery, that Revolution would soon lead them to push their challenge substantially further.

III

THE REVOLUTIONARY WAR had a major impact on slavery—and on the slaves. Wartime disruption undermined normal plantation discipline, and division within the master class offered slaves unprecedented opportunities that they were not slow in grasping. The Revolution posed the biggest challenge the slave regime would face until the outbreak of the Civil War some eighty-five years later; indeed, it appeared for a while as if the very survival of slavery in the new nation was threatened.

The British wasted little time in reaching out to the slaves as potential allies against the American rebels. On November 7, 1775, Virginia's Governor John Murray, Earl of Dunmore, issued a proclamation offering freedom to all slaves who would bear arms against the rebellion. Throughout the South, the offer raised understandable panic among slaveholders already fearful for the loyalty of their slaves; "if the Virginians are wise," noted Washington, "that arch traitor . . . Dunmore should be instantly crushed."[6] Similar concern was evident farther south; three months earlier, Patriots in Charleston had hanged and burned a free black harbor pilot suspected of helping slaves flee to British ships.

As this incident suggests, despite varying responses Americans were unable to come up with a satisfactory way of blunting the British appeal to their slaves. Virginia planter Robert Carter III warned his people that a British victory would result in their being sold into a far more oppressive slavery in the West Indies. A very different approach came from South Carolina Colonel John Laurens, who for both idealistic and pragmatic reasons proposed enrolling up to five thousand slaves in the Patriot army, with freedom promised for them at the war's end; the proposal—scaled back to three thousand slaves—won the eventual endorsement of the colonel's prominent father, Henry Laurens, but was defeated by the South Carolina legislature early in 1782. Some slaves did serve in the Patriot army: Maryland specifically authorized slave enlistments, and several states (North and South) allowed slaves to serve in place of their masters, usually with informal promises of subsequent freedom; New York offered freedom to slaves in return for three years of military service, with a compensatory land bounty to be paid to their owners. Small numbers of *free* blacks served in all states except South Carolina and Georgia, and a few bondsmen enlisted, pretending to be free. Most slaves, however, saw little reason to believe that the War for Independence was their war; it was important to them because it provided many with a new opportunity to escape their own thralldom, not because it pitted the forces of freedom against those of despotism.

Unable or unwilling to compete with the British for the loyalty of their slaves, Southern masters struggled to preserve a threatened way of life. In the Chesapeake region, British depredations of 1775, 1777, and 1781 intensified the existing economic crisis and induced some planters to flee with their slaves to the security of the backcountry or to Kentucky and Tennessee. Wartime destruction was greater still in the South Carolina and Georgia low country. First loyalist planters saw their property plundered by rebel forces; many Tories were able to evacuate their slaves to safer locales (including the West Indies), but others lost some or all of their holdings. Patriots suffered a similar fate after the British captured Savannah in 1778 and Charleston in 1780, and many of the loyalists returned—temporarily, it turned out—to reclaim their slaves. (Some of these slaves wound up fighting the Patriots. At least forty-seven blacks served the British in a Hessian regiment; others worked as scouts, guides, and laborers.)

The destruction, confusion, and loss of authority that accompanied the war provided slaves with numerous opportunities to escape bondage. The absence of able-bodied white males and the proximity of enemy forces produced an abrupt decline in discipline on many farms and plantations throughout the South; slaves were emboldened, and masters complained of a breakdown of order and deference. No mass uprising of slaves occurred in the United States during the American Revolution, the way it did in Saint Domingue during the French, for American slaves lacked the overwhelming numerical advantage enjoyed by their Haitian cousins. Tens of thousands of slaves did, however, take advantage of the wartime disruption to run away. The fugitives faced varying fates.

Dunmore's proclamation unleashed massive flight among slaves in the upper South. On June 25, 1776, nine of Landon Carter's slaves, whom he denounced as "accursed villains," ran away at night, "to be sure," the planter guessed, "to L[or]d. Dunmore"; later he heard a rumor that minutemen shot and killed three of the fugitives. In part because the British governor lacked a land base after December 1775, only a relatively small number of slaves—the usual estimate is eight hundred—reached his forces, and most of these died from disease (especially smallpox); when Dunmore's fleet left the Potomac on August 6, 1776, it carried with it some three hundred fugitive slaves. But these represented only a small fraction of the slaves who had fled, and slaves continued throughout the war to seize any opportunity to run away. Jefferson's "Farm Book" lists some thirty slaves of his who escaped in 1781, with various descriptions such as "joined enemy" or "caught smallpox from enemy & died."[7] Most fugitives fled individually or in very small groups, to avoid detection, but the turmoil and weakened authority that accompanied the Revolution made possible, for the last time until the Civil War, coordinated escapes of whole families and larger groups as well. Upon occasion the population of entire plantations, including all eighty-seven slaves owned by John Willoughby in Norfolk County, Virginia, ran away.

Because disruption was even greater in the lower South, so, too, was opportunity for flight. The scope of both is evident in testimony at the 1807 inventory of a deceased South Carolina planter's estate explaining why his slaves had decreased in number from 172 in 1776 to 132 in 1789: 64 slaves had disappeared one night in 1779, and there followed "years of general . . . calamity, . . . in which all but the particular friends of the British thought themselves fortunate if they could raise provisions, and save their negroes from being carried off."[8] When British forces evacuated Savannah and Charleston at the end of the war, some ten thousand blacks accompanied them. An uncertain future awaited them (and the thousands more removed from New York City): some died, some gained their freedom, and others wound up as slaves elsewhere (usually in the British West Indies).

Estimates vary on the number of people who escaped slavery during the Revolution. Allan Kulikoff has recently suggested that about five thousand slaves from the Chesapeake area and thirteen thousand from South Carolina reached the British, with smaller numbers from North Carolina and Georgia, for a total of some 5 percent of all Southern blacks. (These would have constituted considerably more than 5 percent of black adults and of black males, however, since young adult males were disproportionately represented among the fugitives.) But this figure represents only the tip of the iceberg. Many other slaves fled their owners but did not go over to the British. The extent of the loss to slave owners in the lower South is indicated by the sharp decline between 1770 and 1790 in the proportion of the population made up of blacks (almost all of whom were slaves): from 60.5 percent to 43.8 percent in South Carolina and from 45.2 percent to 36.1 percent in Georgia. Philip D. Morgan has estimated that during the Revolution, South Carolina lost about 25,000 slaves (or about 30 percent of the state's slave population) to flight, migration, and death. When one adds to these imprecise estimates the slaves who were freed by emancipation in the North and private manumissions in the South, one can begin to see the magnitude of the jolt the Revolution provided to American slavery.

The Revolutionary era also brought significant changes to the lives of slaves who did not run away, as both masters and bondspeople strove to make sense of radically new conditions. Some, especially in the North and the upper South, received (or were promised) their freedom (see section IV). Increased autonomy also characterized the daily lives of the majority of Southern blacks who remained slaves. This autonomy took strikingly different forms, however, in the upper and lower South.

In the Chesapeake region, the war dealt an added blow to the already faltering tobacco economy and thus accentuated the surplus of slaves. Slack demand for slaves had many consequences, ranging from the proliferation of private manumissions to the cessation of African imports, but one of the most important was a relaxation in the severity of the slave regime and increased opportunity for individuals—especially males—to escape field work and engage in skilled occupations. In Maryland, according to historian Lorena S. Walsh, "ordinary field hands spent more time in self-sufficient activities such as gardening, hunting, and fishing," while agricultural diversification led to a proliferation of new jobs. "By the end of the century many men were performing a greater variety of tasks," she concluded, "and even on large plantations they sometimes worked on special projects by themselves or with only one or two mates and not always under constant supervision."[9] This relaxation was also facilitated by the increasingly creole character of upper-South slaves, whose behavior no longer seemed so "outlandish" to whites as did that of Africans. The largely acculturated slave population enjoyed considerably more "breathing space" than had Africans whose breaking in was thought to require careful supervision of every move.

Slaves who earned the trust of their masters often received increased freedom to dispose of their "spare" time. Those with particular skills were sometimes allowed to hire themselves out, contracting on their own and paying their masters a fixed weekly fee from their earnings, the remainder of which they kept. Far more common were slaves whose masters, having too many hands, hired them out for odd jobs or seasonal work. Although slaves who were hired out were not necessarily treated better than those who were not—hirers has less direct financial incentive than did owners to take good care of their laborers—slave hiring provided slaves with new experiences, contacts (white and black), and knowledge, and broadened their horizons. Trusted slaves visited friends and relatives on nearby holdings and also increasingly interacted with whites in the revival meetings that converted whites and blacks alike to evangelical Christianity. Increased freedom of action for slaves went hand in hand, ironically, with growing contact between white and black.

This loosening of controls in no way implies that slaves had come to accept their servitude, except in the sense that they made the best of the circumstances in which they found themselves. They continued to run away, with fugitives now for the first time having the prospect of securing freedom in the North. And the Gabriel Prosser conspiracy of 1800, a carefully planned but abortive uprising in which thousands of blacks were to attack Richmond, shows the potential for armed rebellion in even the most trusted, "acculturated" slaves. In a number of ways the Prosser uprising, nipped in the bud after being revealed to authorities by a black informer, bears the mark of the Revolutionary age, for if the uprising's planning was facilitated by the easy association and relaxed controls prevalent at the time, its leaders seem to have been influenced by the era's rhetoric of liberty. Perhaps too much should not be made of the conspirators' ideology. Blind hatred of slavery—and of those responsible for it—motivated participants far more than abstract theories of the social good; as one recruit coolly stated, "I could kill a white man as free as eat." Still, a number of reports indicated that the rebels had planned to spare Quakers, Methodists, and Frenchmen because they were "friendly to liberty."[10] Clearly, many black Virginians were aware of the "outside" world—and of the contradiction between the "liberty" their masters invoked and the slavery they practiced.

Slave autonomy in the lower South manifested itself very differently. The coastal low country of South Carolina and Georgia was dominated by a black majority—with a heavy African component—who often saw little of their owners. In two ways the Revolution acted to accentuate this distinctive pattern. Wartime disruption and the military obligations of whites increased the existing tendency toward owner absenteeism and further isolated the slave population from white Southerners; as one historian put it, "wartime anarchy created a power vacuum in the countryside that allowed slaves to expand their liberty."[11] A postwar surge in slave arrivals from Africa, prompted in part by a conscious effort to make up for the heavy wartime losses and in part by a determination to secure as many laborers as possible while the federal government still tolerated the importation of slaves, reinforced this black isolation and sharply differentiated the low country from the Chesapeake, where the turn of the nineteenth century was a time of growing cultural interaction between white and black. During the late eighteenth century, notable features of low-country slave life—owner absenteeism, slave isolation, the task system, the internal slave economy—became more pronounced, even as Gullah took root as the embodiment of the region's cultural distinctiveness.

The Revolutionary era, in short, saw the further differentiation of upper from lower South, although increased slave autonomy characterized both sections. In the Chesapeake region, an overwhelmingly creole slave population lived in close physical and cultural contact with whites, many of whom exercised relatively loose control over their slaves and expressed heightened concern for their physical and spiritual well-being. In the coastal region of the lower South, most blacks lived in a world of their own, largely isolated from whites, and developed their own culture and way of life; into this world poured tens of thousands of Africans imported in a last surge by labor-hungry planters anxious to beat the anticipated cutoff of the slave trade in 1808. Although these regional distinctions would persist in the nineteenth century, the contrast between upper South and lower South would never be so great as it was during the years immediately following the War for Independence.

IV

THE REVOLUTIONARY ERA also saw an increasing gap between the South as a whole, where slavery survived the challenge to its legitimacy and remained firmly entrenched, and the North, where slavery gradually gave way to freedom, albeit a severely restrictive freedom. Because the Revolution was waged for "liberty," and generated an enormous amount of rhetoric about despotism, tyranny, justice, equality, and natural rights, it inevitably raised questions about slavery, questions that seemed all the more pertinent in view of the determined efforts of slaves to gain their own freedom, and it is no accident that the United States was the first country to take significant (although ultimately limited) action against the peculiar institution. Patriots commonly denounced the "slavery" they suffered at the hands of the British, and insisted that they would rather die than remain slaves; although there was considerable hyberbole in this rhetoric—clearly Patriots did not believe that they were slaves in the same sense their own chattels were—the irony of fighting a war for liberty at the same time that they held one-third of their own population as slaves was not lost upon them. They might not have liked the way British Tory author Samuel Johnson phrased the matter when he asked rhetorically, "How is it that we hear the loudest *yelps* for liberty among the drivers of negroes?" but they were acutely aware of the problem.[12]

Whites in the Revolutionary era were by no means united on the question of slavery. A few Americans became abolitionists, arguing for the immediate and unconditional freeing of all slaves; although abolition societies emerged in the South as well as the North, they were heavily dominated by Quakers and became progressively rarer as one moved farther south. Others took action to end their own association with what they regarded as an immoral practice, providing freedom for their slaves either immediately or (like George Washington) in their wills. Even among the great majority of slave owners who never freed their slaves, however, there was widespread unease about an institution that seemed backward and unenlightened. Many agreed with Thomas Jefferson that slavery was wrong, both for moral and practical reasons, and would if properly curtailed suffer a gradual and peaceful death.

Indeed, the Founding Fathers took a series of steps designed to bring about slavery's gradual demise. As children of the Enlightenment, they typically abjured hasty or radical measures that would disrupt society, preferring cautious acts that would induce sustained, long-term progress; rather than a frontal assault on the peculiar institution, they favored a strategy of chipping away at it where it was weakest. Still, there seemed reason to believe—although time would ultimately prove otherwise—that these acts had contained American slavery and put it on the road to gradual extinction.

Much of the action on slavery during the Revolutionary era occurred at the state level. In the upper South, the state legislatures of Virginia, Maryland, and Delaware revised their laws on manumission, making it easier during the 1780s and 1790s for masters to free their bondspeople. (From 1723 to 1782, private acts of manumission had been illegal in Virginia.) In those states (and to a lesser extent in North Carolina and in the new state of Kentucky), prompted by both principled opposition to slavery and a reduced demand for labor stemming from the downturn in tobacco cultivation, growing numbers of slave owners took advantage of the new laws to free some or all of their slaves. Some masters manumitted only a few select favorites; others, such as George Washington, John Randolph, and Robert Carter III, provided in their wills for the freedom of all their slaves, thereby securing emotional benefit without suffering financial loss. (Legal complications, however, prevented most of Randolph's and Carter's slaves from ever receiving their freedom, and Washington lacked the legal authority to free the numerous "dower Negroes" belonging to his wife, Martha, from a previous marriage; of 277 Washington slaves, 124 belonged to George at the time of his death in 1799, while 153 belonged to Martha.) A smaller number of slaveholders—often Quakers—followed to the end the logic of their antislavery convictions and freed all their slaves immediately. Acts of private manumission freed thousands of blacks in the upper South following the Revolution, and for the first time, especially in Delaware and parts of Maryland, seemed to threaten the very survival of slavery; in Delaware, three-quarters of all blacks were free by 1810 (see table 2 and section V, below).

Farther north, state action was more decisive. Because slaves in the Northern states formed only a small proportion of the population and constituted a minor economic interest, abolishing the peculiar institution in an era that celebrated liberty and natural rights proved relatively easy, although often painfully slow. During the three decades following the outbreak of the Revolutionary War, every Northern state initiated complete slave emancipation. The process varied considerably. In some states, emancipation was immediate: the Vermont constitution of 1777 prohibited slavery, and soon thereafter Massachusetts courts, reacting to a series of freedom suits brought by blacks themselves, interpreted that state's constitution as outlawing slavery, too; as the state's chief justice put it in 1781, "there can be no such thing as perpetual servitude of a rational creature."[13] In most Northern states, however, especially those with a significant slave population, emancipation was gradual, so as to provide as little shock to society (and the masters' pocketbooks) as possible. According to Pennsylvania's law of 1780—the first of five gradual-emancipation acts passed by Northern states—all future-born slaves would become free at age twenty-eight. New York's law of 1799 freed future-born boys at age twenty-eight and girls at twenty-five; New Jersey's act of 1804 (the last emancipation act of a Northern state) was similar, but provided that boys would receive freedom at age twenty-five and girls at twenty-one. Because these gradual-emancipation laws freed no one actually in bondage at the time of their passage, and freed children subsequently born into slavery only when they reached adulthood, the North contained a small number of slaves well into the nineteenth century. By 1810, however, about three-quarters of all Northern blacks were free, and within a generation virtually all would be.

Complementing the abolition acts of individual Northern states was legislation by Congress to restrict the geographical scope of slavery. Because the western territories were largely unsettled (except by Indians), the movement to prohibit the spread of slavery there did not challenge vested interests in the same way that the movement to abolish slavery in existing states did, and received considerable support from those convinced that slavery, although wrong, could not be immediately ended in the South. In 1784, a bill drafted by Jefferson, which would have barred slavery from all the western territories after 1800, was defeated by a single vote. Three years later, the Northwest Ordinance did abolish slavery in a vast area north of the Ohio River known as the Northwest Territory, including the present states of Ohio, Indiana, Illinois, Michigan, and Wisconsin.

The African slave trade, viewed as deplorable even by many defenders of slavery, was also the object of considerable legislation, at both the state and the national level. Widespread opposition to the trade in the North and upper South led the second Continental Congress to pass a resolution opposing slave imports in 1776, and a number of states (including Virginia in 1778) banned such imports on their own. In the upper South, economic depression sharply reduced the demand for new slaves, and the happy convergence of economic interest with principle easily carried the day. Farther south, however, in South Carolina and Georgia, planters suffered from an acute shortage of labor and bitterly resisted what they considered the hypocritical efforts of those who now had enough slaves suddenly to force others to do without.

Although advocates of the slave trade represented a small minority among the Founding Fathers, they were powerful enough to force a compromise on the question at the Constitutional Convention of 1787: the new Constitution prohibited Congress from outlawing the slave trade for twenty years. During this period, labor-hungry planters in the lower South imported tens of thousands of Africans; indeed, more slaves entered the United States between 1787 and 1807 than during any other two decades in history. Still, the general understanding among those who were politically active was that Congress would abolish the slave trade at the end of twenty years, an expectation that was borne out by congressional legislation passed in 1807 and taking effect in 1808. In their usual cautious, roundabout manner, the Founding Fathers succeeded in ending the importation of Africans to the United States; many believed, incorrectly, that this ending would doom slavery in the United States as well.

The Constitutional Convention showed the Founding Fathers at their most cautious with respect to slavery. In drafting the Constitution, they carefully avoided the word "slavery," resorting to a variety of euphemisms such as "other persons" and "person[s] held to service or labor." At the same time, they acceded to slaveholding interests by recognizing the right of masters to reclaim fugitives and by unanimously accepting a compromise formula whereby for purposes of congressional representation a slave would count as three-fifths of a free person, thereby substantially augmenting the political power of the Southern states. In the future, both supporters and opponents of slavery would wrap themselves in the Constitution and claim to be expressing the views of the Founding Fathers. In fact, although most of the decisions taken by the delegates at the Constitutional Convention represented compromises rather than clear-cut victories for pro-slavery or anti-slavery forces, on balance the Constitution bolstered slavery by throwing the power of the federal government behind it.

Still, to many informed Americans in the 1790s, time seemed to be on the side of reason, reform, and progress. The Northern states were in the process of abolishing slavery within their borders. Congress had acted to guarantee that the Northwest would be forever free. The laws of several Southern states had been changed to facilitate private manumissions, and hundreds of slave owners in the upper South were taking advantage of these laws to free some or all of their chattels. And although importation of new slaves remained legal in South Carolina and Georgia, a compromise had been worked out that would end such importation in 1808. In short, a moderate opponent of slavery—like many of the Founding Fathers—had good grounds for being cautiously optimistic. Slavery appeared to be in full retreat, its end only a matter of time.

V

THE REVOLUTIONARY and post-Revolutionary years saw the emergence, for the first time, of a large community of free blacks. They escaped slavery in a variety of ways, ranging from state-enacted emancipation in the North to private manumissions and flight in the South. Some in the upper South were the beneficiaries of sweeping acts by individual slaveholders who, prompted by newly felt moral qualms, freed all their bondspeople; others were objects of selected manumissions by less idealistic masters—most commonly in the upper South but also in the lower South—of particular favorites (including their own children); others still, especially in the border states, were discharged from bondage because they were old and no longer able to perform useful labor. Slaves who were able to earn money could sometimes purchase their own freedom. Fugitives escaped slavery by fleeing to the North, especially from the border states of Maryland, Delaware, and Kentucky, and by blending with free blacks in cities such as Baltimore and Charleston. In addition, during the 1790s and 1800s, hundreds of free, light-skinned refugees from Saint Domingue entered the United States, concentrating in Charleston, Savannah, and New Orleans, much to the alarm of local whites.

In sheer numbers, the growth of the free black population was staggering. Although statistics on free blacks before the Revolution are lacking, it is clear that there were few; as late as 1782, only about 1,800 out of 220,582 black Virginians—less than one per-cent—were free. Between 1780 and 1810, however, the number of free blacks in Virginia surged, reaching 12,766 (4.2 percent) in 1790 and 30,570 (7.2 percent) by 1810. In the United States as a whole, the number of free blacks rose to 59,466 (7.9 percent of all blacks) in 1790 and 186,446 (13.5 percent) in 1810. Over half these free blacks were concentrated in the upper South, where more than 10 percent of all blacks were free by 1810. As a proportion of the black population, however, free blacks were most numerous in the North; by 1810 three-quarters of Northern blacks were free, and by 1840 virtually all were. In the lower South, by contrast, the number of free blacks grew far more modestly, from 1.6 percent of the black population in 1790 to 3.9 percent in 1810. At the latter date in South Carolina and Georgia, only about 2 percent of all blacks were free. (For statistics documenting this section, see table 2.)

It was this post-Revolutionary beginning that provided the basis for the South's free black population in the antebellum period, for after 1810, few slaves were freed. The proportion of blacks who were free grew slightly in the upper South, from 10.4 percent in

1810 to 12.8 percent in 1860, primarily because of a surge of manumissions in Delaware, which by the mid-nineteenth century had become virtually a free state, and in Maryland, which, as historian Barbara J. Fields has shown, was threatening to do so; in 1860, 91.7 percent of Delaware's and 49.1 percent of Maryland's black population was free. In the lower South, by contrast, the proportion of free blacks decreased after 1810, as state after state passed new laws restricting manumission and harrassing those who had been manumitted, and after 1840 the absolute number decreased as well. By 1860, only 1.5 percent of deep-South blacks were free, and half of these lived in Louisiana. In Mississippi, free blacks constituted only 0.2 percent of the population. The great majority of free blacks in the antebellum South were descendants of those who received their freedom between 1780 and 1810.

There were significant regional variations in the status and character of the free black population, both between North and South and within the South. Northern blacks, although free, were objects of both legal discrimination and vicious hostility. Excluded from most public schools, denied the right to vote (except in Maine, Vermont, New Hampshire, Massachusetts, and—if they could meet a property requirement—New York), forbidden by (sporadically enforced) law from entering many states, jeered at and at times physically attacked by whites who refused to work with them or live near them, blacks quickly came to appreciate the difference between freedom and equality. Although their legal rights were usually greater than those of free blacks in the South, and a few of them achieved wealth and prominence, most Northern blacks were relegated to menial occupations such as day laborers and domestic servants. They constituted a highly urban population: more than three-fifths lived in cities at a time when fewer than one-fifth of all Americans did.

Although there were relatively few free blacks in the deep South, their condition was, ironically, in many respects better than that of those in the upper South. An unusually high proportion of them were elite people of "color"—neither physically nor mentally black—who set themselves apart from the mass of slaves. This was especially true of descendants of French and Spanish colonists who lived along the Gulf of Mexico and called themselves "Creoles" to indicate their ancestry. (White descendants of the French and Spanish commonly referred to *themselves* as "Creoles" and refused to use the term to apply to people of African origin. Note that in both of these cases, the meaning of "Creole" differs substantially from that of "creole," used earlier in this book.) In Mobile, Pensacola, and especially in New Orleans, these light-skinned Creoles prided themselves on their wealth, breeding, heritage, and membership in exclusive organizations such as Mobile's Creole Fire Company Number 1 and New Orleans' octoroon balls. Refugees from Saint Domingue brought similar attitudes with them when they settled in New Orleans, Savannah, and Charleston.

The free black population in the lower South, unlike that in the North or upper South, was overwhelmingly light-skinned; in 1860, the census categorized about three-quarters of lower-South free blacks (and more than four-fifths of those in Louisiana) as mulattoes. A majority of these "free colored" were, like their cousins in the North, urban dwellers, although the South was, overall, overwhelmingly rural. Although most of them could hardly be termed wealthy—and many supported themselves through a variety of menial occupations including day labor, domestic service, and prostitution—they occupied many skilled positions, and held a near monopoly on some important service occupations such as barbering. A significant minority, both urban and rural, *were* wealthy. In Louisiana's Natchitoches Parish a colony of free Creoles, descended from an eighteenth-century French settler and an African slave, grew and flourished until by 1860 it contained 411 persons who owned 276 slaves; equally remarkable was the free South Carolina family whose patriarch, cotton gin maker and planter William Ellison, owned 63 slaves in 1840.

The position of elite free blacks in the deep South was never secure, but because they were few in number and seemed so different from the mass of slaves—a difference they strove to accentuate—they usually received at least grudging toleration from prominent whites whose favor they strove to curry. In southern Louisiana especially, but to a lesser extent elsewhere along the Gulf Coast as well as in Charleston and Savannah, many whites followed a practice common in much of Latin America but rare in most of the United States of distinguishing between mulattoes, especially their own sons and daughters, and blacks. As a Louisiana judge ruled in 1850, in allowing a free Negro to testify against whites, many of the state's free population were "respectable" as well as "enlightened by education, and the instances are by no means rare in which they are large property holders . . . , such persons as courts and juries would not hesitate to believe under oath."[14]

The vast majority of the South's free blacks, however—about 85 percent—lived under very different circumstances in the upper South. They were darker, poorer, less urban, and less educated than those farther south; only about one-third were mulattoes or resided in cities. They typically lived on the margins of society, as farmhands, casual laborers, and occasionally small landowners, shunned by most whites and isolated from most slaves. Those who lived in cities—Baltimore and Washington, D.C., contained most of the region's urban free blacks—worked as domestics, day laborers, factory hands, and artisans and usually lacked the elitist pretensions evident in the lower South. Where they were able, they often fraternized with (and sometimes married) slaves.

Wherever they lived, free blacks faced hardship, persecution, and physical insecurity, all of which grew after 1850 as the Fugitive Slave Act increased the risk in the North of being kidnapped into slavery and concerted action in the South threatened more stringent enforcement of existing restrictive legislation; in the deep South, free blacks were sometimes pressured into enslaving themselves to masters of their own choice, and the free black population actually declined. Faced with such implacable white hostility, free blacks turned increasingly inward to their own community organizations, the most important of which were the independent "African" churches that emerged in the 1780s and 1790s; in Philadelphia, for example, the Free African Society, a quasi-religious organization founded in 1787 by former slaves Richard Allen and Absalom Jones, spawned a number of churches, the most influential of which was Allen's Bethel Church, which in 1816 expanded to form the African Methodist Episcopal Church. Overwhelmingly Baptist and Methodist, African churches flourished openly in major cities of the North and were sometimes tolerated in the urban South. Free blacks also set up schools for their children (usually clandestinely in the South) and formed a wide variety of mutual-aid associations to provide members with benefits such as burial and insurance.

During the crisis of the 1850s, free blacks not only turned inward but also increasingly looked outward, as some concluded that white America would never provide a hospitable environment and viewed with increasing favor the prospect of emigration to Liberia. Although only a small number of blacks actually moved to Africa, the heightened interest in emigration was a sign of the growing pessimism that gripped many free blacks during the 1850s, for emigrationist sentiment has always been a key index of black attitudes toward white America, rising during times of particular hardship and receding during periods of hope and progress.

Most free blacks, however, rejected the notion of emigrating to Africa, for they saw themselves as (and indeed were) quintessentially American and looked upon Africa as a distant and savage land. (The idea of sending blacks "back" to Africa drew more support from whites who sought to remove a thorn in the side of the slave regime or to "purify" America than from blacks who sought to improve their status.) In the North, they fought for their own rights by holding "colored conventions" in which they promoted common interests and cautiously demanded equal treatment, and they worked as abolitionists to promote the rights of those blacks still in slavery; in 1829, David Walker stirred (and in some cases alarmed) free blacks throughout America with his "incendiary" booklet *An Appeal to the Colored Citizens of the World*, in which he denounced slavery as a crime against humanity and called for its violent overthrow. Despite all the disabilities they faced, even in the South free blacks were sometimes able, as historian Loren Schweninger has recently demonstrated, to acquire impressive quantities of wealth, often with the help of particular whites who acted as their sponsors and protectors. Although most free blacks in the South remained propertyless, one of every six rural family heads in Maryland and Virginia owned land in 1860, and one in seven urban families in the upper South owned real estate.

However oppressive "freedom" was for blacks in America, it remained far preferable to slavery. Blacks made this preference clear when they "voted with their feet": tens of thousands put themselves in mortal peril to escape slavery, but virtually none voluntarily gave up freedom for bondage.

VI

DESPITE THE HOPES AROUSED during and immediately after the American Revolution, Southern slavery survived the era intact. The reform spirit had never spread very far in the lower South, where most slave owners seemed far more concerned with securing additional African laborers before the 1808 deadline than with the moral ambiguities of holding humans in bondage. And in the upper South, the kind of moderate questioning of slavery that was so pervasive in the 1770s and 1780s declined during the 1790s and early 1800s, as a new orthodoxy increasingly took hold of the region. During the Revolutionary era, the South was home to much of the most liberal social thought in America, as the "great generation" wrestled with the problem of slavery, challenged traditional religious doctrine, and championed a republicanism that when pushed to its Jeffersonian limits had a strong egalitarian thrust. During the post-Revolutionary years, however, the South began a retreat from this liberalism, a retreat that would in the antebellum years leave the section the undisputed home of conservatism.

As in the growth of Revolutionary-era liberalism, a number of factors helped bring about its decline. A reaction against the more radical tendencies present in the American Revolution—spurred in part by revulsion over the excesses of the French Revolution— increasingly led statesmen in the new nation to espouse a conservative strand of republican thought that emphasized protection of property and order rather than equality. (In the Declaration of Independence, Jefferson had substituted "life, liberty and the pursuit of happiness" for John Locke's "life, liberty and property.") By the time of his death in 1809, Thomas Paine, that fiery exponent of republican egalitarianism who had at one time captured the imagination of a fledgling nation struggling against despotism and privilege, was widely reviled as a radical and an infidel; the former hero died in obscure poverty, his funeral attended by only six persons, including a Quaker and two blacks.

A similar trend was evident in Southern religion. Revolutionary-era Southerners had been among the least orthodox of Americans. Calvinist-oriented Northerners had long derided Southerners for not taking their religion seriously enough; Presbyterian tutor Philip Fithian, who spent 1773–74 on the plantation of Robert Carter III, filled his diary with scathing comments about the perfunctory nature of religious behavior among Virginia Anglicans. During the Revolutionary era, this tendency toward religious moderation was supplemented by a new challenge to established tenets that took the dual forms of a rational questioning of Christian faith epitomized by the Deism that captivated many gentry intellectuals, and of an evangelical recommitment to that faith that brought with it an egalitarian emphasis on the equality of all souls, white and black, before God. The 1790s and 1800s, however, saw a sharp reversal of this trend toward religious unorthodoxy, as Deism—and reason in general— lost its appeal to white Southerners, at the same time that evangelical Christianity lost much of its egalitarian thrust. Baptism and Methodism continued their advance throughout the South, but their message was no longer tinged with anti-slavery overtones. Indeed, during the antebellum years, the Southern churches would become bulwarks of the peculiar institution, and Southern religious spokesmen would lead the way in developing arguments in its behalf.

Economic considerations reinforced this new conservatism. If the tobacco crisis that gripped much of the Chesapeake region had facilitated moderate opposition to slavery, Southern economic expansion in the early nineteenth century had the opposite effect, for people are much less likely to question an institution when they are making money from it hand over fist than when they are suffering from hard times. Although tobacco never fully recovered its position of dominance in the upper South, and conditions in much of the Chesapeake remained depressed until the 1830s, the South as a whole experienced substantial economic growth, based primarily on a surge in the planting of cotton (see chapter 4, section II). This surge brought a sharp increase in demand for labor at precisely the same time that the importation of new slaves was being ended, and therefore resulted in a substantial increase in slave prices throughout the South. Ironically, ending the slave trade may have strengthened the commitment of Southern whites to slavery, both by putting upward pressure on slave prices and by removing the most easily identifiable barbarity associated with the slave regime.

The changing intellectual climate of the post-Revolutionary South had a major impact on attitudes toward slavery. Whereas many well-intentioned Southerners in the 1780s could legitimately believe that slavery had been placed on the road to gradual extinction and that "enlightened" sentiment would gradually become more and more opposed to the peculiar institution, a generation later it was clear that this was not to be. Not only did natural population growth among slaves mean that Southern slavery could, unlike slavery elsewhere in the New World, continue to flourish even after African imports were cut off; Southern white opinion moved steadily away from the moderate, rational questioning of slavery shown by many of the Founding Fathers. If these leaders abandoned much of their youthful liberalism, their children revealed little of the moral ambivalence and few of the doubts their parents felt about slavery. The Revolutionary-era challenge to slavery proved to be a short-lived phenomenon.

This development may be clearly illustrated by examining Thomas Jefferson's changing attitude toward slavery. Jefferson never renounced his belief that slavery was wrong, but as he aged he abandoned his youthful conviction that it could readily be abolished. In his original draft of the Declaration of Independence, rejected as too inflammatory by the Continental Congress, he had denounced George III for foisting slavery on the colonies, noting that that monarch "waged cruel war against human nature itself, violating the most sacred right of life and liberty in the persons of a distant people who never offended him." Unlike many others of his generation, however, Jefferson harbored serious doubts that blacks' "depravity" could be attributed entirely to their slave status, and he expressed strong views on what he considered their innate racial characteristics. In his celebrated *Notes on the State of Virginia* (written in 1781–82 and published in 1785), he argued that blacks were physically unattractive—maintaining that they displayed a "preference" for whites "as uniformly as is the preference of the Oranootan for the black woman over those of his own species"—stressed their deficiency in reasoning, and proclaimed that "in imagination they are dull, tasteless, and anomalous."

Jefferson's opposition to slavery always rested more on the harm it did to whites than on the harm it did to blacks, and after the Revolution he grew increasingly cautious in his criticism of the peculiar institution, increasingly concerned about the perils of too reckless an assault on the very basis of the South's social fabric. By 1805, although still believing that anti-slavery sentiment was on the rise, Jefferson admitted that he had "long since given up the expectation of any early provision for the extinguishment of slavery among us." Nine years later, forced to concede that emancipation sentiment was not spreading among the next generation, he had abandoned hope for any near-term end to slavery, contenting himself instead with advocating humane treatment of its victims: "My opinion has ever been that, until more can be done for them, we should endeavor, with those whom fortune has thrown on our hands, to feed & clothe them well, protect them from ill usage, require such reasonable labor only as is performed voluntarily by freemen, and be led by no repugnancies to abdicate them, and our duties to them. The laws do not permit us to turn them loose, [even] if that were for their good."

Even this retreat to benevolent stewardship did not, however, represent Jefferson's ultimate position. By 1819, he had come to identify almost wholly with the defense of Southern "rights" against those who would limit the spread of slavery into Missouri. Espousing the casuistic doctrine that the expansion of slavery would actually weaken the institution, by bringing about its "diffusion," the Sage of Monticello in his more honest moments expressed the Southern dilemma with brutal frankness: "We have the wolf by the ears," he declared in 1820, "and we can neither hold him, nor safely let him go. Justice is in one scale, and self-preservation in the other."[15]

Lacking Jefferson's introspective ambivalence, most Southern whites came to accept slavery as a legitimate if not yet necessarily desirable institution, and the early nineteenth century saw a general hardening of sentiment on the subject. As evangelical Protestants made their peace with the peculiar institution, active support for abolitionism was more and more confined to Quakers, who represented a tiny fraction of the population; 78 percent of the leaders of the North Carolina Manumission Society in the 1790s were Quakers. Panicky reaction to the Saint Domingue revolution of the 1790s and Gabriel Prosser's abortive uprising of 1800 dealt a further blow to what remained of Southern abolitionist sentiment—and organization—among non-Quakers; by the early nineteenth century, abolitionism was virtually nonexistent in the deep South and increasingly limited in the upper South to small pockets of dissenters on the fringes of society.

Private manumissions, by which thousands of blacks had received their freedom in the 1780s and 1790s, also declined precipitously in the nineteenth century (although they never ceased altogether). Concern for order, property rights, and their own economic security exceeded interest in the rights of their slaves among all but the most exceptional slave owners; even Jefferson failed to free his slaves, either during his lifetime or upon his death. Changing attitudes toward manumission were evident not only in the behavior of individuals but also in the actions of state legislatures, which, one after another, beginning with South Carolina in 1800, moved to restrict the slaves' access to freedom. Although state laws varied slightly, those in the lower South typically barred private manumissions without legislative approval, and those in the upper South (such as Virginia's act of 1806) required newly freed blacks to leave the state or face reenslavement. Laws expelling free blacks were not always strictly enforced, but they sent the clear message that most Southern whites regarded the existence of free blacks in their midst as a troublesome anomaly; the only proper status of blacks in white society was that of slave.

Formal defense of slavery did not yet reach the crescendo that it would during the late antebellum period, but here, too, the trend was clear. If the Revolutionary era saw the first sustained attack on slavery in the South, that attack was met by the first sustained defense of it; what is more, whereas the attack was feeble and short-lived, the defense would prove remarkably hardy and persistent. Most early arguments in defense of slavery were tentative and practical and lacked the later boastful assertions that slavery provided the best possible form of social organization. Still, many of the racial, religious, and paternalistic arguments that would flourish during the three decades before the Civil War were already evident in embryonic form during the late eighteenth century. Five pro-slavery petitions, signed by 1,244 persons and presented to the Virginia legislature in 1784 and 1785, asserted that emancipation was "exceedingly *impolitic*" because it would produce "Want, Poverty, Distress, and Ruin to the Free Citizen"; they also appealed to property rights, however, proclaimed that slavery was best for the slaves, pointed to biblical precedent, and warned of "the Horrors of all the Rapes, Murders, and Outrages, which a vast Multitude of unprincipled, unpropertied, revengeful, and remorseless Banditti are capable of perpetrating."[16]

Indeed, the Revolution clearly served to accentuate two themes that would be central to Southern white thought in the antebellum years. One was the racial component in the defense of slavery. Although the Revolution did not immediately democratize American society, it produced an egalitarian republicanism that posed a severe problem for those who would defend slavery: if all men were created equal, how could some hold others in bondage? As Duncan J. MacLeod and other scholars have pointed out, the only logical answer to this question (aside from replying that they could not) was to assert that those held as slaves were somehow so different from free Americans that they were not entitled to the same rights and privileges. Because race was the most easily identifiable difference, it became an increasingly important justification for slavery; the assumption that blacks were not fit for freedom was crucial to the defense of slavery in an era of liberty and equality. Although arguments for the innate inferiority of blacks to whites were not fully elaborated until later, a new racism was one of the ironic byproducts of Revolutionary-era republicanism.

Equally problematical—and significant for the future—was the reconciliation of liberty and slavery, terms that in other times and places have seemed to be diametric opposites. The concept of liberty, like that of rights, assumes for most present-day readers, as it did for most antebellum Northerners, an abstract character. Its origin and early usage, however, were often much more specific and were related to custom, tradition, and interest: just as slaves commonly viewed as theirs by right the little privileges that were extended to them (such as the "rights" to cultivate garden plots and enjoy certain holidays), so, too, colonists put great stock in the "English liberties" they enjoyed by tradition, and viewed the abrogation of those liberties as signs of monarchical despotism.

Although the Revolution fostered an abstracted sense of rights— specific "liberties," enjoyed by specific groups, became a generalized "liberty" belonging to all—many Southerners continued to use the term in the older sense. According to this usage, infringing on their right to own slaves was a violation of their liberty. In this manner, Southerners in the antebellum period were able to portray themselves as both ardent defenders of slavery (that is, of blacks) and equally ardent proponents of liberty (that is, their own). To many Northerners, the simultaneous defense of liberty and slavery seemed patently hypocritical. To defenders of slavery, however, the right to own slaves was *their* most important liberty (the meaning of which came close to the right to pursue one's own interest); indeed, they insisted that to deprive them of the right to own slaves would be to subject them to slavery (just as the Patriots had argued that the British, in infringing on their traditional liberties, were subjecting them to slavery).

Although formal articulation of these arguments was still in its infancy at the beginning of the nineteenth century, it was clear that Southern slavery had survived the multiple threats it faced during the Revolutionary era and, like steel tempered by fire, had emerged from that era stronger than ever. Before the Revolution, Southern whites had generally taken slavery for granted. The Revolutionary ferment, both physical and intellectual, forced them to grapple with the question of slavery's morality and utility and, after a brief period of uncertainty, left them far more committed to the peculiar institution than they had previously been. With emancipation in the North, slavery became ever more deeply identified with the South, Southern interests, and the Southern way of life. The next time Southern whites fought for their "liberty," it would be explicitly for their rights as slave owners.

4

Antebellum Slavery: Organization, Control, Paternalism

I

DURING THE THREE-QUARTERS of a century following the War for Independence, American slavery, although increasingly confined to the South, underwent massive expansion. The 697,897 slaves counted by the first federal census in 1790 increased by more than 70 percent, to 1,191,354, by 1810, two years after the end of legal importation of slaves; during the next fifty years the slave population more than tripled, reaching 3,953,760 in 1860 (see table 3). Geographic expansion was equally striking. Before the Revolution, American slavery, like the non-Indian population, was confined to a string of colonies along the Eastern Seaboard; by 1860, it had spread to nine new states and reached more than halfway across the American continent, into Texas. Because the growth of a vast Southern empire based on slave labor coincided with the gradual emancipation of the North's relatively few remaining slaves, the fate of the South became increasingly associated, both in people's minds and in fact, with that of slavery. In 1750, slavery existed in all the American colonies, and in most of the New World; a century later, the "slave South" stood increasingly alone, joined in the Western Hemisphere only by Brazil and the Spanish islands of Cuba and Puerto Rico. Slavery had become the South's "peculiar institution."

As slavery in the South became more and more distinctively Southern, it underwent further changes, some of which represented continuations of trends previously evident and others of which were new developments. Patterns of behavior that had been tentative became more firmly entrenched as people who were increasingly third-, fourth-, and fifth-generation slaves and masters confronted one another. Masters expressed growing concern for the well-being of their "people," and the material treatment of most slaves improved. At the same time, slave owners renewed their efforts to promote slave dependence and docility, sharply curtailed manumissions, and imposed new restrictions on the actions of both slaves and free blacks. These two trends, although apparently contradictory, were in fact closely linked, for as Southern whites grew increasingly committed to their peculiar institution and took measures to defend it, they also sought to demonstrate, both to themselves and to outside critics, its basic humaneness (and hence its defensibility). Antebellum Southern slavery became both more rigid and more paternalistic; in the process, it also became increasingly distinctive.

II

EXPECTATIONS THAT ENDING the African slave trade would put slavery on the road to gradual extinction proved radically wide of the mark. During the half century after the legal end of slave importation, the slave population of the United States surpassed not only that of any other country in the New World, but, after abolition of slavery in the British colonies in the 1830s, that of all of them combined. This growth was entirely the result of natural increase, for the small number of slaves smuggled into the United States was probably exceeded by the number who escaped from slavery. What is more, although slavery disappeared from the Northern states and seemed well on the road to extinction in Delaware and parts of Maryland, in the South as a whole it showed no sign of retreat: in 1860, as in 1790, slaves constituted about one-third of the Southern population.

The peculiar institution owed much of its persistence in antebellum years to cotton, a crop grown only in very limited quantities in the colonial period. The widespread introduction of steam power in British industry in the late eighteenth century sharply lowered the cost of spinning cotton into yarn and weaving that yarn into fabric, and created a burgeoning demand for American cotton; similar mechanization, although based primarily at first on waterpower, occurred in the Northeastern United States. Prompted by this new demand, planters along the coast of Georgia and South Carolina increased the cultivation of cotton during the post-Revolutionary years. The long-staple cotton raised in the low country, however, could not flourish inland, and substantial production of short-staple cotton, which could, was for years blocked by the time and expense needed to separate its seeds—which clung far more tenaciously to the cotton than did those of the long-staple variety—from the fiber. Given the heightened demand for cotton, invention of an improved cotton gin in 1793 was not entirely fortuitous; had Eli Whitney not come up with a device capable of efficiently separating the seeds from the fiber of short-staple cotton, someone else surely would have. In an immediate sense, however, the invention made possible the emergence of the cotton South.

It is almost impossible to overemphasize the importance of cotton to the antebellum Southern (and indeed American) economy. Annual cotton production rose from about 3,000 bales in 1790 to 178,000 in 1810, and then surged more than twentyfold during the next half century, surpassing 4 million bales on the eve of the Civil War. About three-quarters of this cotton was exported, principally to Britain, and throughout most of the antebellum period, cotton not only constituted the United States' leading export but exceeded in dollar value all other exports combined. Cotton provided the basis for the first significant growth of the factory system in New England and thus played a leading role in that section's industrialization. But for our purposes, cotton was most important because of its close association with slavery. Like tobacco in the colonial Chesapeake region and rice on the South Carolina and Georgia coast, cotton created a seemingly insatiable demand for slave labor.

Cotton cultivation, which required a growing season of at least two hundred frostless days, was confined primarily to the deep South. At the turn of the nineteenth century, this meant Georgia, South Carolina, and the southeast corner of North Carolina, but as Southerners moved west, so, too, did cotton; although the seaboard states continued to grow the crop, as did newly settled states such as Arkansas, Florida, and Texas, production was increasingly concentrated in Alabama, Mississippi, and Louisiana. As early as 1834, those three states grew more than half the nation's cotton, and by 1859, together with Georgia, they produced 79 percent. The share produced by the Carolinas, by contrast, fell from 60 percent in 1801 to 10 percent in 1859.

Nevertheless, cotton boosted the economy of all the slave states, cotton-producing or not. Because cotton created an intense demand for slave labor, it led—in conjunction with the closing of the African slave trade—to a rise in slave prices (and hence in the value of slave owners' property), a rise that accelerated from the middle of the 1840s. The cotton boom also enabled slave owners in the non-cotton-producing states to profit from a commodity they did have in abundance: slaves. During the half century preceding the Civil War, slave owners moved hundreds of thousands of "surplus" slaves west, mostly from non-cotton-producing to cotton-producing states. This long-distance migration represented a major new development: American slaves had been subjected to sale in the colonial era, but relatively few had been removed far from their existing homes. By breaking up existing families and forcing slaves to relocate far from everyone and everything they knew, the long-distance domestic slave trade, which reached significant dimensions just when the international slave trade to America was coming to an end, not only replaced that international trade but also replicated (if on a reduced level) many of its horrors.

While precise statistics are lacking, about one million slaves (or almost twice as many as had crossed the Atlantic from Africa to America) moved west between 1790 and 1860. Most of the departures were from Maryland, Virginia, and the Carolinas; the main importing states were at first Kentucky and Tennessee, but after 1810, when the transfer of slaves to the West accelerated, Georgia, Alabama, Mississippi, Louisiana, and Texas received the most. Although the westward movement fluctuated with the economy—peaking during the 1830s, slowing during the depression of the early 1840s, and surging again during the fifteen years before the Civil War—every decade between 1810 and 1860 saw more than 100,000 slave migrants.

Historians disagree over how most slaves moved. The majority of early migrants from the Chesapeake to Kentucky and Tennessee accompanied masters who left home in search of more lucrative opportunities, took their entire work force with them, and resumed operations in a new locale. This transfer of farms and plantations continued during subsequent decades, although its share in the overall westward movement of slaves declined; in their controversial book *Time on the Cross*, econometricians Robert W. Fogel and Stanley L. Engerman maintained that "about 84 percent of the slaves engaged in the westward movement migrated with their owners." Most other scholars assign far greater weight than do Fogel and Engerman to slave sales. In the most recent book on the domestic slave trade, Michael Tadman has estimated that sales accounted for 60 to 70 percent of interregional slave movements, and that "for slave children living in the Upper South in 1820, the cumulative chance of being 'sold South' by 1860 might have been something like 30 percent."[1]

Throughout the antebellum years, professional slave traders scoured the rural areas of the seaboard states, buying up surplus slaves who were then sent west—usually in overland "coffles" but sometimes by boat—where they were eagerly snapped up both in the countryside and in markets of cities such as New Orleans, Natchez, and Montgomery. For enterprising speculators, the slave trade could be a big business; between 1828 and 1836, partners Isaac Franklin and John Armfield, headquartered in Alexandria, Virginia, purchased and resold more than one thousand slaves annually. A disproportionate number of slaves sold west were youths and young adults aged fifteen to twenty-five, but with the exception of those sent to New Orleans, where the demand was for strong young men capable of working in the sugar fields, traders shipped approximately even numbers of males and females; in this respect, the domestic slave trade differed markedly from the transatlantic trade.

Slaves found the westward movement traumatic, whether they accompanied their owners or traders. Sale of any sort was one of the most dreaded events in the life of a slave, but sale to the Southwest meant being permanently separated from home, friends, and often family members, as well as adjusting to a new owner in a new environment. Narratives of former slaves are filled with heartrending recollections of the slave trade. When young Laura Clark was shipped from North Carolina to Alabama in a wagon with nine other children, she was given candy to keep her quiet and did not understand why her mother was so upset; "I knows now," she added sadly, "and I never seed her no mo' in dis life." Most slaves, however, were well aware of what was going on, and later recalled details of their sale with anguish and bitterness. Anne Maddox, sent at age thirteen from Virginia to Alabama, remembered the horror of the auction: "White peoples were dere from everywhere; de face of de earth was covered by dem." Those left behind suffered as well. Virginian Carol Anna Randall described the sale of her sister as "de saddes' thing dat ever happen to me." Slaves in the upper South heard rumors of a far more brutal slavery in Alabama, Mississippi, and Louisiana, and being "sold down the [Mississippi] river" was both a prevalent fear and a threat that masters used to keep their hands in line.[2]

Although the slave trade was extremely lucrative—Tadman estimated that the traders' average annual rate of profit exceeded 30 percent until the 1840s and after then ranged from 15 to 30 percent—it was never entirely respectable. "Polite" sentiment in the South bemoaned the forced separation of family members and looked down on traders as coarse, crude, and mercenary, "Yankee" traits unbefitting a Southern gentleman. Throughout the antebellum years, thoughtful defenders of slavery gave increasing attention to proposals that would impose restrictions on the slave trade, attention that was not entirely fruitless (see below, section VII). Widespread discomfort with the slave trade—upon which all slave property was ultimately based—highlighted a troubling if usually unarticulated contradiction in the thought of slavery's most eloquent defenders: if buying and selling human beings was wrong, it was hard to avoid questioning the legitimacy of owning them.

In part for this reason and in part because of economic imperatives, distaste for the slave trade was never translated into effective action within the South to abolish or even curtail it; indeed, during the 1850s, powerful voices were raised on behalf of pushing pro-slavery policy to its logical conclusion by reopening the African trade. Throughout the antebellum years, sale of slaves from East to West continued to play a vital role in the flourishing of Southern slavery. The trade not only helped spread slavery westward but also contributed to the economic revival of once depressed seaboard states as money poured in from slave sales and as demand for still more slaves in the West put upward pressure on slave prices. During the years preceding the Civil War, slavery, and the Southern economy that was based on it, seemed to be thriving as never before, and expectations that the peculiar institution would wither away had themselves largely withered away. On the eve of the war, it seemed as if Southern slavery would survive for a long time.

III

ANTEBELLUM SLAVERY was a heterogeneous institution, and the slaves faced a wide diversity of conditions. Some lived on large plantations and toiled under the watchful eyes of overseers and drivers, while others, on small farms, worked beside their owners; some had resident masters with whom they came in frequent contact, while others labored for absentee proprietors whom they rarely saw. Small numbers of slaves, especially in South Carolina and Louisiana, belonged to free blacks, and others even had Indian masters: during the antebellum period, leaders of the Cherokee, Chickasaw, Choctaw, and Creek nations consciously appropriated the culture of white Americans—including the ownership of black slaves. Slaves served as preachers, carpenters, blacksmiths, house servants, drivers, and agricultural laborers, and grew a wide variety of crops, including cotton, sugar, rice, tobacco, wheat, corn, and hemp. They faced variations in region and climate as well as in treatment and in owner disposition; some lived on isolated rural holdings, others were able to visit neighboring farms and plantations, and still others resided in urban areas and enjoyed considerable freedom of local movement and association. Such diversity has contributed to sharp disagreement among historians over the nature of Southern slavery, about which virtually every assertion can be challenged with counterexamples.

Still, although there was no *one* slavery that encompassed the experiences of all slaves and masters, one can outline certain dominant patterns even while recognizing the existence of widespread variation. These dominant patterns and variations existed both *among* slaveholdings, and thus affected the slaves collectively (the subject of this section), and *within* slaveholdings, differentiating some slaves' conditions from those of their neighbors (the subject of section IV).

Antebellum slaveholdings, like those in the colonial period, differed from one another in numerous respects, from location and size to crops grown and methods of slave management. Life on a large cotton plantation in Mississippi, where slaves worked in gangs under the watchful eyes of an overseer and drivers, was very different from that on a small hemp-producing farm in Kentucky, where the master personally directed and toiled alongside his hands, and both were far removed from the slavery experienced by blacks in Baltimore or New Orleans. If anything, the range of variations increased over time, with territorial expansion, the emergence of new crops, increased socioeconomic stratification among Southern whites, and the growth of a significant (although still small by Northern standards) urban population.

Nevertheless, in general, Southern slaves continued to live in a distinctive environment that accentuated close contact between master and slave. Most basic was the ratio of slave to free and black to white, a ratio that served to differentiate the South from Caribbean societies such as Jamaica and Saint Domingue, where slaves formed a huge numerical majority of the population, as well as from such nominally slaveholding regions as colonial Mexico or Massachusetts, where slaves never represented more than 3 percent of the population. In the South as a whole, slaves formed about one-third of the population.

The proportion of slaves varied considerably from state to state, ranging in 1860 from 1.6 percent in Delaware to 57.2 percent in South Carolina. With the exception of the border states of Delaware, Maryland, and Missouri, however, where slavery was in sharp retreat in the late antebellum years, slaves constituted about half the population in the deep South and from one-fifth to one-third in the upper South (see table 3). In some areas—especially along the lower banks of the Mississippi River and in the low country of South Carolina and Georgia—the great majority of the population was slave, and in most of the South, slaves were numerous enough to constitute the heart of the laboring class. But like their colonial forebears, antebellum Southern slaves did not generally live in the kind of overwhelmingly black world that prevailed in much of the Caribbean. In Jamaica, on the eve of emancipation, there were about ten blacks for every white; in the American South, there were about two whites for every black.

This population mix permitted the emergence of some very large plantations but guaranteed that most holdings would be of modest size. There were far fewer economies of scale associated with cotton than with sugar and rice; like tobacco, cotton could be profitably grown on small as well as on large holdings. Cotton plantations were on average somewhat larger than those for tobacco, but the dominance of cotton in the deep South, like that of tobacco in the upper South, meant that most antebellum slaves would not live on huge, Caribbean-style estates. In 1860, only 2.7 percent of Southern slaveholders owned 50 or more slaves, and only one-quarter of the slaves lived on such holdings. Very large plantations were a rarity: a mere 0.1 percent of slave owners held estates of 200 or more slaves, and such estates contained only 2.4 percent of the slaves. By contrast, in Jamaica on the eve of emancipation, one-third of the slaves lived on holdings of 200 or more and three-quarters lived on holdings of at least 50. (Holdings of serfs in Russia were even more concentrated: four-fifths of all serfs belonged to masters who possessed more than 200 bondspeople.)

Regional variations qualify but do not negate the generalization that most Southern slaves lived on holdings of modest size. Exceptions were most likely to be in the deep South, especially along the lower banks of the Mississippi River and in the coastal low country of South Carolina and Georgia; as earlier, the largest plantations were usually those devoted to growing sugar and rice. In sugar-dominated Ascension Parish, Louisiana, half of all slaves lived on plantations containing 175 or more slaves. Such a figure, although noteworthy, was highly atypical even for the deep South, where half the slaves lived on holdings of more than 32; in the South as a whole, the median figure was 23. In rough terms, about one-quarter of Southern slaves lived on very small holdings of 1 to 9, one half lived on middle-range holdings of 10 to 49, and one-quarter lived on large estates of 50 or more (see tables 4 and 5).

Most Southern slaves not only lived on modest holdings but also lived with resident masters. Once again, exceptions prove the rule. The small number of wealthy planters who owned multiple holdings were of necessity absentee proprietors to many of their slaves, and other masters chose to spend much or all of their time away from their slaveholdings, either because of other obligations, such as political office or legal practice, or because of personal inclination. Low-country planters often avoided their estates during the malarial summer months, and elsewhere, too, some very wealthy slave owners, craving the company of fashionable society, kept houses in nearby towns. But far more often than most Caribbean slave owners or Russian serf holders, American masters lived on their rural holdings and considered those holdings home. This resident mentality, which, as we have seen, was already well established in the eighteenth century, became still more entrenched in the nineteenth as political independence and the spread of democratic government reinforced local attachments among the white gentry. As Louisiana planter Bennet H. Barrow put it succinctly, in explaining the need for personal supervision by a planter of his slave property, "if a master exhibits no extraordinary interest in the proceedings on his plantation, it is hardly to be expected that any other feelings but apathy, and perfect indifference could exist with his negroes."[3] Southern slave owners typically felt strong ties to place, which included their governments, communities, landholdings, and slaves.

Because most slaveholdings were relatively small and most masters took a lively interest in running their own estates, slave management usually required little in the way of administrative hierarchy. On farms and small plantations with fewer than thirty slaves —which constituted more than nine-tenths of rural slaveholdings and contained a majority of the slaves—resident masters usually supervised operations personally. They knew the slaves and their capabilities and directed their work informally, with a minimum of record keeping and regimentation of labor. On farms with fewer than ten slaves, which contained a quarter of the slaves but a majority of the owners, masters could typically be found in the field, toiling alongside their slaves while bossing them and casually interacting with them.

Larger estates required more organization. Many planters kept record books in which they listed their slaves and livestock, recorded expenditures and sales, and kept track of agricultural operations, usually through brief daily or weekly entries. Such record keeping became so routine among planters that a number of published record books, complete with spaces for making entries under the proper headings, appeared during the late antebellum period. The most widely used of these, composed by Thomas Affleck, went through several editions in the 1840s and 1850s and offered a number of versions; in addition to *The Cotton Plantation Record and Account Book, No. 1. Suitable for a Force of 40 Hands or Under*, there were cotton plantation books designed for planters with forty to eighty hands and for those with over eighty hands, and two sugar plantation books as well.

Many planters, although by no means all, hired overseers. They came from a variety of backgrounds: some were non-slaveholding whites who lived in the vicinity, while others were planters' sons who fulfilled overseeing duties temporarily, until they could establish themselves as landed proprietors. Increasingly, however, they belonged to a professional group who made their careers managing plantations and boasted of their skill in handling slave labor. On estates with absentee owners, overseers wielded great authority, representing the masters' will; on plantations with resident masters, however, overseers frequently served essentially as administrative assistants, carrying out daily policies set by their watchful employers.

Slaves on large plantations usually worked in gangs, often headed by a slave driver appointed from among the male slaves for his strength, intelligence, loyalty, and managerial ability. The driver functioned as an assistant to the overseer or master, directly supervising agricultural labor. Plantations with more than fifty slaves generally had two or more gangs. A typical arrangement was to divide slaves into plow-hands, who usually consisted primarily of able-bodied men but sometimes included women, and hoe-hands, less fit for strenuous endeavor; on some plantations, lighter work still—for example, weeding and yard cleaning—was assigned to members of a "trash gang" made up of children and others incapable of heavy labor. Very large plantations sometimes exhibited more complex administrative hierarchies that approached those typical of big sugar plantations in the Caribbean (although not the military-like organization of huge serf-holding estates in Russia). In low-country South Carolina and Georgia, absentee planters continued to use the task system, placing their large rice and cotton plantations under the control of "stewards," super-overseers who exercised general authority over two or more estates and in turn ceded day-to-day plantation management to black drivers.

Being an overseer could be a thankless task, for he was likely to be blamed for any of the countless things that could go wrong on a plantation. New overseers often received written instructions from their employers, detailing what was expected of them and warning them to perform their duties diligently or face dismissal. Planters urged overseers to be hardworking, sober, and responsible, to exercise firm control over the slaves but at the same time avoid excessive severity. Equally important, overseers were expected to put their employers' welfare above their own, giving up the temptation to have any sort of social life that would interfere with their responsibilities; as one instruction noted succinctly, "subordination to the master is the first of an overseer's duties."[4] Resident masters instinctively distrusted their hired agents and ceded authority to them grudgingly, constantly checking on and interfering with their plantation management and making sure that everyone knew who was really in charge. Many planters encouraged slaves to report on the misdeeds of their overseers.

It is not surprising, therefore, that dissatisfaction with the performance of overseers was rampant among slave owners. The expressions of confidence that typically accompanied the hiring of a new overseer usually changed within a matter of months to concern and then outrage as the employee's "true" character was revealed; with boring repetitiveness, planters reviled their overseers for being greedy, dishonest, and lazy, mishandling the slaves, and showing a lack of proper respect for their employers. When Haller Nutt returned to his Araby plantation in Madison Parish, Louisiana, after a prolonged absence due to bad health, he heard "most terrible accounts of the severity, cruelty & bad management" of his overseer; although Nutt suspected that some of these accounts were "exaggerated," he soon determined that "far too much has been true," a conclusion strengthened by his discovery that the overseer had overreported the amount of cotton harvested. Noting that "even unti[l] the last my overseer would lie & deceive me," Nutt dismissed him, but conditions remained unsatisfactory; three days later "an examination found the negroes in very bad order for business [,] the mules in worse order than the negroes[,] and the overseer not much better."[5]

Although an occasional lucky slave owner found someone who met his expectations and stuck with him for decades, many more engaged in a never-ending search for the perfect overseer who would work contentedly for a modest salary. Others tired of the search and decided to do without overseers, either temporarily or permanently, exercising managerial responsibilities personally, sometimes with the help of trusted slaves. On some estates, slaves served in the place of overseers, although the term "overseer" was usually reserved for whites.

The overseer problem was very real for wealthy planters, but it must be kept in perspective. The modest size of most slaveholdings and the resident character of most slave owners precluded the emergence of a pervasive managerial crisis in the antebellum South. The majority of slaves did not have overseers, and of those who did, the majority had masters who themselves took the dominant role in establishing and supervising the routine of plantation life. As a consequence, interaction between masters and bondspeople assumed a salience unknown in much of the slaveholding Caribbean and in serf-holding Russia. The intense relationship between slaves and slave owners was at the heart of the distinctive slave society of the antebellum South.

I V

AS EARLIER, slaves in the antebellum period engaged in a broad range of endeavors. They cultivated the South's major crops, cleared land, dug ditches, put up fences, built and maintained houses, unloaded boats, and worked as mill hands. They served their masters in managerial capacities, as drivers and overseers, and cared for their comfort, as cooks, grooms, gardeners, and personal servants. They also attended to the needs of fellow slaves, working as preachers, conjurers, child carers, and "doctors"; as one white physician wrote of the area around Columbia, South Carolina, "On every plantation the sick nurse, or doctor woman, is usually the most intelligent female on the place; and she has full authority under the physician, over the sick."[6]

Widely scattered evidence suggests that in general about three-quarters of the adult slaves worked as field laborers while one-quarter had other duties, but there were many variations on this pattern. There was more specialization of labor on large plantations and in cities than on smaller plantations and farms. Women performed a narrower range of occupations than men, with house service the main alternative to field labor. Occupations that catered to the masters' personal comfort—house servants, grooms, coachmen—were relatively scarce on absentee-held estates. In the deep South, where demand for cotton produced an intense shortage of labor, especially during the 1850s, a higher proportion of slaves was pressed into field labor than in the upper South. And throughout the South, increased importation of manufactured goods from the North and pressure from white artisans who resented the competition acted to reduce the number of slaves (and free blacks) working in skilled crafts, especially from the 1840s.

Field work was arduous but far from constant. The "sunup to sundown" that constituted the basic workday varied with the seasons: not only were there more hours of daylight in the summer than in the winter but there was more work that needed to be done. (During the hottest months, this work was commonly interrupted by a two-hour siesta following the midday meal.) At harvesttime, the pace of work accelerated and slaves often toiled fourteen or more hours per day. Regional variations were also significant: Louisiana sugar planters drove their slaves more relentlessly than most, especially at harvesttime, when many hands worked far into the night; low-country slaves, who were able to control the pace of their own work, often completed their tasks in eight hours or less.

Despite these seasonal and regional variations, the basic pattern of field work was one of long hours of work at a less-than-frantic pace, punctuated by short bursts of intense activity and relieved by opportunities throughout the year for rest and revelry. Although the hours of daylight defined the workday for most Americans who worked the land, whether slave or free, there can be no doubt that the compulsion of the lash enabled slave owners to extract extra work from their laborers. Scholars differ on precisely how this occurred. According to calculations by econometricians Roger L. Ransom and Richard Sutch, free blacks in the deep South worked 28 to 37 percent fewer hours per year in 1879 than slaves had in 1859. By contrast, Robert W. Fogel and economist John F. Olson recently argued that although the gang system enabled masters to drive slaves at a more intensive pace per hour, they actually worked 10 percent fewer hours per year than Northern free farmers; in other words, slaves worked harder, not longer.

Even under gang labor, slaves, like many other preindustrial workers, typically resisted the efforts of their masters and overseers to impose a factory-like work routine, forcing a more relaxed pace through behavior that contemporary whites typically blamed on innate laziness and that more recent scholars have attributed either to a deliberate effort to undermine authority or to a pre-industrial, "peasant" sense of work and time. As Eugene D. Genovese has argued, slaves expected to work at breakneck speed on particular occasions—for example, at corn shuckings and hog killings—but they resisted the attempt to turn them into metaphorical clock punchers and forced their masters to accept a compromise schedule that included elements of industrial discipline (being summoned to work by the sound of a horn, for example) but that also included a lackadaisical work pace and time off for themselves. Unlike house servants, who had to be at the constant beck and call of their masters, field workers almost always had Sundays to themselves, whether to pray, to play, to rest, or to work on their garden plots and attend to other chores. Although masters occasionally forced hands to work on Sundays, especially at harvesttime, it was universally understood that this violation of the slaves' customary right—and throughout the antebellum South, state law—was justified only by exceptional circumstances. Indeed, many masters required of their slaves only half a day's work on Saturday, while others *paid* their hands for Sunday field work.

There has been some scholarly disagreement over the status of slaves who had occupations other than basic agricultural labor, and their relationship with the "ordinary" slaves who toiled in the fields. Slave owners—and visitors to the South—often saw house servants and craftsmen as members of a slave "aristocracy," an elite distinguished from the mass by superior training, manners, and "intelligence." Frances Kemble, an Englishwoman who despite spending a year on her husband's rice plantation never became reconciled either to slavery or to life in low-country Georgia, found the field hands "the more stupid and brutish of the tribe"; the skilled craftsmen, however, showed "a greater general activity of intellect, which must necessarily result from even a partial degree of cultivation," and the head driver was intelligent, kept a clean house, and held himself "a good deal aloof from the rest."[7] Historians, too, have traditionally stressed the divisions between elite and common slaves, maintaining that the former took pride in their superior status and sometimes identified more with their masters than with their fellow bondsmen.

There is considerable evidence pointing to the existence of tensions resulting from such stratification among slaves. Resentment of drivers, often seen as brutal agents of planter rule, was common, and black oral tradition as well as autobiographies left by former slaves reveal very real hostility to house servants who acted as spies on the slave community. "Domestic slaves are often found to be traitors to their own people," asserted autobiographer Henry Bibb; Austin Steward agreed that typically servants were either "greatly envied" or "bitterly hated." Former servants sometimes had a different perspective; as one pointedly remarked, "Honey, I wan't no common eve'day slave, I hoped [helped] de white folks in de big house."[8]

Historians have become increasingly aware, however, of the ambiguities connected with "elite" slave status. As in the colonial period, "privileged" occupations usually brought slaves disadvantages as well as very real benefits. House servants, and most other slaves whose jobs involved promoting the masters' comfort rather than their profit, typically ate and dressed better than field hands and were spared the worst rigors of backbreaking labor, but they also faced far more galling supervision and often lived isolated from the slave community. Their unusually intense relationships with whites brought both ties of affection and constant meddling in their personal lives. Frederick Douglass recalled the incessant punishment inflicted on "old Barney" and "young Barney," father and son who served as grooms to his owner, "for in nothing was Colonel Lloyd more particular than in the management of his horses." Stressing the different worlds of field hand and house slave, Northern traveler Frederick Law Olmsted argued that "slaves brought up to house-work dread to be employed at field-labour; and those accustomed to the comparatively unconstrained life of the negro-settlement, detest the close control and careful movements required of the house-servants." Although he exaggerated the gulf separating the two worlds, Olmsted understood that house service was no unmixed blessing to slaves.[9]

Indeed, historian John W. Blassingame has suggested that far from regarding house servants and drivers as slave aristocrats, most slaves placed them near the bottom of the social hierarchy. Viewing those who served whites as members of the elite, he argued, represented the perspective of the masters; the slaves, by contrast, awarded highest status to those who served the *black* community: preachers, conjurers, folk doctors, midwives, entertainers, the literate, rebels. Such an interpretation has the virtue of underlining the subjective nature of status—the slaves' view of social stratification was not necessarily the same as their owners'—and the caution with which one must approach the subject of inter-group attitudes among slaves. At the same time, however, I believe that it continues to overemphasize the social divisions among slaves, which, although real, remained limited.

Despite occupational diversity among slaves, there were at least four factors that restricted both social stratification among slaves and attendant group tensions. First, most slaveholdings were too small to allow for much specialization of labor. A plantation with twenty slaves, for example, was likely to have only ten to twelve able-bodied adult workers, half male and half female; such an estate would not have its labor force divided into different groups and could not spare slaves to work exclusively as carpenters, blacksmiths, gardeners, nurses, or preachers. Slaves possessing these skills would perform them when needed, in addition to engaging in other endeavors, including field work. Planters owning more than thirty slaves needed to pay greater attention to labor organization, but only those with well over fifty slaves were likely to have formal division between house and field workers, or large staffs with specialized occupations. The modest size of most slaveholdings stipulated relatively homogeneous conditions for the majority of slaves.

Equally important, those slaves lacked the kind of economic base—ownership of property, inheritance of wealth—that spurred stratification among free people. They cultivated their owners' land, lived in cabins put up under their owners' direction, and received food from their owners as well. Although many slaves were allotted garden plots on which they could grow vegetables and raise chickens, and some were able to sell these products or barter them for small luxuries, these plots and goods were privileges that could be granted or removed at a master's discretion rather than property to be passed from generation to generation; as a result, conditions did not allow for the kind of property inequality among slaves that typically existed among peasants under serfdom, or even (with the partial exception of coastal South Carolina and Georgia) the more limited kind that existed in parts of the Caribbean, where slaves had greater access to primitive market conditions. The enforced dependence of Southern slaves (elaborated in greater detail in sections V and VI below) produced a general economic equality among them; indeed, there were usually greater differences in material well-being from plantation to plantation than among slaves on any given plantation.

Two kinds of job mobility also reduced the degree of entrenched stratification based on occupation and status. The first resulted from the prevalence of both slave sales and slave hiring. Slave hiring was a widespread practice in much of the antebellum South, one that facilitated the meshing of supply and demand for slave labor, enabling masters to profit from surplus slaves while persons with short-term labor needs could fill them relatively inexpensively. Unlike self-hire, which was limited to a small number of trusted slaves with special skills (and, because of the independence it allowed slaves, was illegal in most of the South), the rental of slaves by owners to hirers was common and touched a wide range of slaves; according to estimates made by Fogel and Engerman, 6 percent of rural slaves and 31 percent of urban slaves were on hire in 1860 (with a far greater percentage experiencing hire over a protracted period of time). Being hired out was not necessarily advantageous to slaves. On the one hand, it reduced their isolation and provided them with differing experiences, but on the other, it often took them away from friends and family and placed them under the authority of someone who lacked the owner's incentive to treat them decently; the hirer–slave relationship was far more fundamentally utilitarian than that between master and slave.

Together with slave sales, however, hiring did tend to reduce permanent status differences among slaves, by increasing the likelihood that any particular condition under which a slave lived was temporary. Most slaves experienced one or more changes in status during their lifetime: as the accounts of virtually all ex-slave autobiographers reveal, they were sold, inherited, hired out, moved from one region to another, taken from countryside to city and back again, assigned new occupations. Under such circumstances, it made little sense to pull rank or discriminate sharply on the basis of occupation or status, for who knew where they would live and what they would do tomorrow? The diversity of conditions that individual slaves typically experienced thus prevented the emergence of sharp social divisions among them.

Life-cycle mobility strongly reinforced this diversity. Many slave occupations were highly age-specific. Few able-bodied males between fifteen and forty years of age, for example, served as house slaves; domestic servants were overwhelmingly composed of boys, old men, and women. (Even among female servants, the young and old prevailed.) Except on a small number of unusually large estates, and in sophisticated cities such as Charleston and New Orleans, house servants therefore constituted less an elite stratum than a contingent of slaves at a particular stage of their life cycle. Boys and girls were often taken into the "big house" to serve their masters, but few of them spent their whole lives as domestics. The great majority of males, and many of the females as well, were sent to the fields when they came of age, and stayed there until they were no longer able to perform heavy labor. Then they might be "retired" to jobs requiring less strenuous exertion, such as housework, gardening, cooking, and looking after children. Such mobility also existed, although to a somewhat lesser extent, in craft work, which masters frequently assigned to men with physical disabilities that precluded their participation in gang labor.

In short, although there was an extraordinary variety of slave experiences, the slave population was relatively undifferentiated in terms of economic and social status. Slaves performed numerous occupations under widely varying conditions, but except on atypically large estates those conditions did not encourage the emergence of sharp social divisions among them. The dependent status they shared, together with the limited opportunity for specialization of labor and the substantial degree of occupational mobility, meant that antebellum Southern slaves formed a population that paradoxically was marked by great uniformity even as it exhibited great diversity. Despite the multiplicity of different slave experiences, much more united the slaves than divided them.

V

ANTEBELLUM SLAVE RELATIONS were marked by a dualism inherent in slavery: slaves were at the same time both objects and subjects, human property held for the purpose of enriching the masters and individuals with lives of their own. But this dualism was especially pronounced in the antebellum South because conditions there accentuated personal relations between master and slave to an extent rarely seen in other slave-owning societies. Slavery served mercenary goals in the South, as it did elsewhere, but it did far more than that; to most masters, slavery represented a civilization or way of life that ordered their very existence.

The distinctive way in which Southern slave owners looked upon and dealt with their slaves has recently been characterized by the term "paternalism." This concept is useful, but it is important to specify what it does and does not mean, for it has generated widespread confusion. Slave-owner paternalism involved not a good, painless, or benign slavery—all contradictions in terms—but a slavery in which masters took personal interest in the lives of their slaves. The typical Southern slave owner knew his or her slaves by name and interacted with them on a frequent basis, not only directing their labor but also looking after their welfare and interfering in their lives. Masters saw their slaves not just as their laborers but also as their "people," inferior members of their extended households from whom they expected work and obedience but to whom they owed guidance and protection. Not all masters took their paternalistic responsibilities seriously, but the small size of slaveholdings and the resident character—and mentality—of slaveholders produced unusually close contact between master and slave and fostered among many slave owners a strong paternalistic self-image. They spoke frequently of their "love" for their slaves, and although such assertions contained considerable hyperbole, they also expressed the very real conviction that there was more to slavery than profit and loss. If the seeds of this paternalism were already widely sown in the eighteenth-century Chesapeake, with the simultaneous emergence of a largely resident planter class and a predominantly creole slave population, its full blossoming occurred throughout much of the South during the half century before the Civil War.

Antebellum Southern publicists increasingly bombarded the reading public with admonitions to take good care of their people, looking after their physical needs, spiritual welfare, and general happiness. As Presbyterian minister (and Georgia slave owner) Charles C. Jones argued in *The Religious Instruction of the Negroes* (1842), blacks "were placed under our control . . . not exclusively for our benefit but theirs also," so they could receive moral and religious uplift; "we cannot disregard this obligation thus *divinely imposed*, without forfeiting our humanity, our gratitude, our consistency, and our claim to the spirit of christianity itself." Although there was a strong propagandistic element to such public discourse—defenders of slavery were eager to prove to the outside world the humane nature of the slave regime—the profusion of essays, speeches, and sermons on the "Christian responsibilities" of slave owners inevitably influenced the general consciousness and behavior of Southern whites at large. What is more, similar themes are evident in the *private* correspondence of slave owners, including their instructions to overseers. As rice planter P. C. Weston informed his overseer, "his first object is to be, under all circumstances, the care and well being of the negroes. The Proprietor is always ready to excuse such errors as may proceed from want of judgment; but he never can or will excuse any cruelty, severity, or want of care towards the negroes."[10]

Although not all masters followed exhortations to take good care of their people, the actual material condition of antebellum slaves was in general superior to that of their colonial forebears. An abundant supply of food enabled masters to provide their slaves with a plentiful if not nutritionally balanced diet, and the periodic famines that afflicted the poor in much of the world were unknown in the South; as Frederick Douglass grudgingly noted, "not to give a slave enough to eat, is regarded as the most aggravated development of meanness even among slaveholders."[11] The peck (eight quarts) of cornmeal and two and a half to four pounds of pork or bacon per week that became the widely accepted standard ration for healthy adult field hands were supplemented by numerous items that varied according to season and region, many of which—including chickens, vegetables, fruit, opossum, fish, and shellfish—slaves grew on their garden plots or hunted and gathered from the forests and waterways. Some masters dispensed small luxuries such as sugar, coffee, and even whiskey to their people, or allowed them to trade the products of their garden plots for such items.

The abundance of food that most slaves received helped sustain them in comparatively healthy condition. True, seasonal variations and the prevailing ignorance of elementary principles of nutrition produced a slave diet that by today's standards lacked balance and was at times deficient in basic vitamins; the nutritional composition of food given to young children was especially inadequate and contributed to a high rate of infant mortality. But such dietary deficiency was more a function of the state of antebellum medical knowledge than the nature of antebellum slavery; no one had yet heard of vitamins, and most Southerners, white and black, consumed nutritionally unbalanced diets.

Recent research on height, historically closely related to nutrition, suggests that for their time, Southern slaves were relatively healthy; scholars associated with Robert W. Fogel have estimated that although adult antebellum slaves were on the average an inch shorter than Northern whites, they were three inches taller than newly imported Africans, two inches taller than Trinidad-born slaves, and one inch taller than Englishmen in the nineteenth-century British Royal Marines. The crude death rate among antebellum slaves averaged about 30 per 1,000, a figure somewhat higher than that of white Southerners (primarily because of the higher infant mortality rate among slaves) but similar to the rate of many Western Europeans and substantially lower than that of Caribbean slaves. (In general, the least healthy slaves were those in the swampy low country of South Carolina and Georgia and in the sugar-producing parishes of southern Louisiana.) Protected by the sickle-cell trait, black Southerners suffered much less than whites from malaria but succumbed more often than whites to cholera, tetanus, and sudden infant deaths that contemporaries frequently blamed on "smothering."

Slave housing and clothing were generally crude but functional. Spurred on in part by the proliferating slave-management literature, which contained frequent appeals to provide slaves with clean, dry cabins, antebellum slave owners in fact paid considerably more attention to slaves' housing than their colonial precursors, who had often left them to find sleeping spaces for themselves in barns, sheds, lofts, or, weather permitting, out of doors. During the decades preceding the Civil War, it became standard to provide each slave family with a small wooden cabin, typically sixteen by eighteen feet, and, in part because of concern for slave health, to insist that it be regularly cleaned. Field hands typically received four coarse suits of clothes per year—pants and shirts for the men, dresses for the women, and long shirts for the children—that were usually "homespun" by the slave women or sewn by them from rough "Negro cloth" that Northern textile mills manufactured expressly for sale to Southern slave owners. (During the late antebellum years, however, an increasing proportion of slave owners purchased ready-made clothes for their slaves.) Slave women also used their spare time to sew dressy clothes for use on Sundays and special occasions. Shoes, although regularly distributed, fit so poorly and were so uncomfortable that many slaves chose to go barefoot much of the time.

Unlike slaves' housing and clothing, which were primitive even by contemporary standards, their medical care exceeded that of Southern whites, most of whom rarely if ever saw physicians. Like other antebellum Americans, slave owners lacked knowledge of how to deal effectively with most diseases, but they worried a good deal about the health of their people—who represented valuable investments—and took whatever action they thought necessary to maintain it. Although they realized that slaves sometimes shammed illness in order to escape work, masters (and less often overseers) paid considerable attention to slaves' medical complaints, prescribing rest and a wide range of home remedies. On one of George Noble Jones's two absentee-held plantations in central Florida, all but one of thirty-one working hands missed some work because of illness in 1841, and the majority missed ten or more days. Thirteen years later, the overseer on Jones's other plantation plaintively begged his employer to "pleas send me Webersters Medical Dictionary as I cant git one hear."[12]

In cases of serious illness, slave owners frequently sent for doctors. Slaves living on large plantations, some of which contained "hospitals" of their own, were especially likely to be treated by specialists, and the records of some planters reveal considerable expenditures for medical care; in 1853, the doctor's bill for numerous visits to Robert F. W. Allston's Waverly estate in South Carolina came to $390.21. "We have had upwards of 50 cases of measles," read a typical diary entry of Louisiana planter Leonidas Pendleton Spyker, who frequently summoned a doctor to his Morehouse Parish plantation. "On yesterday we had 16 grown negroes lying up—today 14."[13] The treatment doctors provided usually included liberal bleeding and administration of "vomits," and often did not differ appreciably from the kind of treatment administered by masters themselves; it is not surprising, therefore, that some masters found patients reluctant to submit to their prescribed treatment, or "stubbornly" preferring their own home remedies. The medical care that slave owners provided did not significantly improve the health of their slaves, but it did reflect the widespread concern of masters for the well-being of those slaves.

Such concern was evident in numerous other endeavors, for the lives of the masters were intimately bound with those of the slaves. Slave owners followed the major events in the life history of their people—births, marriages, deaths—but they also often paid attention to more mundane events and interacted with their slaves on a daily basis, reading the Bible to them, providing small favors, nursing the sick. "I walked over to the quarters this morning before breakfast, to see a sick woman, found her quite sick," Mississippian Eliza L. Magruder recorded in her diary in January 1846; five days later she noted that "Aunt Olivia went . . . to the quarters, found one of the negroes very sick; Elizabeth had a baby this afternoon." Slave owners held parties, barbecues, and dances for their slaves, to celebrate seasonal events such as completion of the harvest, to mark local occurrences such as weddings, or simply to provide a break in the normal work routine; throughout the South, it became a common practice to allow slaves a weeklong holiday between Christmas and

New Year's (a time when most holdings had little essential work to do). Although Frederick Douglass ascribed the prevalence of Christmas revelry to a cynical effort on the part of slave owners to provide "safety valves, to carry off the rebellious spirit of enslaved humanity," he and other slaves looked forward eagerly to holiday festivities, and kept fond memories of them.[14]

One of the most noteworthy signs of the spread of paternalism among antebellum slave owners was their growing interest in their slaves' religious lives. A number of factors combined to foster this interest, including the wave of evangelical revivals known as the Second Great Awakening that swept much of the country during the first half of the nineteenth century, the increased receptivity of creole slaves to Protestant proselytizing, and the conviction of some white Southerners that religion would be a stabilizing force among the slave population. Most basically, however, the effort to bring Christianity to the slaves was a function of the intense interaction that existed between resident masters and slaves. Slave owners who strove to order virtually every aspect of slave life paid particular, and increasing, attention to their religious behavior.

This attention was expressed in both organized and unorganized form. A "mission to the slaves," spearheaded by the major Protestant denominations, gained momentum from the 1830s, and saw the formal enlistment of growing numbers of bondsmen and -women in white-controlled churches, especially Baptist and Methodist; on the eve of the Civil War, half a million slaves were officially church members, and most of the remainder received at least some exposure to Christian worship. As historian John Boles has recently argued, antebellum blacks received a warmer welcome from churches than from any other major white organization in the South (which no doubt in part explains their increasing receptivity to Christianity). Fearing that literacy would promote excessive independence among slaves, most (although not all) slave owners opposed teaching their people to read or allowing them to attend Sunday school, thereby subverting the central Protestant tenet that each individual must be able to read the Bible. Instead, many masters read the Bible to their slaves, prayed with them, encouraged them to attend church, and arranged special services for them. Like many other former slaves, Solomon Northup, a free man who spent twelve years in bondage in Louisiana after being kidnapped in Washington in 1841, recalled how his master "would gather all his slaves about him, and read and expound the Scriptures."[15]

The close contact between master and slave that underlay slave-owner paternalism was pervasively shaped by the intimacy of child-hood comradeship. White and black children on farms and plantations commonly played together, a source of some anxiety for planters who worried that their children's deportment and pronunciation would be corrupted by excessive contact with young slaves, and of amazement to many visitors to the South, who marveled at the close and easy relationships they saw between white and black. "I am struck with the close cohabitation and association of black and white," wrote Frederick Law Olmsted from Virginia; "negro women are carrying black and white babies together in their arms; black and white children are playing together . . . ; black and white faces are constantly thrust together out of doors, to see the train go by." On the train near Olmsted sat a white woman and her daughter together with a black woman and her daughter, all of whom "talked and laughed together; and the girls munched confectionary out of the same paper, with a familiarity and closeness of intimacy that would have been noticed with astonishment, if not with manifest displeasure, in almost any chance company at the North."[16]

Although youthful friendships almost always yielded to the reality of class power as children reached their teens, growing up together and continuing to live together inevitably shaped the attitudes of masters and slaves and set the stage for the continuing relationship between them. Blacks and whites often lived in different worlds, but they were by no means strangers to one another, and intense personal ties persisted among adults. Most owners had personal favorites among their slaves—a former playmate, a serving girl who grew up with (and shared secrets with) her mistress, a trusted assistant who helped run the plantation—in whose lives they took special interest. But many masters took interest in the lives of *all* their slaves. "I have no overseer, and do not manage so scientifically as those who are able to lay down [written] rules," wrote a small planter in the influential *DeBow's Review*; "yet I endeavor to manage so that myself, family and negroes take pleasure and delight in our relations."[17] This planter might have been surprised to learn that his slaves did not fully share his pleasure and delight, but his outlook was typical of that held by large numbers of antebellum slave owners, who looked upon their slaves as far more than a source of income, and who thought that those slaves looked upon them as far more than exploiters of labor.

VI

SOUTHERN SLAVES suffered an extraordinary amount of interference in their daily lives. Of course, such interference was rooted in the very existence of slavery, for masters everywhere assumed the right to direct and control their slave property. But the unusually close contact that existed between masters and slaves in the antebellum South meant that whites there impinged to an unusual degree on slave life. White influence did not destroy slave autonomy—as we shall see in the next chapter, slaves strove mightily to protect their families and communities from outside interference—but for most slaves, such autonomy was sharply circumscribed. The pervasive presence of white Southerners shaped the everyday lives of the slaves.

Slaves could hardly turn around without being told what to do. They lived by rules, sometimes carefully constructed and formally spelled out and sometimes haphazardly conceived and erratically imposed. Rules told them when to rise in the morning, when to go to the fields, when to break for meals, how long and how much to work, and when to go to bed; rules also dictated a broad range of activities that were forbidden without special permission, from leaving home to getting married; and rules allowed or did not allow a host of privileges, including the right to raise vegetables on garden plots, trade for small luxuries, hunt, and visit neighbors. Of course, all societies impose rules on their inhabitants in the form of laws, but the rules that bound slaves were unusually detailed, covered matters normally untouched by law, and were arbitrarily imposed and enforced, not by an abstract entity that (at least in theory) represented their interests, but by their owners. Slaves lived with their government.

This closely governed nature of slave life represented a central feature of slave-owner paternalism, as masters who cared for their slaves in a variety of ways also strove to shape virtually every aspect of their lives, treating them as permanent children who needed constant direction as well as constant protection. The slave owner's "design for mastery" was to a considerable extent a function of the close master–slave contact that pervaded the antebellum South: given the arbitrary power they enjoyed over their slaves and convinced that they knew what was best for those slaves, few masters could resist the temptation to meddle in their lives. Some slave owners were quite explicit about what was at stake; as Barrow succinctly noted, it was important to make the slave "as comfortable at Home as possible, affording him What is essentially necessary for his happiness—you must provide for him Your self and by that means creat[e] in him a habit of perfect dependence on you."[18] Over and over, slave owners returned to the metaphor of slaves as children, stressing that they needed loving and firm but above all consistent management if they were not to be spoiled.

Slave owners adopted a wide variety of measures, including suppressing independent religious activities, limiting contact with slaves on neighboring holdings, and interfering with the naming of children, in order to undercut slave autonomy. Although custom dictated that slaves be allowed garden plots for their personal use, many masters agreed with Barrow that this privilege fostered "a spirit of traffic[k]ing" and therefore either forbade slaves to sell and barter produce raised on their plots or banned such plots altogether, giving slaves cash handouts instead. Routine preparation of meals provided even greater risk for masters who would be truly dominant, and produced considerable debate among them over optimum policy. Whereas slaves preferred a system that allowed them maximum control over the cooking and consumption of their food, owners typically worried that the slaves would, "like children," quarrel over food supplies or consume too much at once; in any case, one planter explained, "there are always some negroes on every place who are too careless and indolent to cook their food in a proper manner." One widely touted solution was frequent dispensation of food— although weekly distribution of rations was common, some anxious masters insisted on daily handouts—combined with careful supervision of its preparation, or better yet, use of a plantation cook.[19]

The efforts of paternalistic masters to destroy every vestige of slave independence, and the limitations of those efforts, are evident in the administration of James Henry Hammond, who in 1831 acquired Silver Bluff, a South Carolina estate with 147 slaves. Disturbed by the degree of autonomy he found among his slaves, as well as by their poor work habits and health, Hammond took energetic measures designed to impose his order on Silver Bluff, measures detailed in the careful "instructions" he later composed for the estate's overseer. He shifted his work force from the task to the gang system, hired itinerant white ministers to preach to his people in place of the independent black services they were accustomed to holding, banned his slaves from trading with or visiting neighbors, placed all children younger than eleven under the care of a nurse, and insisted on naming some babies himself. Although he strove to encourage family life among his slaves, and refrained from separating family members, he also pervasively interfered with their families, requiring couples to secure his permission before marrying, forbidding off-plantation marriages, and punishing sexual infidelity. (Hammond was something of an expert on infidelity: a prolonged affair with two of his slaves put serious strains on his marriage, and his "intimacy" with four of his own nieces blew up in a scandal that derailed his political career and led to his ostracism by polite society.) Divorce was allowed, but Hammond imposed a penalty of up to one hundred lashes on separating couples, and forbade either spouse to remarry for three years.

Hammond's "design for absolute control" was not entirely successful. Like other slaves, those at Silver Bluff were never reduced to the childlike, subservient beings their master sought to create; as Hammond's biographer Drew Gilpin Faust wrote, "they retained, in a manner only partially visible to Hammond, essential aspects of black communal life and autonomy." Nevertheless, Hammond did succeed in putting his stamp on life at Silver Bluff and forcing the slaves to confront the reality of close supervision of their activities. His kind of paternalism profoundly influenced, but did not totally shape, slave life and culture.[20]

Amid the myriad ways in which slave owners interfered in the lives of their slaves, two created particular resentment. Most basic was punishment, and slaves used this criterion above all others in rating their owners: a "good" master was one who rarely or never subjected his people to corporal punishment, while a "bad" master was one who did so incessantly, cruelly, and for trifling or nonexistent offenses. Slave owners spanned the full range from gentle humanitarians who abjured use of the lash and whose fortunate charges were sometimes termed "free" by neighboring slaves to sadistic psychopaths like Hoover, the North Carolinian who beat his pregnant slave Mira "with clubs, iron chains, and other deadly

weapons" over a period of four months, during which he also over-
worked, starved, and "burnt her" until she died.[21]

The vast majority of slave owners fell between these extremes:
convinced that their slaves were like children, these masters took
it for granted that maintaining orderly behavior required the threat
and at least the occasional application of "correction." At the same
time, like proverbial parents, they gave lip service—and sometimes
more than that—to the need to avoid excessive severity and to make
sure that slaves understood under what circumstances they would
be punished. "Much whipping indicates a bad tempered, or inat-
tentive manager, & will not be allowed," declared Hammond in a
typical instruction. "The Overseer must never on any occasion—
unless in self defence—kick a negro, or strike with his hand, or a
stick, or the butt-end of his whip."[22] Throughout the South, publicists denounced as un-Christian masters who mistreated those
placed under their authority, and stressed the need for "moderate,"
predictable punishment for offenses that were clearly spelled out.
Such guidelines were dictated not simply by the much-vaunted
"love" that masters felt for their slaves, but also by intensely practical considerations: observant slave owners learned by experience
that continual, random, or extreme punishment was likely to be
counterproductive, producing confusion and seething resentment
rather than cheerful and orderly deportment.

Nevertheless, almost all masters punished, most more than they
would have been willing to admit. By far the most common punishment was whipping, and it was a rare slave who totally escaped
the lash. A whipping could be a formal occasion—a public, ritualized
display in which a sentence was carried out in front of an assembled
throng—or a casual affair in which an owner, overseer, or hirer
impulsively chastised an "unruly" slave. Either way, the prevalence
of whipping was such a stark reminder of slave dependence that to
the bondspeople (and abolitionists) the lash came to symbolize the
essence of slavery.

Many owners resorted to additional methods to inflict pain and
maintain order, methods that included stocks, private jails, and public humiliations, as well as fines and deprivation of privileges, and
that less commonly embraced harsher physical tortures. Bennet H.
Barrow, who denounced his neighbor as "the most cruel Master I
ever knew of" for castrating three of his slaves, devised numerous
measures to keep his own people in line, including confinement in

stocks, "whipping frolics" in which all his slaves were subjected to the lash, and humiliating men by making them wear women's clothing or exhibiting them "during Christmas on a scaffold in the middle of the Quarter & with a red Flannel cap on." Slave patrols (or "paddyrollers"), which whites formed to maintain local order, aroused particular fear among blacks, because these groups lacked any incentive to avoid unnecessary cruelty and often in fact engaged in erratic acts of violence against defenseless slaves. "Paddyrollers was mean ez dogs," recalled one ex-slave pointedly.[23]

Despite the widespread expressions of repugnance for arbitrary and excessive punishment, on a day-to-day basis flesh-and-blood masters—and overseers—were rarely able to adhere to the kind of rational and restrained punitive system that their most articulate spokesmen advocated; the despotic power of master over slave that inhered in slavery, together with the close contact between master and slave that inhered in *American* slavery, undercut the evenhanded application of rules and regulations in slave punishment. It was simply too easy for whites to react to the innumerable annoyances that slave relations produced by striking out at those in their power, and slave narratives are filled with accounts of "unjustified" punishment, administered haphazardly or without cause. On this question, as on so many, a huge gap in perception separated the slaves and the masters: few slaves recognized the order and regularity that their masters sought and saw in their system of discipline; what to the masters was the prudent application of moderate chastisement for the well-being of the slaves themselves to the bondspeople often appeared as arbitrary and unpredictable.

Next to punishment, interference in the family lives of slaves stood as the starkest reminder of their dependent status. Legally, slave families were nonexistent: no Southern state recognized marriage between slave men and women, and legal authority over slave children rested not with their parents but with their masters. In practice, slaves lived in families, whether recognized by law or not, and historians have recently devoted considerable attention to exploring how those families shielded their members from the worst rigors of bondage (see chapter 5, section III). Still, slave-owner paternalism combined with the slave family's lack of legal standing to render that family subject to unwanted intervention at every stage of the life cycle, as masters convinced that they knew what was best for their people strove to regulate their families as well. Not all slave owners took advantage of every opportunity to interfere in the family lives of their slaves, and some made special efforts to avoid such interference, but few could entirely resist the temptation to meddle.

Slave marriage, although unrecognized in law, received considerable attention from slave owners. In an effort to promote "morality," stability, and a rapidly expanding slave population, virtually all masters endeavored, sometimes with the aid of financial bounties or other material incentives, to encourage early and long-lasting marriages among their slaves. They differed, however, in their regulatory zeal. Although a few chose mates for young slaves and forced them to live together, most masters expected men and women to find their own spouses and secure their permission (usually readily granted) before marrying. Some slave owners, like Hammond, punished slaves who engaged in extramarital sex or sought to divorce, or even forbade divorces entirely. Others avoided, or abandoned as useless, all efforts to regulate their slaves' marital behavior; "I attempted it for many years by preaching virtue and decency, encouraging marriages, and by punishing, with some severity, departures from marital obligations," explained one Mississippi planter, "but it was all in vain."[24]

One kind of slave marriage that particularly troubled most owners was marriage "abroad," that is, to someone with a different owner. Made necessary by the prevalence of small and medium-sized holdings with a paucity of eligible mates, the practice was common throughout the South; typically, husbands would receive weekend passes to visit their wives and children, leaving home after a half day of work on Saturday and returning on Monday morning. Virtually all slave owners professed to deplore off-plantation marriage, because it gave (usually male) slaves a ready opportunity to be away from their masters, but their policy toward it was by no means uniform. Owners of small farms often had little choice but to allow it. Large planters had more options: some adopted a hands-off policy, others discouraged marriage abroad without actually prohibiting it, and still others, like Barrow, flatly ruled it out because "it creates a feeling of independence, from being, of right, out of the control of the masters for a time."[25] Still, the practice continued, a clear reminder to slave owners of the limits to their ability totally to control the lives of their slaves.

The close contact that existed between masters and slaves worked special hardship on slave women, who were vulnerable to sexual as well as labor exploitation. Southerners, both white and black, were sensitive on the subject; pro-slavery polemicists typically greeted abolitionist portrayals of the South as a hotbed of license and debauchery with either stony silence or outraged denial, while blacks who reminisced in autobiographies or interviews were reluctant to reveal family skeletons in an era of prudish standards. Still, those who dealt at all frankly with the subject noted—albeit from very different perspectives—the prevalence of interracial sex. South Carolina ideologue William Harper turned it into a virtue, insisting that it helped account for the absence of Southern prostitution and the purity of white women. Patrician diarist Mary Boykin Chesnut, by contrast, countered that in fact "we live surrounded by prostitutes . . . Like the patriarchs of old our men live all in one house with their wives and concubines, and the mulattoes one sees in every family exactly resemble the white children." Chesnut's resentment was directed at the wrongs she saw committed against *white* women made to suffer in silence their husbands' barely concealed dalliances with slaves, but to the equally bitter ex-slave autobiographer Harriet Jacobs, the victims were *black* women forced to endure the shameful indignities "inflicted by fiends who bear the shape of men." As Chesnut and Jacobs recognized, and Harper implicitly conceded, no slave woman was safe from unwanted sexual advances.[26]

Of course, not all advances were entirely unwanted. There were slave women who maintained long-term relations with white men that came close to common-law marriages (on rare occasions, slave men had such relations with white women), and others who voluntarily formed liaisons of more limited duration. Over several years, James Henry Hammond carried on affairs with two of his slaves, refusing to break them off even when they were discovered by his wife; these affairs, like others that took place within the context of the ever-present power that planters wielded over their "people," were based on more than overt use of physical force even if from the slaves' perspective they represented less than fully consenting relationships. Like many (but not all) masters in such relations, Hammond was especially solicitous of his slave lovers and children, warning his white son Harry to take good care of them and never sell "any of my children or possible children."[27]

Far more often, however, slaves who had sex with whites did so against their will, whether the victims of outright rape or of the powerlessness that made resistance to advances futile and the use of force in such advances unnecessary. (It should be noted that slave women were also easy targets of *black* sexual aggression. Although a slave's rape of a white woman was a capital offense, his rape of a slave woman was ignored both by state laws and in most cases by slave owners; the disapproval of other slaves—and fear of retribution at their hands—constituted the main deterrent to sexual abuse of slave women by slave men.) Sex between white men and black women was a routine feature of life on many, perhaps most, slave-holdings, as masters, their teenage sons, and on large holdings their overseers took advantage of the situation to engage in the kind of casual, emotionless sex on demand unavailable from white women. What was routine and casual to white men caused anguish to black women, anguish graphically described by Harriet Jacobs in her searing autobiography, *Incidents in the Life of a Slave Girl.* "I cannot tell how much I suffered in the presence of these wrongs," she wrote, "nor how I am still pained by the retrospect."[28]

The ultimate and most dreaded form of interference in slave family life was the forced separation of family members. Although many slave owners strove to keep families together, separation remained a pervasive feature of the slave South. Good intentions alone proved insufficient to protect slaves against the dictates of economic interest, anger, or plain thoughtlessness; there were simply too many instances when it "made sense" or was "necessary" for masters with the best of intentions to separate their slaves. Most slave owners may have disliked the idea of separating their people—and some refused to do so under normal circumstances—but when push came to shove, few put their slaves' happiness above their own self-interest.

There were numerous occasions, by no means all involving sale, in which slaves were forcibly removed, either temporarily or permanently, from their loved ones. Children were taken from their parents and sent to serve in the "big house"; children and adults were hired out to employers who lived far enough away to make home visits difficult or impossible; slaves who belonged to wealthy masters were moved from one plantation to another, and those with owners in financial straits were "loaned" to creditors. Slaves who married abroad faced likely separation from their spouses if one of the owners moved.

Sale, however, produced the most wrenching—and permanent—disruption of families. Historian Michael Tadman has estimated that in the upper South about one first marriage in three was broken by forced separation and close to half of all children were separated from at least one parent. (Families in the lower South, which was a net importer rather than exporter of slaves, were torn apart much less often.) The interregional slave trade was the largest single producer of these separations, but slaves found themselves on the market on a variety of occasions. One of the most common of these was the death of a slave owner, with the attendant division of his or her estate among heirs and creditors. Although some slaves were truly attached to their owners and grieved at their deaths, much of the proverbial distress at their masters' passing reflected anxiety over their *own* fate rather than sadness over that of their owners.

Whatever its cause, the forced separation of men, women, and children from their relatives and friends constituted the most devastating experience of bondage for the slaves, and the most embarrassing for the masters. It also indicated the fragility and elasticity of their paternalistic pretensions. Slaveholder paternalism encompassed behavior with sharply divergent implications: the paternalistic master dispensed supervision and punishment together with love and protection, and could easily cross the line from benevolent patriarch to despot (and back again). So long as their authority was unquestioned, most slave owners could accentuate their "soft" side, represented by honor, duty, and noblesse oblige. But even under the best of circumstances, paternalism was often indistinguishable from petty tyranny; the same master who nursed the sick, read the Bible to his "people," and expressed real affection for a childhood chum or a beloved "nanny" could also drive, whip, and sell with steely determination. If absolute power proved essential to the paternalist's sense of duty, the loss of that power threatened to turn benevolent paternalists into domineering bullies.

Articulate defenders of slavery resorted to a variety of stratagems to come to grips with the horror of breaking up families. They denied its prevalence, maintaining that they and most of their friends never engaged in it; they insisted that victims of the slave trade suffered only briefly, because blacks lacked whites' capacity for forming deep, long-lasting relationships; and they derided traders as coarse, crude, and unfeeling, Yankees at heart rather than true Southerners. These responses testified to the contradictions of an intrusive slaveowner paternalism under which infliction of pain and humiliation was integrally linked with the slaves' care and supervision. So, too, did the assertion of Anna Harris some three-quarters of a century after the end of slavery that she had never allowed a white person to enter her house. "Dey sole my sister Kate," she explained. "I saw it wid dese here eyes. Sole her in 1860, and I ain't seed nor heard of her since. Folks say white folks is all right dese days. Maybe dey is, maybe dey isn't. But I can't stand to see 'em. Not on my place."[29]

VII

SLAVE-OWNER PATERNALISM accentuated a dualism already present in slavery: slaves were both persons and property. During the antebellum years, this dualism, and the tensions that accompanied it, became more pronounced, as slave owners strove both to protect their property interests and to create an order that conformed to their notions of morality and benevolence. As a result, as the passage and application of laws relating to slavery reveal, Southern slavery became more restrictive at the same time that it became more protective.

Law must be approached with considerable caution as an indication of actual slave treatment or conditions. The absence of legal recognition for slave families hardly meant that those families did not exist, nor did the inability of slaves legally to own property prohibit many masters from recognizing slaves' possessions as their "own." Neither laws protecting nor laws restricting slaves were always enforced, and the vast majority of crimes committed by and against slaves were handled informally on farms and plantations, without resort to the judicial system. Nevertheless, the character and conduct of slave law can provide important insights into the thinking of the master class, for if laws do not always indicate how slavery actually functioned, they do indicate how authorities *wanted* it to function.

Over the course of the antebellum period, Southern lawmakers passed a great deal of legislation designed to secure the subordination of slaves—and also of free blacks—to white authority. Although such legislation (and its enforcement) varied from state to state, and tended to be more draconian in the deep than in the upper South, the overall trend was clear: legislators sought to strengthen slavery by plugging existing loopholes that threatened the orderly working of the system. Thus the states imposed increasingly severe limits on slave movement and assembly—usually slaves were forbidden to preach or even assemble away from home except in the presence of a white, and planters were required to make sure that their holdings were at all times supervised by competent white personnel—and paid increasing attention to buttressing the slave patrols that would enforce these limits. They passed laws to prevent slaves from trading, hiring themselves out without white supervision, and possessing liquor or unauthorized weapons; most imposed severe restrictions on teaching slaves to read or write. These laws were aimed at combatting any sign of independence on the part of the slaves, at ensuring that slaves would remain totally under the control of their masters and white society at large.

This effort received its clearest manifestation in new laws directed at those slaves who sought to become free. Unlike Cuba and Brazil, where the proportion of blacks who were free soared in the nineteenth century, the Southern United States (with the exceptions of Delaware, Maryland, Kentucky, and Missouri) made it increasingly difficult for slaves to become free, and most required those who *were* freed to leave their borders. Most of the deep-South states forbade manumission except by specific legislative act taken to reward individuals for "meritorious service"; an 1852 Louisiana law requiring emancipated slaves to leave the United States within twelve months was superseded in 1857 by a complete prohibition on manumissions. Courts differed in their treatment of slave owners' wills that directed the manumission of slaves, but the trend was in the direction of overturning them. As the chief justice of the Alabama Supreme Court ruled in 1838, there was a "want of authority to confer freedom by will" because doing so constituted a transfer of property (themselves) to the slaves, whereas slaves lacked "the capacity to take property."[30] Freedom, even if only for a small number of blacks, represented a potent threat to the concept of total slave dependence.

Much of this restrictive legislation, however, was haphazard, inconsistent, and sporadically enforced. Freed blacks were usually able to evade laws requiring them to leave their state, and slaves continued, often with the support of their masters and other whites, to trade and to hire themselves out without supervision. As Janet Duitsman Cornelius has recently noted, white Southerners were divided over attempts to prevent slave literacy, for "restrictions ran counter to the centuries-old tradition that the word of God should be accessible to all people and that Bible literacy would promote order, decorum, and morality."[31] Most states passed laws designed to keep slaves illiterate, but these laws were surprisingly vague, inconsistent, and ineffective, and were poorly enforced. Only four states—Virginia, North Carolina, South Carolina, and Georgia—had laws on the books throughout the last thirty years of slavery totally prohibiting teaching slaves to read and write; other states had such laws for briefer periods or banned the teaching of *assembled* slaves but not individuals.

Even as Southern authorities moved to strengthen slavery by ensuring total slave subservience, they also sought to strengthen slavery by making it more humane. The notion that slave owners could do whatever they wanted with their slaves, that slaves had no rights that masters were bound to respect, was anathema to many Southern whites convinced that theirs was a just—and good—society. Because slaves were to be kept dependent, they were vulnerable and needed special protection. Reformers were not successful in securing all the legal guarantees for slaves that they sought—efforts to legalize slave marriage and to prevent the splitting of families by sale came to naught—but the law did increasingly reflect the perceived need to protect slaves as well as regulate them.

The slave trade, widely recognized as the most embarrassing component of slavery, received considerable attention from state lawmakers. Even before the federal prohibition on the African slave trade, most individual colonies and states, motivated primarily by racial fears and economic concerns but in the Revolutionary era also by ethical qualms, had at least temporarily banned the importation of new slaves. Such action persisted in the antebellum period. Despite their intense demand for slave labor, many states of the deep South passed laws designed to curtail the operations of professional slave traders; Georgia banned the commercial importation of slaves from 1817 to 1853, and Alabama, Mississippi, and Louisiana imposed similar bans for much briefer periods. Upper-South states, too, passed laws against the importation of slaves from other states, although only Delaware prohibited exporting slaves to those states. Ethical concerns also spurred efforts to *regulate* the slave trade. Several states discouraged the separation of families, and in 1829 Louisiana forbade the sale of children under the age of eleven apart from their mothers.

As such measures suggest, antebellum legislation gave considerably more attention than had colonial-era slave laws to regulating the masters as well as the slaves. The Alabama slave code of 1852 typified the trend. Although much of the lengthy code consisted of provisions designed to ensure the slaves' subordination, it also contained measures setting guidelines for their treatment and limits to their mistreatment. "The master must treat his slave with humanity, and must not inflict upon him any cruel punishment," the document intoned; "he must provide him with a sufficiency of healthy food and necessary clothing[,] cause him to be properly attended during sickness, and provide for his necessary wants in old age." The lawmakers urged that slaves should, "if practicable," be sold only in families, and flatly prohibited sale of children under five apart from their mothers.

The code went on to list, and detail punishment for, a variety of specific offenses against slaves. Anyone killing a slave "with malice aforethought" was guilty of "murder in the first degree," while someone inadvertently killing a slave through excessive punishment "is guilty of murder in the second degree, and may be guilty of murder in the first degree." A slave owner or his subordinate who imposed "cruel punishment" or "treats [a slave] in any other way with inhumanity"—it was up to the jury to decide what these terms meant—was to be fined between twenty-five and one thousand dollars. Anyone compelling a slave to perform field labor on Sunday was subject to a ten-dollar fine.[32]

The practical consequences of such provisions were mixed. Because no slave state allowed slaves to testify against whites, the vast majority of whites who committed non-capital offenses against slaves escaped detection, let alone punishment; where such whites were brought to trial, it was usually because other whites sought their prosecution, as, for example, with an overseer who mistreated his employer's slaves. Laws forbidding the slave trade were easily evaded, and the buying and selling of slaves continued unabated. Still, efforts to regulate the trade were not totally without effect. Before passage of Louisiana's 1829 law prohibiting sale of children under age eleven apart from their mothers, 13.3 percent of the slaves shipped to New Orleans by Virginia-based traders Franklin and Armfield consisted of such children; after 1829, Franklin and Armfield abruptly halted these sales. Throughout the South, public sentiment reinforced legislation to discourage the separate sale of very young children. Similarly, although most crimes committed against slaves went unpunished, whites were occasionally tried, convicted, and punished—typically with ten-year jail sentences—for murdering slaves. Laws prohibiting cruelty to slaves were easy to evade, but the very existence of these laws was indicative of the kind of community sentiment that acted to curtail although by no means eliminate the worst abuses against them.

Equally significant was the care with which courts deliberated the fate of slaves accused of crimes against whites. Of course, most infractions committed by slaves never reached court, and in times of widespread public anxiety, such as following a slave insurrection, trials sometimes resulted in the hysterical meting out of vengeance upon anyone suspected of guilt. But as legal historians such as Mark V. Tushnet, Daniel J. Flanigan, and Edward L. Ayers have recently stressed, slaves charged with killing or physically assaulting whites often received serious trials. "Blacks accused of major offenses could expect procedural fairness," noted Ayers; "once slaves entered the higher levels of the judicial machinery, in particular, they were treated much like whites." Like whites, guilty blacks were sometimes acquitted on technicalities; in 1857, for example, the conviction of a Louisiana slave for stabbing a white man was overturned on appeal, because the law in effect at the time of the offense had since been repealed.[33]

Thoughtful Southern jurists were well aware of the dualism of antebellum Southern law, as an agency of both repression and protection of slaves. Repression inevitably came first: as Georgian Thomas R. R. Cobb noted in his 1858 book, *An Inquiry into the Law of Negro Slavery in the United States of America*, "the right of personal liberty in the slave is utterly inconsistent with the idea of slavery," and the law's preeminent obligation was to secure the slave's subordination. At the same time, however, Cobb observed that precisely "on account of the perfectly unprotected and helpless position of the slave, . . . the courts should, and do, feel themselves to be his guardian and protector." Like many other Southern spokesmen, he worried that the slaves' utter dependence, essential though it was, left them vulnerable to abuse, and he favored broadening their legal protection by, among other things, making the rape of a slave woman an indictable offense. He blithely asserted, however, that "the occurrence of such an offence is almost unheard of[,] and the known lasciviousness of the negro, renders the possibility of its occurrence very remote."[34]

These comments reveal much about the nature—and limits—of slave-owner paternalism. To men like Cobb, it was the slaves' very powerlessness that accentuated the need to look after them; protection represented the flip side of total slave dependence. Even as they sought to promote that dependence, many pro-slavery ideologues were troubled by the arbitrary power of master over slave that it entailed, for as good republicans they well knew the potential for abuse that lay in such power. But for most of them, it was the potential rather than the actual misuse of power that was problematical; they were convinced that the system—and most slave owners—was good, and that abuses under it were rare.

The slaves' view was very different. If the *possibility* of arbitrary treatment of slaves proved troubling to articulate defenders of slavery, it was the incessant *reality* of such treatment that impressed the slaves. The slaves were profoundly influenced by slave-owner paternalism, and as we shall see in the next chapter, they expressed toward the masters some of the same ambivalent feelings the masters held toward them. Ultimately, however, the slaves had a very different perspective on master–slave relations from that of their owners. That difference underlay much of daily life in the slave quarters.

5

Antebellum Slavery:
Slave Life

I

MASTERS NEVER ACHIEVED the total domination they sought over
their slaves. Despite the efforts of slave owners to regulate all their
activities, the slaves lived in a world that was influenced but by no
means totally controlled by the slaveholders' regime. Because paternalistic Southern masters interfered in the daily lives of their
"people" more than masters typically did in the Caribbean, Brazil,
or Russia, the independence of slave life was unusually restricted
in the antebellum South. Nevertheless, the slaves managed to develop their own semi-autonomous way of life, to interact with one
another on a basis that reflected shared values and customs. Slaves
at work were closely regulated, but away from work, they lived and
loved, played and prayed, in a world largely unknown to the masters.

Until recently, it was also a world largely unknown to historians.
During the past two decades, however, as historians in general have
abandoned an almost exclusive focus on the rich, famous, and powerful to pay attention to the lives of ordinary Americans—women,
blacks, immigrants, laborers, farmers, families—students of slavery
have probed with increasing sophistication the world of the slaves.
Considering slaves as subjects in their own right rather than merely
as objects of white action, historians have striven to reconstruct their

"internal" lives, including their families, religion, social organization, folkways, values, and resistance to oppression, and have in the
process dramatically revised our understanding of the peculiar institution.

II

A BRIEF AND SIMPLIFIED historiographical survey provides a useful
introduction to this development. Until fairly recently, most historians of slavery paid far more attention to the behavior of the
masters than to that of the slaves; slaves, the vast majority of whom
were illiterate and therefore left no written records, appeared in
their works primarily as objects of white action. Scholars differed in
many of their evaluations of slavery—some portrayed it as benign,
whereas others depicted it as harshly exploitative—but with the
partial exception of a tiny number of black and Marxist scholars,
they focused far more on what slavery did to the slaves than what
the slaves did themselves.

During the first half of the twentieth century, a major component
of this approach was often simple racism, manifest in the belief that
blacks were, at best, imitative of whites. Thus Ulrich B. Phillips,
the era's most celebrated and influential expert on slavery, combined
a sophisticated portrait of the white planters' life and behavior with
crude passing generalizations about the life and behavior of their
black slaves. Noting that "the planters had a saying . . . that a negro
was what a white man made him," Phillips portrayed the plantation
as a "school constantly training and controlling pupils who were in
a backward state of civilization"; through this educational process
the slaves "became largely standardized into the predominant plantation type." He proceeded to list "the traits which prevailed" as
"an eagerness for society, music and merriment, a fondness for
display . . . , a not flagrant sensuality, a receptiveness toward any
religion whose exercises were exhilarating, a proneness to superstition, a courteous acceptance of subordination, an avidity for praise,
a readiness for loyalty of a feudal sort, and last but not least, a
healthy human repugnance toward overwork." Content with asserting such traits rather than demonstrating them, Phillips devoted
most of his attention to the way planters managed their slaves, not
to the slaves themselves.[1]

Although such overt expressions of racism became less prevalent in the 1930s and 1940s and downright unfashionable in the 1950s, the tendency to treat slaves as objects persisted. As this persistence reveals, commitment to racial equality could be just as compatible with objectifying the slaves as was belief in white superiority. Indeed, because stressing the cruelties of slavery usually led to focusing on the injuries done to slaves, it could easily reinforce rather than subvert a historical model in which white slave owners and their agents acted and black slaves were acted upon. Thus, although Kenneth M. Stampp's "neo-abolitionist" book *The Peculiar Institution* (1956) differed sharply from Ulrich B. Phillips's *American Negro Slavery* (1918) in its overall evaluation of slavery, its main subject remained the treatment—now the *mis*treatment—of slaves. Stampp took the slaves far more seriously than did Phillips, but the sources that Stampp relied upon—plantation records, letters and diaries of slave owners, travel accounts written by Northern and European visitors who almost invariably stayed with white hosts—revealed more about the behavior and thought of the masters than of the slaves, whom he portrayed as "culturally rootless people."[2]

The depiction of antebellum slaves as victims reached its peak in Stanley M. Elkins's 1959 volume, *Slavery: A Problem in American Institutional and Intellectual Life,* one of those rare historical works that not only arouse intense controversy but also promote sharp reversals of historical interpretation. Noting the absence of slave rebellions in the American South equal in size or duration to those in Brazil and the Caribbean islands, Elkins argued that the unusually harsh conditions faced by Southern slaves produced a "closed" environment that stripped them of their native African culture, prevented the emergence among them of any meaningful social relations, and turned them into childlike "Sambos" who almost completely internalized the values of their masters. Unlike the monarchy and the established Church in Latin America, both of which supposedly protected slaves from the worst abuses of bondage, nothing came between master and slave in the South; slavery there was, like the Nazi concentration camp, a "total" institution that rendered its victims psychologically defenseless. The Southern slave who, "for his very psychic security, had to picture his master in some way as the 'good father,' " was transformed into an emasculated, docile Sambo who came to identify with that very master.[3]

Despite its ingenuity, the Elkins thesis soon came under withering attack from critics who blasted it as contrived, illogical, and unsupported by empirical evidence. Historians of Latin American slavery disputed the notion that the Church and Crown always mitigated the severity of slavery, and comparative historians pointed to the superior health and unique natural population growth of American slaves to rebut the argument that the conditions they endured were far harsher than those in the rest of the Americas. Other scholars disputed the utility of Elkins's concentration-camp analogy, suggested that apparent Sambo-like behavior was explicable without recourse to theories of slave infantilization (as a result of role-playing, for example), and noted that after the Civil War the actions of emancipated blacks were hardly childish or docile. Research by scholars seeking to test the Elkins thesis provided increasing evidence that antebellum slaves lived not in a totally closed environment but rather in one that permitted the emergence of enormous variety and allowed slaves to pursue important relationships with persons other than their masters, including those to be found in their families, churches, and communities. By the 1970s, although historians such as Robert W. Fogel and Stanley L. Engerman had borrowed Elkins's idea that the slaves internalized their owners' ideals (the Protestant work ethic, according to Fogel and Engerman), the Sambo thesis lay in tatters.

Ironically, however, that thesis—and the controversy it provoked—played a major role in redirecting historical scholarship on slavery. As historians sought to rebut Elkins's assertion of slave docility, they found it necessary to focus far more than they previously had on the slaves as subjects in their own right rather than as objects of white treatment. The effort to test the Sambo thesis thus combined with the new historical interest in the lives of ordinary people to bring the slaves themselves to center stage in the drama of slavery. This new focus came to full fruition during the 1970s, as historians produced an avalanche of works seeking to rediscover the slave experience. For the first time, that experience became the major (although by no means the only) focus of historical research on antebellum Southern slavery.

As the focus of historical attention shifted increasingly to the slaves, historians found themselves forced to exploit "new" kinds of historical sources, which had previously been little used, to shed light on the slaves' world. Scholars probed archaeological remains, analyzed black folklore, and toiled over statistical data culled from census reports and plantation records, but in their efforts to explore slave thought and behavior they found two kinds of sources especially useful: autobiographies of former slaves (some written after escape to the North and some after emancipation) and interviews with former slaves, the most extensive collection of which was taken under the auspices of the Federal Writers' Project during the 1930s. It is largely on the basis of these sources that historians have redirected their attention to the slaves, a redirection that has been more productive for the antebellum South than anywhere else because historical records that illuminate slavery from the slaves' vantage point are far more abundant for the slave South than for any other slave society.

Using slave sources to explore the slaves' "consciousness"—their thought, ideology, values, and identification—is a task of enormous difficulty, because these sources, although highly revealing, are also often highly problematical. Because most of them illustrate the late antebellum period, they encourage scholars either to focus on that period or to generalize from it about earlier times, in the process losing sight of significant changes that occurred over time. Equally serious are problems associated with interpreting autobiographies that were often written as deliberate acts of abolitionist propaganda and interpreting recollections of very old men and women about their youth three-quarters of a century earlier, especially when most of those recollections were elicited in interviews conducted by white Southerners in an era of black racial subordination. Historians have at times been too eager to take slave autobiographies and interviews at face value—an inappropriate approach with any historical document—and to construct on their basis an idealized version of slave behavior.

Nevertheless, when used with proper caution and sensitivity, and supplemented with additional evidence (including inferences drawn from actual behavior), autobiographies and interviews constitute an extremely important window on the minds of the slaves and have enabled scholars of the 1970s and 1980s to revise radically our understanding of American slavery. Although these scholars do not agree with one another in all particulars, the great majority of them have abandoned the victimization model in favor of an emphasis on the slaves' resiliency and autonomy. As I suggest below, I believe that some of these arguments for slave autonomy have been overstated and eventually will be modified on the basis of future evidence. It is clear, however, that whatever such modifications may occur, we have in a relatively short time learned an enormous amount about the lives of those who were for too long ignored in the study of slavery: the slaves. Those lives are the subject of this chapter.

III

HISTORIANS EXAMINING the lives and behavior of antebellum slaves have disagreed on numerous points, but they have been virtually unanimous in finding that Elkins erred in depicting a world in which slaves had no "meaningful others" aside from their masters. Of course, slaves lived under widely varying conditions, and some may have experienced the totally controlled, "closed" system described by Elkins. For the vast majority, however, slavery never provided such a hermetically sealed environment; beings who were in theory totally dependent on their masters were able in practice to forge a semi-autonomous world, based on a multiplicity of social relationships, which accentuated their own distinctive customs and values. In this endeavor, they looked for support most of all to their families and their religion.

Families provided a crucial if fragile buffer, shielding slaves from the worst rigors of slavery. Although the transatlantic slave trade, exceptionally high mortality rates, and the excess of men over women among newly imported slaves decimated African families, the emergence of a predominantly creole slave population created the basic preconditions for family re-creation. A new African-American family structure took root in the eighteenth century and spread throughout the South, along with slavery, in the nineteenth. Those families were not, of course, untouched by slavery. Even under the best of circumstances, slave families lacked the institutional and legal support enjoyed by those that were free, and in extreme cases masters could not only hinder but prevent the development of normal family relations; Frederick Douglass, taken from his mother as an infant, recalled it as "a common custom, in the part of Maryland from which I ran away, to part children from their mothers at a very early age."[4] But historians now know that in the South as a whole, separation of young children from their mothers was relatively unusual. Antebellum slaves lived in families, legally recognized or not, and the majority of slave children grew up with their mothers and—somewhat less often—their fathers. Slave owners were usually aware of, and considered themselves strong supporters of, slave families. Motivated by both a paternalistic concern for the well-being of their "people" and a calculating regard for their own economic interest, slave owners paid increasing attention to the family lives of their slaves. Antebellum masters usually assigned one slave family (much less often two) to a cabin, grouped slaves according to families in plantation censuses, and promoted "family morality" among their people in a variety of ways, including punishing adultery and divorce, insisting on early marriage, allowing (or not allowing) marriage "abroad," and less often purchasing spouses of favored servants. The actions of the masters were in many ways contradictory: they not only supported slave families but also disrupted them, through forced separations and forced sex. Still, their actions as supporters served to some extent to limit the impact of their actions as disrupters, and to make possible, despite the hostile environment, a family life among slaves that was vital if constantly at risk. Indeed, historians Robert W. Fogel and Stanley L. Engerman have gone so far as to attribute the strength of antebellum slave families primarily to the support they received from slave owners.

Most other historians have stressed the actions of the slaves themselves in building and defending their families, often against overwhelming odds. As a result of research by Herbert G. Gutman and other scholars, we now know a great deal about the structure of slave families. Like most other Americans and Western Europeans (but unlike many Eastern Europeans, Asians, and Africans), Southern slaves usually lived in nuclear (or "simple") households: father, mother, and children. In the most recent study of slave families, Ann Patton Malone, who examined a sample of 19,329 slaves in Louisiana between 1810 and 1864, found that 73 percent of these slaves lived in simple households composed either of married couples with or without children or of single parents with children, and an additional 18.3 percent lived alone; only 8.7 percent of the slaves lived in more complex "multiple," "extended," or "non-nuclear" households. Throughout the South, families were large, with the average woman giving birth to about seven children over the course of her childbearing years and the typical slave cabin containing four to seven residents at any given time. Marriages, unless broken by sale, were usually long-lasting. Families constituted a fundamental survival mechanism, enabling the slaves to resist the kind of de-humanization that Elkins believed they underwent. Slaves may have owed their masters instantaneous and unquestioned obedience, but in the bosoms of their families they loved, laughed, quarreled, schemed, sang, and endured, much as free people did.

Slave families exhibited a number of features that differentiated them from prevailing norms among white Southerners and revealed the degree to which those families were created by the slaves them-selves. Slaves used naming practices to solidify family ties threat-ened with rupture, naming children after fathers and grandfathers especially frequently because male relatives were more likely than female to be sold away. Although whites did not acknowledge (or often even know of) the practice, many slaves took surnames, for the sake of family unity as well as family dignity; as former slave Robert Smalls testified in 1863, although "among themselves they use their titles [surnames] . . . before their masters they do not speak of their titles at all."[5]

The slaves' marital standards differed in significant ways from those of their owners. Although slaves expected each other to be faithful in marriage, they did not put much stock in the prevailing Victorian notion of premarital sexual abstinence; sexual experimen-tation before marriage (not always with the ultimate spouse) was widespread and aroused little stigma among them. Unlike Southern planters, however, slaves strictly adhered to marital exogamy, shun-ning marriage with first cousins. As this practice indicates, living in nuclear families did not preclude the existence of extended kinship networks among slaves, who often exhibited impressive awareness of and attachments to more distant familial relations.

The role and status of women in slave families were also distinc-tive. Recent research has dispelled the once common stereotype of a prevalent slave "matriarchy," predicated on weak ties of affection between slave men and their families. Still, for at least two reasons, slave families were less male-dominated than free families typically were in the nineteenth century. First, slave men lacked the legal authority over their wives that free men possessed. When free women married, they lost a variety of rights, including the right to own and dispose of property, and became legally subordinated to their husbands. Because slave families lacked legal status, however, women who married were not automatically subjected to legal de-basement; slave husbands had no more property rights than did their wives, who maintained "equal or near equal status with their husbands."[6] Second, slave women were more likely than their husbands to be "home." They ran away, were sold off, and were hired out far less often than men; in marriages abroad, it was the husbands rather than the wives who typically traveled to visit their families on weekends. For these reasons, mother-headed households, although not the norm, were relatively common; Malone found that about one-third of the nuclear households in Louisiana were headed by a single parent, in the vast majority of cases the mother. In short, slave women provided basic continuity to families—and communities—faced with disruption.

Children growing up as slaves faced contradictory experiences that reveal both the importance and the fragility of family life under slavery. Young children often enjoyed substantially greater freedom than their elders. Although very large plantations sometimes had nurseries, most children received relatively little supervision; with their parents and older siblings at work, they spent much of their time playing among themselves—and often with local white children. "The first seven or eight years of the slave-boy's life are about as full of sweet content as those of the most favored and petted *white* children of the slaveholder," recalled Frederick Douglass; noting that "he literally runs wild," Douglass portrayed the "slave-boy" as "a spirited, joyous, uproarious, and happy boy, upon whom troubles fall only like water on a duck's back."[7] Some black autobiographers and interviewees later remembered that as children they were literally unaware of being slaves. (The relative freedom afforded many slave children is one reason that the Federal Writers' Project interviews must be used with extreme caution in reconstructing the lives of adults; two-thirds of those interviewed were born after 1850 and were thus ten years old or younger at the outbreak of the Civil War.)

Still, children were hardly untouched by slavery. In a variety of ways, masters interfered extensively in their lives, bringing some to the "big house" to serve as domestics and assigning others "light" chores that became increasingly onerous until they were put to regular field work, usually between the ages of eight and twelve. Slave owners insisted on naming some slave children, against the wishes of (and sometimes competing with names awarded by) their parents, and exposed children to their version of Christianity. Slave owners also sometimes taught household "pets" how to read and write:

abouc 5 percent of slaves (two-thirds of them male) interviewed by the Federal Writers' Project recollected being taught to read under slavery, most often by sympathetic whites. (Other slaves, however, learned to read on their own or with the help of other blacks, *in spite of* the strenuous efforts of their owners to keep them illiterate.)

Slave children learned at an early age that they had to conform to the wishes of two sets of authorities—their parents and their owners—both of whom were involved in their upbringing. Such competing claims on their loyalty could be confusing. Evidence of the masters' authority was readily apparent in their dealings with adult slaves; children who saw their parents verbally or physically abused without resisting could not fail to draw the appropriate lesson about where real power lay. At the same time, parents struggled to provide their children with love and attention and passed on family lore as well as customs and values. With the help of friends and relatives, parents sang to their children, told them stories, exposed them to their version of Christianity, and brought them up to be extremely careful of what they said in front of whites. As children aged, they became increasingly aware of their unfree status, sometimes gradually through incremental discoveries, sometimes at once through a traumatic event—a whipping, a comment by a white playmate, sale of a loved one—that brought home the reality of their situation.

Although families provided slaves with a basic refuge from the horrors of slavery, this refuge was always insecure. Masters who preached the importance of family life subverted their own message by constantly interfering with their people's families: they sold, raped, and whipped, and even under the best of circumstances they insisted on their right, as paternalistic guardians, to direct the upbringing of children. Slaves struggled valiantly to lead "normal" lives, and in doing so they relied most heavily on their families, but their lack of power vis-à-vis their masters rendered those families extremely vulnerable. Although we have learned a great deal about the structure of slave families, we have learned much less about their inner dynamics—how slaves actually interacted with one another at home—and it is a mistake to assume, on the basis of widespread stereotypical assertions in slave narratives, that those families were always loving. Pointing to "overzealousness in revising earlier misconceptions concerning the compositions of the slave family and community," Ann Malone has recently warned against the current scholarly tendency to see the slave family as "the cozy American family unit of mom, dad, and the kids."[8] Her warning is pertinent. Slaves had their own households, in which they were husbands, wives, parents, children, friends, and lovers, but as Elizabeth Fox-Genovese has forcefully argued in her recent book *Within the Plantation Household*, those same slaves were also members of their *masters'* households and could never totally escape their dependence on their masters. Slave families thus reflected simultaneously both the determined efforts of their members to achieve a measure of autonomy and the fragility of that autonomy.

IV

LIKE SLAVE FAMILIES, slave religion exhibited fragile autonomy and evolution over time. During most of the colonial period, white efforts to proselytize among blacks were sporadic, and first- or second-generation African-Americans were at best indifferent to the Christian message; the second half of the eighteenth century saw widespread conversion of blacks to Christianity, a process that accelerated in the religious revivals of the early nineteenth century; by the late antebellum period, evangelical Christianity had emerged throughout the South as a central feature of slave life. The slaves' exposure to Christianity was uneven: some lived in isolated areas without ready access to religious services, and others were subject to the arbitrary whim of masters who prevented them from attending church. But antebellum slaves increasingly experienced a number of overlapping—sometimes competing—religious influences, from paternalistic masters who prayed and read the Bible with their "people," from white religious denominations that mounted a "mission to the slaves," and from the "invisible church" that operated quasi-secretly among the slaves themselves. Most mid-nineteenth-century slaves, unlike their ancestors a century earlier, were devoutly Christian.

Like slave families, the "invisible church" possessed a number of distinctive features that reveal how blacks adapted white forms to their own needs. Slaves who assembled in the quarters, in open-air "hush arbors," and in space sometimes provided by white churches spurned the lectures they received elsewhere on obedience to authority as a central tenet of Christianity in favor of a religion of the oppressed that promised them deliverance from their earthly troubles. White ministers from staid denominations that appealed primarily to upper-class parishioners had special difficulty in attracting slaves: Presbyterian minister Charles C. Jones noted that when he lectured a group of slaves in Liberty County, Georgia, on the Christian virtue of obedience, "one half of my audience deliberately rose up and walked off with themselves, and those that remained looked anything but satisfied." Similarly, Harriet Jacobs recalled how when an Episcopal clergyman began holding separate services for blacks in Edenton, North Carolina, "his colored members were very few, and also very respectable"; soon after, displeased with the injunction that "if you disobey your earthly master, you offend your heavenly Master," "the slaves left, and went to enjoy a Methodist shout." White Methodists and Baptists had far more success with the slaves than did Presbyterians and Episcopalians, but they, too, often found blacks leery of what they heard. "Dat ole white preacher jest was telling us slaves to be good to our marsters," recalled former slave Cornelius Garner. "We ain't keer'd a bit 'bout dat stuff he was telling us 'cause we wanted to sing, pray, and serve God in our own way."[9]

The religious services of the slaves differed appreciably from those provided for them by whites. Accounts of Moses leading his people out of bondage replaced injunctions to obey authority. Although self-called black preachers, often illiterate and almost always ignorant of the fine points of theology, stressed the importance of virtuous behavior, they ignored the traditional Protestant emphasis on human depravity; the slaves' Christianity was a religion of the heart in which they could lose themselves in ecstatic joy, their God a redeemer and friend with whom they could communicate on a personal basis. A high level of emotional fervor characterized Southern evangelical Protestantism, whether white or black, but black Baptists and Methodists took this "enthusiasm" to a level that often shocked white observers—especially those of "genteel" backgrounds, whose religious behavior was likely to be more restrained—and derided white Christianity as stuffy and bloodless. Presbyterian minister R. Q. Mallard opined that a black revival meeting he witnessed in 1859 lacked any true religion, for it consisted of "one loud monotonous strain, interrupted by . . . groans and screams and clapping of hands," but many slaves believed their *masters* lacked true religious feeling: "You see," one explained later,

" 'legion needs a little motion—specially if you gwine feel de spirret."[10]

Despite the distinctive features of the black Christianity that emerged in the slave quarters, that Christianity was marked by pervasive white influence and indeed was itself a sign of the degree to which the masters impinged on the lives of their slaves. Differences between black and white religious practices were significant because those differences reveal the slaves as subjects whose behavior helped shape their own lives rather than merely as passive victims of white action, but from a broad view those differences must be regarded as relatively minor. Not only did the slaves adopt the general religion of their masters—Christianity—but they also adhered to the same specific (usually Protestant) denominations. Antebellum Southern blacks were, like antebellum Southern whites, most often Baptists and Methodists, with much smaller numbers of Presbyterians, Episcopalians, Catholics, and members of other sects. There were differences between black and white Baptists and between black and white Methodists, but there were also differences between black Baptists and black Methodists, or for that matter between white Baptists and white Presbyterians. American Christianity constituted an amorphous and highly heterogeneous religion, within which slaves found it easy to develop their own variants while remaining part of the mainstream.

Equally important, the shared religious heritage of white and black Southerners provided important bases of contact between them. Much of this contact occurred within the confines of slave-owner paternalism, as masters increasingly embraced the "mission to the slaves." Much of it, however, transcended the master–slave relationship and thrust blacks and whites together as believers in an environment that at least temporarily subverted consciousness of class and race. If the religious exposure of some slaves consisted primarily of slave owners reading the Bible to them, praying with them, and arranging for special services where they heard of Christian duty to obey their masters, that of others included attending interracial revival meetings as well as services that exhibited a high level of Christian fellowship. Several recent historians have emphasized the degree to which many white and black Southerners shared not just similar religious views but common religious experiences. "[T]he normative worship experience of blacks in the antebellum

South was in a biracial church," suggested John B. Boles; although slaves usually sat in segregated slave galleries, "black and white co-worshipers heard the same sermons, were baptized and took communion together, and upon death were buried in the same cemeteries."[11]

Whether slaves worshipped separately or with whites, historians have recently been so impressed by the force of slave religion that they have may well have exaggerated its universality and slighted some of its contradictory implications. Many slaves lacked access to regular religious services, either because they lived in remote areas or because they had owners who regarded their religious aspirations with distaste. Bennet H. Barrow's plantation diary (1836–46), for example, is filled with expressions of disgust at the religious enthusiasm of both whites and blacks; he frequently forbade his slaves to attend nearby religious meetings, and when sixteen slaves temporarily ran away from a neighboring plantation he blamed the flight on their owner's "having them preached to for 4 or 5 years past," an action that constituted the "greatest piece of foolishness any one [was] ever guilty of." Other slaves were simply uninterested in religion, and, in the words of slave autobiographer Henry Bibb, "resort[ed] to the woods in large numbers on [Sundays] to gamble, fight, get drunk, and break the Sabbath." Although Bibb expressed typical nineteenth-century outrage at such desecration of the Sabbath, many slaves eagerly looked forward to their day "off" as a time to work on their garden plots, spend time with their families, and simply relax.[12]

Christianity had to compete for the slaves' time and attention not only with secular concerns but also with a host of pre-Christian beliefs and practices that persisted even among ardent Baptists and Methodists. Slaves commonly resorted to potions, concoctions, charms, and rituals to ward off evil, cure sickness, harm enemies, and produce amorous behavior. Dellie Lewis, interviewed in the 1930s for the Federal Writers' Project, described some of the magic tricks she had learned from her midwife grandmother, tricks that included both folk remedies such as prescribing cloves and whiskey to ease the pain of childbirth and magic rituals such as putting a fresh egg at the door of a sick person to prevent anyone from entering the room. "If you is anxious fo' yo' sweetheart to come back f'um a trip," she added, "put a pin in de groun' wid de point up an' den put a aig on de point. When all de insides runs outen de aig yo' sweetheart will return."[13]

Although educated whites derided such "superstition" and slave autobiographers seeking to appeal to "enlightened" nineteenth-century sensibilities wrote of it with extreme embarrassment, magic, conjuring, and folk medicine continued to exercise a powerful hold over most antebellum slaves—at the same time that those slaves also considered themselves practicing Christians. Indeed, it was not uncommon for slaves to develop practices that fused Christian and non-Christian elements, as in the method described by autobiographer Jacob Stroyer of watching how a Bible turned when hung by a string to determine whether an accused person was guilty of stealing. One reason slaves were so easily able to combine belief in Christianity with belief in conjurers, witches, and spirits is that many apparently saw little difference between the two; noting that his father was a root doctor who could cure the sick, George White explained that he, too, knew "all de roots" and could "cure most anything," but he added that "you have got to talk wid God an' ask him to help out."[14]

The particular combination of Christian and pre-Christian religion that coexisted in the slave quarters originated, of course, in the contact and interaction of African and European cultures and was one component of the new, African-American culture that resulted from the enslavement of blacks in America. This combination bore striking resemblance, however, to the mixture of Christian and pre-Christian beliefs embraced by many of the European immigrants to America in the seventeenth and eighteenth centuries, when, as historians such as Jon Butler have recently stressed, adherence to Christian theology constituted a thin veneer beneath which flourished widespread belief in magic and the occult. The similarity between the pre-modern worldviews held by whites and blacks in the South facilitated the continuing interaction between them in the antebellum period, in both Christian and non-Christian manifestations. It was by no means unknown for lower-class whites to consult black conjurers.

Slave magic and slave Christianity coexisted, but appropriated different spheres. Magic was most often directed at a concrete and immediate goal: to cure an illness, punish a rival suitor, prevent an overseer from applying the lash. Christianity was inevitably more abstract, more long-term in orientation: the rewards it promised were not in this world but in the next. As such, it exercised diverse and contradictory influences. It provided enormous comfort to an oppressed people, but in doing so it offered them an escape that could temper their real-world response to oppression. Why struggle to improve conditions in this world when the virtuous would receive everlasting happiness in the next?

Although slave owners had long disagreed over the likely impact of Christianity on their slaves, by the late antebellum years the vast majority had concluded that religion would make them more docile and obedient rather than more troublesome. Although the evidence is mixed, they may well have been correct. At times, Christianity could produce the fervor of a Nat Turner determined to wreak vengeance on the wicked. It could also create a culture of collaboration, one that emphasized rendering unto Caesar what was Caesar's. More often than either of these, however, it appears to have fostered in the slaves both a sense of short-term resignation and fatalism and a belief in eventual freedom. Under existing conditions, deliverance was something to be prayed for and awaited, not worked for and created. Under different conditions, however, that deliverance could certainly be helped along.

V

THE SLAVE COMMUNITY has become one of the central—albeit least well defined—concerns of recent historians of slavery. Eager to rebut images of slave passivity and docility, many of these historians have elevated the slave community to an all-embracing agency that gave order to the slaves' lives, expressed their deepest aspirations, and prevented their complete victimization. In the process, they have offered a real corrective to previous, one-sided interpretations that treated slaves largely as objects of white action rather than as subjects in their own right. At the same time, however, they have often reified "slave community," a slippery and emotionally laden term unused in antebellum years and used with varying (often unspecified) meanings today; "as the word is currently used, . . ." Clarence E. Walker has recently suggested, "[community] is a romantic construct that obscures more than it reveals."[15] They have also come dangerously close to replacing a mythical world in which slaves were objects of total control with an equally mythical world in which slaves were hardly slaves at all.

Any evaluation of the problem of "community" must come to grips with two partially distinct but interrelated questions, those of autonomy and communality. The first of these involves the degree to which the slaves were able to secure control of their own lives, while the second involves the degree to which, in doing so, they acted on the basis of mutuality and collective interests. Resolving these questions is difficult, because levels of slave autonomy and communality were by no means synonymous (substantial autonomy did not necessarily imply substantial communality), because neither was constant over time or space, and because behavior, sharply limited by physical constraints, was closely linked to but never entirely a function of thought. The historian needs to distinguish between the elusive bundle of mental processes that represented the way slaves thought—"consciousness," "worldview," "ideology," "mentality"—and the behavioral patterns that represented the way they acted.

As the existence of slave families and slave religion indicates, large numbers of slaves throughout the antebellum South were able to forge ties other than the master–slave relationship that was central to slavery, in the process creating social and cultural formations that were essentially peripheral to that relationship even though they operated within its overall context. For the majority of slaves who lived on or near plantations, it was the slave quarters that provided the setting and the opportunity for leading lives partially free from white supervision. Composed of cabins grouped together to form a slave "village," the quarters was typically set a considerable distance from the master's "big house," to shield planter families from the intrusive presence of a large slave population. This isolation of the quarters, although primarily for the convenience of the masters, provided an important measure of privacy to the slaves, affording them a real if insecure refuge from the outside world.

Within the quarters, slaves engaged in a myriad of "leisure" activities that belied their condition as human property. When the master's work was done, they ate, sang, prayed, played, talked, quarreled, made love, hunted, fished, named babies, cleaned house, tended their garden plots, and rested. They strove to fill their lives with pleasurable activities that would enable them to transcend their status as slaves. "Whoopee, didn' us have good Sa'dd'y night frolics and jubilees," remarked ex-slave Abraham Chambers in a typical recollection. "Some clap and some play de fiddle, and, man, dey danced most all night."[16] Christmas, harvesttime, corn shucking, and hog killing provided occasions for celebrations that slaves eagerly anticipated and long remembered.

Away from the immediate control of white authorities, slaves developed their own traditions and customs that reflected shared values. Forged out of varying combinations of African and European cultural practices, these customs differed over time and space. In southern Louisiana, voodoo, a syncretic, highly ritualized religion based on African beliefs fused with elements of French Catholicism, flourished, but it was unknown in most of the South; in the low country of South Carolina and Georgia, Gullah, reinforced by geographic isolation and a huge slave majority, fostered a distinctive slave culture, for, as historian Charles Joyner has pointed out, "speech communities, to an even greater extent than political communities, imply a shared culture and world view."[17]

Nevertheless, common experiences—and the domestic slave trade—shaped a shared cultural mainstream in much of the slave South. Slaves dressed up for church on Sundays, favoring bright colors to distinguish their appearance from the normal workaday attire. They sang spirituals and work songs, often using an antiphonal, call-and-response pattern of African origin. They told stories that, like folktales elsewhere, were filled with ghosts, spirits, talking animals, and didactic lessons for the young. They put great emphasis on proper wedding and funeral ceremonies, which, as in traditional peasant cultures, provided occasions for marking key points of transition in the human experience and assumed enormous symbolic importance. In many of these ways, the slaves approached a kind of peasant autonomy, developing their own folkways even while under conditions of severe economic and political dependence.

It is important, however, to keep in mind the limitations to this slave autonomy. What is at issue is not whether slaves developed their own customs and cultural activities but the nature of those customs and activities: the degree to which they were able to operate free from white influence and the degree to which they indicated communal values and behavior. Because historians for many years paid little attention to the slaves' internal lives, accentuating the strength of the "slave community" served as a much needed historical corrective in the 1970s and 1980s. In their efforts to dispel the stereotype of slave passivity, however, many scholars lurched to the other extreme, lacing their writings with an evocative language of celebration in which terms like "community," "culture," "kinship ties," "solidarity," and "human dignity" replaced those suggesting victimization, and presenting such a felicitous portrait of life in the quarters that slavery itself seemed to fade into the background. "To understand the nature of education in the slave quarter community is to come to grips with the paradox of the 'free slave,' . . ." wrote historian Thomas L. Webber in 1978. "By passing their unique set of cultural themes from generation to generation, the members of the quarter community were able to resist most of white teaching, set themselves apart from white society, and mold their own cultural norms and group identity. While still legally slaves, the black men, women, and children of the quarter community successfully protected their psychological freedom and celebrated their human dignity."[18] I believe that an even-handed appraisal must not only incorporate the important revisionist work of the past two decades but also come to grips with the insecurity of slave life, the limits to slave autonomy, and the particular character that "community" assumed among the slaves. These stemmed both from the inherent realities of slavery in general and from the specific characteristics of Southern slavery in particular.

The nature of slave life in the South changed significantly over two and a half centuries. Some of the most emphasized communal features of that life—for example, the central role of slave Christianity—developed relatively late and were dominant characteristics only during the last years of the slave regime. Others— most notably African cultural influences—were strongest early, when the arrival of new slaves from Africa perpetuated knowledge of traditional ways, but gradually weakened in most of the South among slaves who were second-, third-, and fourth-generation Americans. By ignoring these changes over time, telescoping the slave past can distort the reality of slave life at any specific moment and suggest the existence of a generalized communal culture whose constituent parts did not always coexist.

A comparative perspective makes clear some of the particular limitations to both slave autonomy and slave communality in the antebellum South. Some of these limitations were demographic. The relatively small size of most Southern holdings, together with the high population ratio of whites to blacks, meant that most Southern slaves came in contact with whites far more often than did those in Jamaica or Saint Domingue. Reinforcing these demographic realities was the paternalistic meddling of resident masters who, as we have seen, strove to order virtually every element of their slaves' lives. Southern slaves persistently endeavored to augment their social autonomy, taking advantage of every opportunity provided them to manage their own affairs in their own ways, but in their efforts to maximize their day-to-day independence they faced unusually severe limitations, even for slaves. Slaves in Saint Domingue and Jamaica lived in a world that was overwhelmingly black, a world in which European planters felt intensely uncomfortable and from which they frequently retreated; serfs in Russia lived in a world that was even more overwhelmingly peasant, one alien to and usually avoided by their noble masters. Southern slaves, by contrast, lived in, and had to adjust to, the world of their masters.

The slaves' status as societal outsiders impeded their ability to carve for themselves the kind of autonomy typically enjoyed by dependent peasants. Even where the dependence of such peasants was most extreme—as in Russia, where serfs were in many ways indistinguishable from slaves—peasants were typically regarded as constituting the lowest element of society, and enjoyed certain clearly delineated rights (either by law or custom), including the right to marry, hold land, and form communal organizations. Students of peasant life in diverse areas of the world have recently emphasized "community" as an organizing principle of rural life. Communities had geographic, economic, and political bases; they were marked by intense attachment to place, a corresponding distrust of outsiders, a sense of collective interests (often centered on property rights), and the formation of institutions designed to protect those interests. Above all, a village community was composed geographically, by people living in one locality and having a sense of a shared past and mutual responsibility. "To belong to a rural community," sociologist Victor V. Magagna has stated, "was to belong to a specific place with a particular history."[19]

Slaves, by contrast, generally lacked the economic and institutional bases for "community," as well as the local attachments that accompanied them. They did not constitute the bottom level of society so much as outsiders to it; that society provided no formal recognition of what tradition sanctified as theirs by right. It is for this reason that historian James Oakes insists that slavery was "a qualitatively distinct form of subordination" that left its victims far less control over their lives than other forms of unfree and quasi-free labor.[20] In short, slaves did not really form communities in the sense that peasants did. As I will suggest in section VII, however, they did develop a common identification that substituted for—and has often been confused with—a sense of community.

If slaves in general were unable to achieve the kind of folk autonomy typically enjoyed by dependent peasants, *American* slaves faced obstacles that in important respects made their struggle for independence especially difficult. In much of the Caribbean, and to a lesser extent in Brazil, slaves approached a "proto-peasant" status based on a substantial degree of economic independence. Assigned "provision grounds" in much the same way that Russian serfs were allotted land, slaves cultivated their "own" land, providing their own sustenance and selling the surplus in flourishing local markets; in the process, they acquired their "own" property as well as a strong sense of their rights and privileges. Southern slave owners, however, rarely allowed their slaves this kind of economic independence. Historians such as Ira Berlin and Philip D. Morgan have recently explored the development of an internal slave economy in the South, noting the widespread existence of garden plots—which slaves came to regard as theirs by right—as well as the buying, selling, and bartering by slaves that ensued. But the internal economy faced severe limitations in the antebellum South, where, as we have seen, slave owners assiduously strove to keep their people in a state of complete dependence. Commercial activity on the part of slaves was most highly developed in the low country of South Carolina and Georgia, where the task system and widespread owner absenteeism created particularly favorable conditions, but even there it was on a modest scale by Caribbean standards. In most of the South, although masters often allowed their slaves to have garden plots, those masters usually kept control of slave provision, took pains to limit garden plots to at best a supplementary role, and imposed severe restrictions on any commercial activity on the part of the slaves.

Economic dependence did not, of course, totally preclude the development of social and cultural autonomy among the slaves; even under the most adverse of circumstances, slaves strove in countless small ways to wrest as much control of their lives from their masters as they could. The conditions under which they lived, however,

subjected them to unusually pervasive outside influence as paternalistic masters strove to control their every action. Those conditions
also impeded collective action on their part and fostered an ethos
in which individuals struggled to find their niche and make the best
of a bad situation.

Slave folktales offer suggestive if sometimes elusive clues to the
consciousness of the quarters. Through stories of talking animals,
ghosts, and magic as well as those offering semi-realistic depictions
of plantation relations, slaves entertained one another, expressed
fears and longings, and presented their children with didactic lessons
on how to get along in a dog-eat-dog world. A number of scholarly
debates have swirled over the origins, transcription, and interpretation of these tales, but researchers have properly seen their very
existence as strong evidence of autonomous slave behavior and consciousness. Animal trickster tales, in which small but smart animals
typically outsmart those that are large and dumb, as well as stories
centered on persistent rivalry between "Old Master" and his slave
John or Jack, provided only thinly disguised reference to surrounding
social relations and enabled the slaves to poke vicarious fun at their
masters, themselves, and the world in which they lived.

But in addition to pointing to slave autonomy, those tales also
offer revealing hints concerning the slaves' mentality and suggest
the limits to their communal consciousness. Notably absent from
Southern slave folklore are stories depicting heroic behavior—stories
of dragon slayers, popular liberators, or people who sacrificed themselves for the good of the whole. Rather, the dominant themes are
trickery, subterfuge, and securing as much as possible of a desired
item (often food) for oneself. Justice, fair play, and compassion for
one's rivals rarely emerge as desirable characteristics. In short, sur-
viving in a heartless world assumes overriding importance; as historian Michael Flusche perceptively argued, "The recurring themes
of these stories suggest that slavery tended to engender an atomistic,
individualistic world view among the slaves and that the slaves' sense
of community was more complicated than simple unity in the face
of white oppression."[21]

The existence of antisocial behavior in slave folktales should not
be surprising; such behavior is present in the folktales of many
peoples and does not necessarily indicate an acceptance of antisocial
values. (The slaves' Christianity did emphasize idealism and heroic
figures such as Moses.) The highly competitive and aggressive be-

havior featured in so many slave stories, however, should serve to alert us to a notable fact: the grubby reality of day-to-day social relations in the quarters—with all the conflicts and jealousies that inevitably exist in human relations even under the best of circumstances—has been almost totally unexplored by historians interested in demonstrating the vitality of the slave community. Slaves struggled against overwhelming odds to build decent lives for themselves and took pleasure when they could in their friends and families. They were also human beings, however, and exhibited the full panoply of human failings, including their share of theft, violence, jealousy, deceit, wife beating, and child abuse. Slaves successfully resisted being turned into docile, obedient creatures of their masters' will; they did not turn the "slave community" into utopia.

VI

AN EXAMINATION of the ways in which Southern slaves resisted their thralldom and struggled to improve their condition helps clarify the nature of their social outlook as well as their social relations. Conducting such an examination is tricky, because it must rely heavily on behavior—frequently reconstructed on the basis of fragmentary evidence—to explore thought, while at the same time avoiding the tendency to inflate every minor expression of pique into a sign of covert revolutionary activity. Perhaps in part for this reason, there has been remarkably little good historical work done on the resistance of Southern slaves. Nevertheless, because the very act of resisting authority involved expressing sentiments that were normally unvoiced, that resistance—its forms and frequency as well as its character and consequences—can provide revealing insights into the worldview of the slaves.

Concrete political realities (that is, power relationships) shaped the specific patterns of resistance in the slave South. The high ratio of whites to blacks, the relatively small size and dispersed nature of slaveholdings, the presence of well-armed resident masters who took an active interest in local affairs, and—with the important exceptions of the War for Independence and the Civil War—the region's political stability combined to create conditions that were extremely unfavorable for armed rebellion. It is hardly surprising, then, that American slaves engaged in few such rebellions, and that those few were by international standards small and easily suppressed. Some of the most noted "conspiracies," including those led by Gabriel Prosser in Virginia in 1800 and by Denmark Vesey in South Carolina in 1822, were nipped in the bud before any outbreak of violence by a combination of white vigilance and black informers; others, such as that in New York City in 1741, may have existed only in the minds of panicked whites.

The handful of insurrections that actually came off were invariably local outbreaks that were quickly crushed with a minimum of armed force; none lasted more than a couple of days, threatened more than local havoc, or overcame the repressive efforts of local authorities. These revolts included the Stono rebellion of 1739, in which several dozen slaves near Charleston killed a number of whites but were routed the same day by armed planters; a larger but more obscure effort in 1811 in which some two hundred slaves tried to march on New Orleans before meeting the same fate; and, most famous of all, the Turner insurrection of 1831, which for two days produced panic—and fifty-nine deaths—among whites of Southampton County, Virginia, before local residents succeeded in capturing or killing most of the seventy-odd rebels. (Their charismatic leader, Nat Turner, managed to hide out in the woods eluding his pursuers for more than two months before being seized, tried, and hanged.)

Although these and other outbreaks sowed fear in the hearts of slaveholders and served as sources of inspiration for slaves (and generations of their descendants), they never came close to threatening the security of the slave regime. Nothing in the South remotely resembled the Haitian insurrection in which the slaves took advantage of the French Revolution to wage a triumphant revolutionary war of their own, or the massive "peasant wars" of the seventeenth and eighteenth centuries in which hundreds of thousands of Russian serfs joined other downtrodden peasants, cossacks, and town dwellers in protracted although ultimately unsuccessful assaults on established authority. In contrast to Russia and Haiti (and, to a lesser extent, much of the Caribbean and Brazil), the South had a balance of forces that was profoundly inhospitable to massive collective resistance. The waves of repression that followed each insurrection, conspiracy, and rumored conspiracy simply reinforced what was obvious to most slaves: under existing conditions, armed revolt was folly.

Absence of massive rebellion, however, hardly indicated passive acceptance of slavery. In a wide variety of ways, slaves expressed their dissatisfaction with the conditions they were forced to endure. Most common, but also most difficult to isolate, was a collection of acts that historians have labeled "silent sabotage" or "day-to-day resistance," acts through which slaves, without threatening the security of the slave regime, caused considerable aggravation to individual slave owners. Throughout the South, slaves dragged their feet, pretended to misunderstand orders, feigned illness, "accidentally" broke agricultural implements, and stole coveted items (especially food) from their owners, viewing such appropriation as "taking" what rightfully belonged to them. In noting that the slaves commonly adhered to "the agrarian notion . . . that the result of labour belongs of right to the labourer," Frederick Law Olmsted drew attention to a fact widely recognized by slaves and slave owners alike; as former slave Charles Ball put it, "I was never acquainted with a slave who believed, that he violated any rule of morality by appropriating to himself any thing that belonged to his master, if it was necessary to his comfort."[22]

Silent sabotage had ambiguous implications. It provided an accessible outlet through which slaves could express their frustrations with relatively little risk, but it also served to foster patterns of behavior that accentuated dissembling and shirking, and to reinforce among whites the notion that blacks were by nature lazy, foolish, and thieving. A pervasive irritant to masters, it represented a borderline form of resistance that did not directly challenge authority and that merged imperceptibly with the impulse common among slaves and non-slaves alike to get away with something.

Far more clear-cut were two intermediate forms of resistance that, unlike rebellion, occurred with great frequency and, unlike silent sabotage, represented direct challenges to slave owners and their employees. Of these, running away was by far the most common. In the antebellum period, unlike the colonial, the existence of free states to the north served as a powerful magnet to those who dreamed of escaping bondage. Reaching the North could be a task of almost herculean proportions requiring endurance, evasion of slave catchers, and deception of suspicious whites. Fugitives resorted to a variety of imaginative devices to achieve their goals. Frederick Douglass borrowed the identification papers of a free black sailor and took a train from Baltimore to Wilmington, Delaware, and then a boat to Philadelphia, all the time worrying that the considerable contrast between his friend's description and his own appearance would lead to his detection; Henry Box Brown had himself shipped in a crate from Richmond to Philadelphia. Some runaways received food and shelter from sympathetic blacks and whites—the fabled "Underground Railroad"—on their trek to freedom, and others were fortunate enough to have the guidance of a "conductor" such as Harriet Tubman, who, following her own escape from bondage, returned repeatedly to Maryland's Eastern Shore to shepherd others to freedom.

Most fugitives to the North, however, made the journey alone, on foot, traveling by night and resting by day and taking care to avoid blacks as well as whites because, as William Wells Brown later put it, "twenty-one years in slavery had taught me that there were traitors even among colored people."[23] Perhaps one thousand runaways per year managed to reach the North during the late antebellum years, the great majority young males from the upper-South states of Maryland, Virginia, Kentucky, and Missouri; many more attempted the feat but suffered capture (and return home) in the process. Despite conditions that rendered escape to the North extraordinarily difficult, tens of thousands of slaves showed their hatred of slavery by "voting with their feet" for freedom.

An even larger number of fugitives remained in the South. As in the colonial period, most runaway slaves hid out within a few miles of their homes. A few managed to elude capture for prolonged periods, either on their own—by holing up in caves and other rural retreats or by making their way to cities and merging with the free black population—or in groups of escaped slaves known as maroons that found refuge on the frontier and in unsettled internal areas such as the Great Dismal Swamp along the border between Virginia and North Carolina. But long-term survival on the loose was relatively rare in the antebellum South: the increasing density of settlement, improved communication, and the local hegemony of resident masters facilitated the capture of fugitives, and maroon colonies in the South never rivaled those in Brazil, Surinam, or Jamaica in numbers, size, or durability.

The vast majority of fugitives were temporary runaways. Most large plantations and many smaller holdings as well suffered from persistent truancy, as dissatisfied slaves "took off," lurking in the

woods, visiting friends and relatives, or sometimes concealing themselves in outbuildings on their owners' plantations. Some such vagrants returned home on their own, tired and hungry, after a few
days of uneasy freedom; others were eventually tracked down by
irritated masters and overseers or turned in by loyal slaves hoping
for a reward; still others proved more elusive. "I am sorry to hear
of your having so many runaways from the plantation," wrote a
member of a prominent South Carolina planting family to his
brother, describing his own unsuccessful attempt, accompanied by
"a parcel of overseers and professional negro hunters with nine
dogs," to find fugitives who were hiding out in an area "known to
be a safe and unmolested refuge for runaways." Advising his brother
to use dogs to track down his truants, the letter writer warned that
"the utmost secrecy and caution should be observed, as it is *extremely*
difficult to prevent the runaways from being informed of a search
after them being in preparation."[24]

Slave owners complained vociferously about the "thoughtlessness" and "ingratitude" of truants, but many masters and overseers
took temporary flight as a virtual given, a routine annoyance that
went with the job of slave manager and underlined the need for
constant vigilance. Slave owners rarely bothered to advertise for
slaves thought to be in the vicinity (the way they did for those
headed North), or to hire slave catchers to track them down. Although slaves who repeatedly absconded and those whose prolonged
absence caused their masters unusual aggravation and expense could
expect to be severely punished, runaways who returned home
quickly on their own sometimes received little more than verbal
harangues or "light" whippings.

More threatening, although less common, was a second form of
intermediate resistance, through which slaves directly confronted
masters and their assistants by force. Slave owners, embarrassed by
such blatant challenge to their authority, rarely described these confrontations in detail, and their precise frequency is impossible to
gauge. Nevertheless, ex-slave interviews and autobiographies, as
well as judicial records and oblique references in planter journals,
point to a surprisingly widespread pattern of small-scale confrontations in which slaves offered physical resistance to owners, overseers,
and hirers. At times, such resistance resulted in the death of the
assaulted white authority, but murder was rarely the goal of these

slaves who assaulted white authorities; slaves occasionally conspired, either individually or with comrades, to do away with hated whites—poison, arson, and "accidents" were the preferred methods—but the far more numerous direct confrontations were usually opportunistic encounters involving less planning than impulsive response to intolerable provocation. Confrontations were often followed by flight as resisters, pondering the likely consequences of their actions, opted to give their enraged targets a chance to cool off.

Although slave confrontations had numerous scenarios, they typically occurred when bondsmen, and less often bondswomen, felt that they were being pushed too far and determined to resist. In Alabama, a slave named Abram claimed to be sick and "moved off slowly" when ordered to work by the overseer, who for good measure gave him a lash with his whip; the enraged Abram grabbed the whip and a gun from the overseer, knocked him to the ground, bit off a piece of his ear, and in turn received a knife wound as they struggled. Virginian William Lee got tired of the beatings he suffered from his mistress, who would hold his head between her knees and "whack away" on his back, so he grabbed her legs and "bodily carried ole missus out an' thro' her on de ground jes' as hard as I could." Frederick Douglass, hired for a year to an abusive "slave breaker" named Edward Covey, suffered mistreatment in silence for six months before finally refusing to submit to more and resisting when Covey attempted to whip him; the two men struggled with each other for a prolonged period before Douglass's adversary "gave up the contest." Although Covey chided the recalcitrant slave, proclaiming, "I would not have whipped you half so much as I have had you not resisted," Douglass noted in his autobiography that "the fact was, *he had not whipped me at all.*"[25]

If it is impossible to determine exactly how often slaves took part in the kind of confrontation with which Douglass challenged Covey, it is clear that such action, together with the flight in which Douglass also engaged, represented by far the most characteristic, and significant, forms of direct slave protest. Indeed, these two forms of resistance occurred so often, and with such consistency, that they may be regarded as pervasive features of antebellum slavery, features that clearly give the lie to assertions of general slave contentment. They also provide significant clues to understanding the worldview as well as the world of the bondspeople.

VII

LIKE SLAVE FOLKLORE, slave resistance can tell us much about autonomy and communality in the antebellum South. One of the most striking characteristics of that resistance—aside from its very existence—is that it was largely the work of individuals. If collective forms of resistance such as rebellion and marronage were minor features of Southern society, the types of resistance that *were* widespread featured slaves who acted alone or in very small groups rather than as communal representatives. Slaves learned by experience that such individual resistance—although by no means risk-free—had the greatest chance of success.

This was true of both confrontations and flight. Physical confrontation initiated by a large group of slaves was indistinguishable from revolt in the eyes of most slave owners, and invariably called forth swift and merciless response. Slaves who challenged a group of whites also faced almost certain repression, because the nature of the conflict transformed it from a struggle between two individuals into an affront to the honor of those challenged; however they might respond in private, masters could not tolerate public assaults on their authority. Slaves who ran away found that they could travel most safely in a white-dominated world either alone or in pairs; larger groups of fugitives inevitably risked attracting attention and lost mobility. In short, the particular conditions under which Southern slaves lived permitted a significant degree of individual resistance but severely discouraged collective protest.

This should not be taken to imply an absence of cooperation among slaves resisting authority. Slaves joined together to pilfer their masters' larders, as well as, less often, to burn their barns and poison their food. Despite the existence of slave informers, many bondspeople protected those accused of criminal behavior if that behavior was directed at whites rather than at other slaves, and slave owners trying to identify the perpetrators of vandalism or theft often ran into a wall of silence when they questioned their people. Fugitives rightly feared being betrayed by slaves seeking to curry favor with authorities, but some runaways received food, shelter, and guidance from sympathetic blacks, both slave and free; Harriet Jacobs hid for seven years in the attic of her grandmother, a respected free black woman who kept her secret and eventually helped her escape to the North.

But although there was extensive cooperation among slaves resisting authority, this cooperation was almost always that of individuals. Slaves lacked any kind of institutional body like the Russian peasant commune, which represented a whole village or estate and made decisions on behalf of all peasants. Decisions to flee or confront authorities were not reached communally, through collective deliberation, but individually, through private deliberation; indeed, slaves planning to escape usually took care *not* to inform others and thus risk their chance at freedom. Although occasionally a large group of slaves, unexpectedly caught by a slave patrol in a forbidden nighttime revelry, might put up spirited if futile resistance, virtually never in the antebellum South did all the slaves on a plantation decide collectively to go on strike or run away, as serfs often did in Russia. The pattern of slave resistance in the antebellum South thus points to a complex environment that permitted extensive cooperation among slaves but at the same time severely limited the kinds of communal behavior that were possible.

Examining when and why slaves resisted yields equally significant observations. The trigger for slave flight and confrontations almost always consisted of a violation by white authorities of commonly accepted standards of behavior. No matter how much they detested slavery, the balance of forces—and the need to get on with their lives, even under harsh conditions—prevented slaves from engaging in constant struggle against it; resistance was by no means random, or constant across time and space. Certain actions by slave owners and their agents, however, were clearly intolerable. These included most notably excessive or unjustified punishment—that is, punishment that exceeded "normal" parameters or that was meted out for misdeeds not actually committed—but also a host of other breaches of civilized treatment, including separation of family members, sexual assaults, and arbitrary or erratic management. The death of an owner was also a particularly stressful time for slaves, because no one could be sure what would follow; estates were often broken up to pay off debts or satisfy claims of heirs, and at the very least the slaves would have to adjust to a new owner, who would want to establish his or her own authority and would be likely to have new ideas of how things should be done. It is not surprising, then, that such death occasioned heightened concern on the part of slaves, concern that could manifest itself in real (if ambivalent) grief as well as flight and resistance to new rules and regulations.

Although there were variations in the circumstances surrounding decisions to run away or confront whites—confrontations and temporary flight were frequently impulsive acts, immediate responses to unacceptable behavior, whereas flight to the North more often came after considerable thought and even preparation—these decisions almost always rested on specific grievances that triggered the determination to act. In their autobiographies, fugitive slaves typically combined assertion of what Henry Bibb called "a longing desire to be free" with reference to some catalyst, most often involving punishment, that caused them to act on that desire; Bibb decided to flee in 1835, when his Kentucky mistress began abusing him physically, "every day flogging me, boxing, pulling my ears, and scolding." As this example suggests, abuse of a slave accustomed to relatively lenient treatment was especially likely to provoke resistance. Frederick Douglass found hirer Covey's abuse especially hard to take because he had been used to the privileged life of a house servant in Baltimore; Isaac Throgmorton, sold to Louisiana after enjoying considerable freedom as a barber in Kentucky, found "all the privileges were taken from me" and decided to escape to the North.[26] But virtually any substantial change was unsettling and therefore conducive to resistance, both because it threatened established procedures and because it reminded slaves that those procedures were by no means immutable.

In short, although a general hatred of slavery and yearning for freedom underlay slave resistance, particular circumstances provoked individual decisions to resist. Despite their bitter detestation of bondage, on a day-to-day level most slaves came to terms with their conditions—because they had little choice—striving all the while to maximize their autonomy and preserve as "rights" the little privileges they were allowed to enjoy. When those rights were violated, however, slaves were likely to respond. Their resistance thus points both to a shared if never precisely defined understanding of what was acceptable and what was unacceptable within the general framework of a hated system, and to a conservative mentality under which slaves for the most part grudgingly made their peace with an oppressive reality but, when pushed too far, resisted behavior that violated that understanding.

If most slave resistance represented specific responses by individuals to intolerable situations rather than revolutionary efforts to overthrow the system, the consequences were nevertheless often

far-reaching. Unlike armed revolt, which invariably called forth severe repression, flight and confrontation produced highly variable
—indeed, unpredictable—results. Slaves who struck whites or ran
away too often could find themselves brutally whipped, sold down
the river, or even killed, and most could expect to receive at least
some physical punishment for their insolence. Many, however, were
decidedly more fortunate. Some fugitives reached the North, and
others remained on the loose for protracted periods in the South.
Still others, together with slaves who confronted white authorities,
gained ameliorated treatment for themselves even under slavery.
Every slave owner, overseer, and hirer had to consider, on a daily
basis, how individual slaves would respond to specific treatment and
whether a particular action—a whipping or a new rule—was worth
the risk of the response it might provoke. Slaves who gained a
reputation for standing up to authority often gained a measure of
respect and tolerance from white authorities and secured for themselves greater freedom of action.

This was true both of "ungovernable" slaves—the proverbial
"bad niggers" who made it clear that they would not let anyone
touch them without trouble—and of those who lashed out at or ran
away from tormentors after meekly submitting to their oppression.
It was common knowledge among both whites and blacks that there
were a few slaves who were so "mean" that it was not worth messing
with them; although whites sometimes made special efforts to
"tame" such recalcitrants, many masters and overseers decided that
discretion was the better part of valor and gave free rein to those
who did not make too much trouble. But as Frederick Douglass and
numerous other slaves showed, under the right circumstances previously tractable slaves could also prove remarkably resistant; what
is more, their resistance could have equally beneficial results. During
the six months that Douglass remained with Covey after their fight,
Covey never again tried to whip him. Douglass drew the appropriate
lesson, generalizing that "he is whipped oftenest, who is whipped
easiest."[27]

By standing up to and running away from their masters, then,
individual slaves helped set limits to their own oppression. They
also helped set limits to the oppression of their fellow slaves, for no
slave owner or overseer could ever be entirely sure in which apparently compliant soul there secretly lurked the heart of a "bad nigger," and rather than find out the hard way, it did not hurt to give

slaves an occasional benefit of the doubt. Slave resistance never seriously threatened the security of the regime, but such resistance constituted an important part of the slaves' efforts to shape their own lives.

Patterns of slave resistance, like slave folklore and recollections, thus point to the complex, even contradictory, nature of the consciousness that developed in the quarters as the slaves managed to carve for themselves a partially autonomous world even while subject to extensive white controls. Intense individualism coexisted with widespread cooperation among individuals. Associative behavior was pervasive as slaves interracted with one another in their families and churches, as well as through friendships and self-help networks. At the same time those slaves lacked the communal institutions—and loyalties—that typically united peasant villagers throughout much of the world.

Of course, antebellum Southern slaves, like people everywhere, felt diverse, overlapping attachments: to self, family, friends, locality, class, and ethnicity. But evidence suggests that they usually identified most strongly at the two extremes, as individual and family members on the one side and as slaves—or even blacks—on the other, with relatively weak intermediate ties to local "communities." Plantation residents lacked, for example, the intense sense of oneness with each other that Russian serf villagers exhibited, a sense of oneness that often produced equally intense suspicion of and even hostility to all outsiders, including serfs from neighboring villages.

Except in isolated areas, the slaves' geographic mobility combined with their lack of institutional autonomy to reduce local distinctions and attachments and create instead a common slave culture with which residents of widely scattered farms and plantations could identify. Just as the slaves' attenuated occupational differentiation reduced status conflict on given holdings, so, too, did the absence of sharp geographic-based differences make it easier for slaves to see themselves as one with other slaves, and indeed with other blacks in general, whether slave or free.

Racial identification among slaves drew strength from several sources. Because slaves constituted an overwhelming majority of the black population in most of the South, the line separating white from black approximated that separating free from slave, and it was easy for slaves, and their masters, to confuse race with class. Slaves and slave owners alike commonly used racial terminology: if a master spoke of "my negroes" (or "my niggers") to refer to his or her slaves, those slaves also called each other "niggers" or "colored folk" and looked upon whites in general as their oppressors. "White folks jes' naturally different from darkies," explained one ex-slave. "We's different in color, in talk and in 'ligion and beliefs. We's different in every way and can never be spected to think or live alike."[28] Such views drew support from the virulent white racism of many non-slaveholding whites, as well as from the close ties—including, at times, those of kinship—that existed in much of the South between slaves and free blacks.

Substituting for a communal identification with one's local group, then, was a generalized racial consciousness that at times approached but never quite merged into class consciousness. The use of "brother," "sister," "aunt," and "uncle" as terms of endearment commonly applied to blacks whether physically related or not suggests an outlook that incorporated all blacks as members of a kind of giant extended family, or community of the whole. So, too, do the patterns of slave resistance, which, despite their individual manifestation, showed such consistency in form and origin that they clearly reflected shared values that existed among blacks across the South.

VIII

THE COMPLEXITY of slave identification in the antebellum South reflected a world full of contradictions and ambiguities. In describing this world, historians have largely swung away from a model of victimization to one of autonomy, from a view of slaves as objects acted upon to one of independent beings defying the theory of slavery by leading their own lives. A balanced appraisal must recognize the validity as well as the exaggeration of both these models: slaves were subjects who strove with considerable success to carve for themselves areas of partial autonomy within a system designed to exploit their labor, but they were also victims of that system and the power relations that went with it. If the slaves helped make their own world, they nevertheless remained slaves, and the "internal" lives they forged in the quarters operated within the confines of the political, economic, and social hegemony of white slave owners who interfered in the daily lives of their "people" far more intrusively than most masters did elsewhere.

The complexity of this world and of the social relations it engendered is suggested not just in the self-identity of the slaves but also in their judgments—as expressed in subsequent autobiographies and oral interviews—of their owners. Slavery itself they remembered as a barbaric institution, and most had bitter memories of particular injustices they had endured. "I kin tell you things about slavery times dat would make yo' blood bile, but dey's too terrible. I jus' tries to forget," Amy Chapman told an interviewer. After describing a series of tortures, she abruptly stopped, declaring, "I ain't never tol' nobody all dis an' ain't gwine tell you no mo'." Delia Garlic's memories were equally painful: "Dem days was hell," she recalled bluntly.[29]

But many former slaves tempered their overall condemnation of slavery with fond recollections of particular experiences and sympathetic portrayals of particular owners, and testified to the pervasive nature of slave-owner paternalism. "Slavery did its best to make me wretched," wrote Josiah Henson, "but, along with memories of miry cabins, frosted feet, weary toil under the blazing sun, curses and blows, there flock in others, of jolly Christmas times, dances before old massa's door for the first drink of egg-nog, extra meat at holiday times, midnight-visits to apple-orchards, broiling stray chickens, and first-rate tricks to dodge work." Like numerous other autobiographers, Charles Ball distinguished sharply among his various owners, terming one of three masters he had in Maryland "an unfeeling man" but praising the other two and declaring that "my mistresses, in Maryland, were all good women"; although his Georgia master once gave him a brutal whipping—for no reason except that he had not received one since childhood—Ball recalled that he "really loved" that master; and when he died "I felt that I had lost the only friend I had in the world."[30]

A remarkably common pattern in the recollections of former slaves juxtaposed benign judgments of their *own* masters with harsh denunciations of the cruelties of neighboring slave owners and of slavery in general. Mandy McCullough Cosby of Alabama was typical of many ex-slaves in contrasting her owner, who was "good to his black folks" and rarely resorted to the lash, with other masters: "on some places close to us," she remembered, "they whipped until blood run down." Lillian Clarke of Virginia told a similar story:

although her parents received kind treatment from their owners, the master on the adjoining plantation was "mighty mean to his slaves."[31] The pattern was by no means universal: some ex-slaves had nothing good to say of their masters, and others presented at best mixed portraits. It was widespread enough, however, to be highly significant, as well as to be recognized by a number of ex-slaves themselves, who commented, frequently with some embarrassment, on the vicarious pride that many bondsmen took in the wealth, power, and benevolence of their masters. As Frederick Douglass noted, it was common for slaves to fight over who had the best owner, for "they seemed to think that the greatness of their masters was transferable to themselves."[32]

This juxtaposition of general condemnation of slavery with expressions of affection for particular slaveholders is subject to a variety of interpretations, most of which cannot be explored here. In some cases, blacks who sang the praises of their owners were no doubt protecting themselves against possible trouble: one could never be sure when criticism of a white might be considered rude or uppity, and prudent discretion dictated extreme caution when discussing slavery and slave owners in front of whites. But the pattern is evident in such a broad array of ex-slave testimony, encompassing such a variety of genres—antebellum autobiographies left by fugitives who escaped to the North as well as those written after the Civil War by blacks who remained in the South, narratives dating from the 1860s and those dating from the 1930s, interviews conducted by whites and those conducted by blacks—that it is impossible to attribute it exclusively to dissembling.

Slavery as a system was intrinsically exploitative, brutal, and unjust, and on a general level virtually all slaves detested it and longed for the day when they would be free. On an individual, personal, and day-to-day level, however, many slaves experienced pleasure as well as pain, and had contacts with whites that extended far beyond the exploitation of labor. The American version of this exploitative, brutal, and unjust system developed under conditions that at the same time left the slaves room to develop their own vital but fragile subculture and produced particularly intense, and contradictory, relations between masters and slaves, relations that were marked by affection and intimacy as well as by fear, brute force, and calculation of self-interest.

6

The White South:
Society, Economy, Ideology

I

SLAVERY AFFECTED the whole South, not just the slaves. Because the antebellum South was part of the United States, Southerners inevitably had much in common with other Americans, including shared history, language, religions, and political institutions. But Southerners, both white and black, also differed from other Americans. Because the antebellum South was a slave society, not merely a society in which some people were slaves, few areas of life there escaped the touch of the peculiar institution. What is more, the centrality of slavery to the South became increasingly pronounced during the half century preceding the Civil War.

During the past two decades, scholars have probed with new sophistication the pervasive impact of slavery on the antebellum South. Slavery undergirded the Southern economy, Southern politics, and, increasingly, Southern literary expression. Slavery also buttressed the religious orthodoxy that set the South apart from the North, undermined the growth of a variety of reform movements, and helped shape virtually every facet of social relations, from the law and schooling to the position of women. By the eve of the Civil War, slavery virtually defined the South to both Southerners and

Northerners; to be "anti-Southern" in the political lexicon of the era meant to be anti-slavery, to be "pro-Southern" meant to be pro-slavery. Few in either North or South doubted that the South's way of life was a reflection of that section's slave-labor system. When the challenge to that system appeared too great, Southern political leaders demonstrated the extent to which they identified slavery as central to their world by taking their states out of the Union and into war.

II

THE SLAVE-LABOR SYSTEM of the antebellum South was a bundle of contradictions. Established in obscurity without substantial opposition, it generated intense controversy among contemporary Americans and subsequent scholars. Rooted in the lust for profits, it fostered a paternalistic ideology that denigrated crude materialism as a "Yankee" vice. Inextricably linked to the North—and the wider world—through international markets, it produced an intense attachment to section, state, and locality that belied the growing economic interdependence of the modern world. A great success story in terms of economic growth, it left the South seriously underdeveloped both economically and socially. Directed by men whose progenitors had been forward-looking innovators, it ended up in the hands of reactionaries who distrusted reform and feared the future. Predicated upon denial of freedom to a substantial proportion of the population, it was defended by men who talked endlessly of their passionate commitment to "liberty." No wonder it has been so hard for historians to come to terms with slavery as a socioeconomic system, or to agree on how that system shaped the South.

Historians have long debated the question of Southern "distinctiveness." During the first half of the twentieth century, many scholars viewed slavery as a minor irritant that was needlessly blown out of proportion by irresponsible agitators, and portrayed the South as a prototypically American democracy of "yeoman farmers." This view found additional support among "consensus" historians whose emphasis on shared American experiences and values reached its peak of influence in the 1950s; as Charles G. Sellers explained in the introduction to a book of essays by nine prominent historians published under the suggestive title *The Southerner as American* (1960), "The authors believe that the traditional emphasis on the South's differentness and on the conflict between Southernism and Americanism is wrong historically . . . We all agree that the most important fact about the Southerner is that he has been throughout his history also an American."[1]

Although a significant minority of scholars have continued to stress the similarity between antebellum North and South, an increasing number of historians (including the author of this book) believe that those who have played down Southern distinctiveness have seriously understated the impact of slavery on the antebellum South. Unlike most historians of the 1950s and early 1960s, those of recent years have more often embraced a view of the American past that high-lights conflict and discontinuity than one that features consensus and continuity; exploring differences among Americans—whether class, racial, ideological, or geographic—has increasingly replaced a search for shared national characteristics. Equally important has been the changed perspective on slavery and race. The racism that suffused American scholarship during the first half of the twentieth century made it easy for historians to dismiss slavery as a significant issue and to argue that Northerners and Southerners, Americans all, "should" have been able to settle their minor differences amicably, without resort to arms. As scholars began to take seriously the history of African-Americans, however, they found it impossible to relegate slavery to the role of an insignificant, peripheral nuisance. The point is not that the South was totally different from the North, and to the extent that the old debate over Southern distinctiveness en-couraged defense of either "similarity" *or* "difference" as a Southern model, it has outlived its usefulness. Southerners were Americans, who shared a common history with other Americans. At the same time, however, Southerners lived in a slave society whose history differed in important ways from that of other Americans.

Central to the debate over Southern distinctiveness, and to ex-ploring the dualism of slaveholding society, is the commercial ori-entation of Southern slavery. From the early years of European settlement, Southern agriculture was overwhelmingly geared toward production of staple crops for market. Commercial exploitation of agriculture, the very *raison d'être* for the introduction of forced labor in the colonial period, intensified in antebellum years with the spread of cotton cultivation. The vast majority of slaveholders produced marketable crops, and they were intensely conscious of the prices they received for those crops, as well as the prices of slaves, land, and other factors of production. Historians have paid a good deal of attention recently to the "market revolution" that signaled the growth of capitalist relations in the antebellum North, but it is in the slave South that market-oriented agriculture appeared first and remained most pervasive.

Noting this commercial orientation, some historians have portrayed slaveholders as Southern versions of Northern industrialists, capitalists par excellence who directed "factories in the field" with businesslike efficiency. This view of slavery as quintessentially capitalistic, a view that has long been central to the thinking of those who would play down Southern distinctiveness, has received forceful restatement in recent years by econometricians Robert W. Fogel and Stanley L. Engerman, who stressed not only the efficiency, profitability, and businesslike character of antebellum slavery but also the degree to which slave owners succeeded in instilling modern industrial work habits in their slave workers. The idea of slavery as a particular variant of American capitalism also dominated the early writing of James Oakes, who in *The Ruling Race* (1982) stressed the grasping, aggressive, profit-maximizing behavior of Southern slave owners.

This interpretation, although based on important and observable features of the peculiar institution, provides a seriously incomplete and therefore one-sided picture of slavery—as well as of the slave owners and the slaves themselves. Markets did undergird the slave economy, but they were markets of a particular type, limited primarily to the sale of agricultural commodities (the most important of which was cotton). A second kind of market, that for labor power (i.e., labor hire), was largely lacking. Slave owners engaged in extensive commercial relations, selling cotton (and other agricultural products), buying items both for personal consumption and for use in their farming operations, borrowing money, and speculating in land and slaves, but the market was conspicuously absent in regulating relations between the masters and their slaves. In other words, relations of exchange were market-dominated, but relations of production were not. It is recognition of this crucial distinction that has led James Oakes to repudiate his former position on the similarity between the social orders of antebellum North and South. "A highly developed market economy was a precondition to the emergence of any slave society," observed Oakes in *Slavery and Freedom* (1990). "Yet master and slave formed what was, at bottom, a nonmarket relationship."[2]

It is hardly surprising, then, that slave owners exhibited complex, dualistic tendencies, nor that this dualism in many ways characterized Southern society as a whole. Planters and would-be planters were aggressively materialistic, and their behavior often seemed indistinguishable from that of Northern capitalists. Despite their participation in the world of capitalism, however, slave owners differed fundamentally from Northern capitalists because the master–slave relationship, which was so central to their lives, was not a part of this world. As Elizabeth Fox-Genovese and Eugene D. Genovese put it in their thoughtful essay "The Janus Face of Merchant Capital," antebellum slavery was a "hybrid system" whose dominant planter class was both "based on slave relations of production and yet deeply embedded in the world market . . . In this essential respect, the Old South emerged as a bastard child of merchant capital and developed as a noncapitalist society increasingly antagonistic to, but inseparable from, the bourgeois world that sired it."[3]

This fundamental dualism—the juxtaposition of extensive commercial activity in an economy based on non-capitalist productive relations—helps account for the existence of so many apparently contradictory features of the antebellum South. On one level, the section seemed to partake fully of the liberal bourgeois spirit of the era. Political democracy, and the accompanying democratic rhetoric that exalted the "common man," swept the South as well as the North during the first half of the nineteenth century. At the same time, however, slavery inevitably exerted a powerful influence on the nature of the Southern social order. In but not of the bourgeois world, slave owners struggled to make sense of momentous changes that threatened to undermine everything they knew. If at times they embraced some of these changes, they increasingly came to view most as alien and unwelcome. A profound conservatism gripped the Old South during the last years of the slave regime, as concern for order—and class prerogatives—outweighed any lingering attraction for social experimentation.

III

AN EXAMINATION of Southern economic performance during the decades preceding the Civil War illustrates the peculiar, hybrid nature of slave society. In some ways, economic growth in the South followed quintessential American patterns. Southerners, like Northerners, pushed west, speculated in land, carved farms out of the wilderness, shipped agricultural products to markets in the East and abroad, and enjoyed the fruits of unprecedented prosperity. Not only did the Southern economy grow rapidly but, measured in terms of per capita income (the output of goods and services divided by the population), its growth rate between 1840 and 1860 slightly exceeded that of the North. "If we treat the North and South as separate nations and rank them among the countries of the world, the South would stand as the fourth most prosperous nation of the world in 1860," concluded Robert W. Fogel. "The South was more prosperous than France, Germany, Denmark, or any of the countries of Europe except England."[4]

Such a conclusion, although technically accurate, provides an incomplete and distorted picture of the slave economy. Antebellum Southern economic growth was impressive, but it was based largely on increased production and export of a small number of staple crops (the most important of which by far was cotton). Unlike the Northern states, which experienced the early stages of a vigorous transformation that altered the very structure of economy and society, the Southern states produced more by putting more land into cultivation; quantitative growth did not lead to qualitative development. Southern wealth, like that of modern Saudi Arabia, was based on the fortuitous ability to export ever-increasing quantities of a highly prized commodity, but did not indicate a developed economy.

Indeed, what most struck Northern and European travelers to the South in the 1850s was not Southern prosperity but Southern backwardness. Landscape architect Frederick Law Olmsted, who spent fourteen months roaming the South preparing articles for *The New York Times*, described the section as a degraded land of poverty, illiteracy, ignorance, inefficiency, and lethargy in which slavery impeded economic development while corroding everyone's manners and morals. New York Senator William H. Seward concurred. "It was necessary that I should travel to Virginia to have any idea of a slave State," he stated. "An exhausted soil, old and decaying towns, wretchedly-neglected roads, and, in every respect, an absence of enterprise and improvement, distinguish the region . . . Such has been the effect of slavery."[5] Informed defenders of the South, although disagreeing with Northern and European critics over the moral implications, usually agreed with them that the South was far poorer than the North. Some sectional boosters turned this poverty into a virtue, rejoicing that Southerners were not cursed with the crude mercenary traits that characterized Yankees; others, such as New York Democrat Thomas P. Kettell, author of an 1860 tome entitled *Southern Wealth and Northern Profits*, used Southern poverty as a weapon to indict Northern perfidy, insisting that the South would have been wealthier than the North were it not for the thieving ways of Northern middlemen who, like giant economic leeches, drained off the South's hard-earned wealth.

Olmsted, Seward, and Kettell were hardly impartial observers. All three had a vested interest in noting Southern backwardness, the first two because it testified to *slavery's* harmfulness and the third because it indicted *Northern* behavior. But they, and numerous other contemporaries like them, captured a basic truth not fully reflected in statistics on the growth rates of per capita income: the South's economic development was simply not keeping up with that of the North. Contemporary observations of Southern economic backwardness, present in significant numbers from the 1830s, proliferated sharply in the 1840s and 1850s as it became increasingly obvious that the South was not sharing in the economic transformation that was accelerating in the North. In the colonial era, the Southern colonies had been widely recognized as the most valuable "plums" in America, prized for their fertile soil, mild climate, abundant natural resources, and production of highly valued staple crops; on the eve of the Civil War, the Southern states were widely recognized as trailing far behind the North in economic development.

The signs were virtually everywhere. Even measured in terms of per capita income, the statistic most supportive of Southern development, the Southern economy lagged significantly behind the Northern: in 1860, the South's per capita income stood at $103, while the North's totaled $141. In most other respects, the contrast was considerably more striking. Although the South's industrial production increased during the 1840s and 1850s, the section failed to undergo the industrial transformation that swept the Northeast during those years, and Southern manufacturing capacity declined from

18 to 16 percent of the nation's total. Much of the industry that did exist in the South consisted of refineries that finished the section's *agricultural* products—sawmills, gristmills, sugar and tobacco processing plants—although in an especially striking sign of manufacturing underdevelopment, the South continued to send almost all of its cotton to the North and to Europe for spinning and weaving.

Other indices tell the same story. Northern bankers, insurers, and shippers provided most of the credit and transportation that greased the wheels of the cotton economy. The South badly trailed the North in railroad construction, literacy (even excluding blacks), and education; unlike the Northern states, which established vigorous public school systems in the antebellum years, the Southern states made only perfunctory stabs at educating the population at large, and it was not until after the Civil War that most Southern children, white or black, had even limited access to school. In part because the South attracted far fewer European immigrants than did the North, the Southern share of the country's total population decreased from 44.2 percent in 1830 to 35.3 percent in 1860. (Because the Southern population failed to keep pace with the Northern, using per capita income figures masks the full extent of the Southern economic lag.)

The distinctive character of the slave economy is perhaps nowhere more evident than in the lack of Southern urbanization. Throughout the North, economic transformation led to the growing concentration of manufacturing and commerce. Big cities such as New York and Philadelphia became urban giants struggling to integrate the tens of thousands of new residents who poured in from surrounding rural hinterlands as well as from abroad; during the decade of the 1850s alone, New York's population (including Brooklyn) surged from 612,000 to over one million, and Philadelphia's leaped from 340,000 to 565,000. Meanwhile, new western cities burgeoned practically overnight—Chicago, nonexistent in 1830 and containing only 29,000 residents in 1850, boasted a population of 109,000 in 1860—while the growth of numerous smaller cities such as Buffalo, Detroit, Cleveland, Pittsburgh, and Milwaukee testified to the urban transformation of Northern life. By 1860, just over one-quarter of all Northerners lived in a town or city containing more than 2,500 persons, a level of urbanization over twice that of 1830, and in the Northeastern states the urban population stood at 35.7 percent.

Despite a slow growth in the South's urban population, the gap

between North and South increased sharply during the late antebellum years as the urban revolution bypassed the South. In 1860,
only 9.6 percent of all Southerners lived in a town or city with 2,500
people, and even this figure overstates the level of urbanization in
most of the South. In 1860, there were five Southern cities with
more than 50,000 inhabitants, but only one of these, New Orleans
(with 168,675 inhabitants) was located in the deep South. Baltimore,
Maryland (212,418), St. Louis, Missouri (160,773), and Louisville,
Kentucky (68,033), were all on the periphery of the South, looking
northward economically and culturally, and Washington, D.C.
(61,122), also on the South's northern perimeter, owed its size to
being the nation's capital; these were border cities, Southern in
name only. Excluding New Orleans, a cosmopolitan city with French
and Spanish roots that flourished as a port near the mouth of the
Mississippi River, the largest cities in the deep South were Charleston, South Carolina, and Mobile, Alabama, with 40,522 and 29,258
residents respectively in 1860. The great interior of the South was
almost totally rural.

The low level of Southern urbanization reflected not only the
section's lack of modernization but also the slave system that undergirded its economy and social order. Although there were slaves
in Southern cities, in general slavery and urban life made a poor
mix. The sharp rural demand for labor restricted the number of
slaves kept in cities, especially during the booming decade and a
half preceding the Civil War. Equally important, many slaveholders
viewed cities with deep suspicion as places likely to corrupt, and
undermine the subservience of, their slaves. "There are, you may
say, hundreds of Negroes in this city who go about from house to
house—some carpenters, some house servants, etc.—who never see
their masters except at pay day, live out of their yards, hire themselves without written permit, etc.," Charles C. Jones, Jr., son of
a distinguished Presbyterian minister, complained to his father from
Savannah in 1856. "This of course is very wrong, and exerts a most
injurious influence upon the relation of master and servant." He
added pointedly, "Savannah is the last place in the world for servants
inclined to evil."[6]

Jones was right. As historian Richard C. Wade showed in his book
Slavery in the Cities (1964), urban slavery was often a very different
beast from its rural counterpart. Slaves in cities were simply harder
to control. They rubbed shoulders with free blacks, who by word

as well as by their very existence spread subversive notions about alternatives to bondage. They found it easy to barter, gamble, pick pockets, loiter, and frequent "grog shops," where they congregated with other slaves, free blacks, and lower-class whites in "promiscuous" assembly that sent shivers through the hearts of proper masters. Many were able to hire their own time and live largely unsupervised except when at work. In short, unlike the isolated plantation, the city was not conducive to maintaining slave discipline. "A city slave is almost a freeman, compared with a slave on the plantation," Frederick Douglass noted bluntly.[7]

Slave owners strove to keep to a minimum the number of their urban slaves, especially men, whose labor was in great demand on plantations and whose ability to take advantage of opportunities for independent life in cities seemed particularly threatening; in most cities, slave women outnumbered men. Most urban slaves were domestic servants; others served as dock workers, skilled craftsmen, washerwomen, factory hands, and day laborers. Often they lived lives that were the envy of rural blacks, and it is not surprising that fugitive slaves from the countryside sometimes headed for a nearby city where they could hope to lose themselves in the anonymity of urban life as well as partake of forbidden pleasures. But relatively few slaves experienced life in the city. Between 1840 and 1860, the proportion of slaves declined in every "major" Southern city, and in the two largest Southern cities, Baltimore and New Orleans, the absolute number of slaves declined as well. In 1860, slaves made up only 7.3 percent of the population in the eight largest Southern cities, and in the South as a whole only about 5 percent of all slaves lived in a town or city of at least 2,500 persons. If cities were peripheral to antebellum Southern life, they were even more so to antebellum Southern slavery. (See table 6 for statistics on urban slavery.)

Southern economic underdevelopment must be understood in world perspective. Recent historians of slavery in areas as diverse as Cuba, Brazil, and the British West Indies have concurred with historians of the Southern United States that slavery was not, as many scholars formerly believed, economically moribund in the decades preceding its abolition, and that that abolition cannot be explained simply in terms of rational economic decisions to abandon unprofitable systems. (Some recent experts on Russian serfdom have reached the same conclusion.) Slavery was not gradually dying out;

the slave economy of the Southern United States was particularly dynamic, and, except in some of the border states, showed no signs that it was on its last legs in the 1850s.

But that slave economy grew, like other slave economies, in a distinctive way: nowhere did slavery prove compatible with socio-economic modernization. Increased production for export of agricultural commodities did not lead to the kind of capitalist transformation that marked the economies of Britain and the Northern United States, but indicated instead the existence of semi-colonial economic relations under which increased staple production masked continued structural backwardness. Enslavement of the laboring population did not impede Southern economic growth, but it did shape that growth along particular lines that could occur within the contours of a planter-dominated social order. The internal (or home) market—constrained by the slave status of one-third the population, the paucity of urban residents, and the self-sufficiency of many farms and plantations—provided little stimulus to industrialization. More important still, the slave regime could tolerate and even embrace limited urbanization and industrialization, but it could never accept the ideals that underlay capitalist transformation, because central to those ideals was economic "freedom," including the freedom of laborers to contract for wages.

IV

UNLIKE MOST OTHER SLAVE REGIMES, that in the antebellum South had to accommodate a substantial number of free whites who did not own slaves but who claimed political equality. Like free blacks, these non-slaveholding whites were in a sense an anomaly in a slave society whose most important social relation was that between master and slave. Because of their numbers, however, they were a far more problematical anomaly. Put most simply, in most Southern states the majority of whites were neither slave owners nor close relatives of slave owners. Their majority status in a society organized around slavery—and in a political system increasingly organized around the defense of slavery—created enormous tensions, tensions that were contained but never fully resolved. Slave owners had to be concerned not only with the loyalty of their slaves but also with that of their non-slaveholding white neighbors.

Non-slaveholding Southern whites were a diverse lot. They included impoverished subsistence farmers who scratched a marginal existence from the unproductive soil of hill country and pine barrens and were derided by their social betters as shiftless "poor whites," "hillbillies," "crackers," and "rednecks," as well as more prosperous "yeoman farmers" who supplemented subsistence agriculture with limited production for market and won praise for their stereotypical sturdy independence. Some non-slaveholders lived in cities, where they ranged from immigrant day laborers to skilled artisans and merchants; some worked as overseers for planters; some were the sons and daughters of planters, who had not yet established their financial security but would one day be slave owners themselves; a few were wealthy but chose not to purchase slaves because they found slave owning either unethical or inconvenient.

Despite this diversity—and that within the slaveholding class as well—an enormous gulf separated slaveholding from non-slaveholding whites in the antebellum South. As historian Gavin Wright demonstrated, the average wealth of slaveholders in the Cotton South in 1860 ($24,748) was 13.9 times the average wealth of non-slaveholders ($1,781); slaveholders owned 93.1 percent of the region's agricultural wealth. What is more, the gap between slaveholders and non-slaveholders widened as slave prices rose during the late antebellum period and opportunities for non-slaveholders to acquire slaves diminished; the proportion of Southern white families owning slaves decreased from about 36 percent in 1830 to 26 percent in 1860 (although in the deep South slave ownership remained more widespread). The rural South was a region of sharp—and increasing—economic stratification in which a decreasing minority of the white population directly benefited from slavery.

Why did non-slaveholders, who constituted an increasing majority of the white population in an era of universal white manhood suffrage, tolerate, and often support, the continued existence of slavery? To explore this much-debated question is to explore the nature of antebellum Southern society and of the slaveholding hegemony that characterized it. To begin with, although only one-quarter of all Southern whites owned slaves in 1860, a far higher proportion had an indirect interest in slavery. As James Oakes demonstrated, the boundary between slave owner and non–slave owner, although becoming more difficult to breach, was never totally impervious. Ambitious yeoman farmers scrimped and saved in order to mark their status by purchasing slaves of their own; although far more dreamed of acquiring slaves than ever succeeded in doing so, there was considerable movement (in both directions) across the slave-owning line, as successful farmers strove to join the "gentry" while small slave owners were forced to sell off their human property to cover unmanageable debts. For other white Southerners, non-slave-holding status was a temporary phenomenon that marked a particular, youthful stage of the life cycle rather than a permanent condition; before establishing their financial well-being, children of small slave owners—and even sometimes of planters—could typically expect to spend some time as young adults without slaves. Still other non-slaveholding whites had relatives who owned slaves, and hence perceived themselves as members of the slaveholding class by extension. In short, the number of white Southerners with an economic stake in slavery was far greater than the number who owned slaves at any given time. When such potential slave owners are added to the number of actual slave owners, the proportion of Southern whites with an investment in slavery may have approached half in the South as a whole and substantially exceeded half in the deep South.

Among those who lacked this investment, racist fear could act as a powerful deterrent to anti-slavery. As far back as the 1780s, Thomas Jefferson had expressed the conviction that there was no place for free blacks in a white America; in the antebellum years, as historian George M. Fredrickson has emphasized, the triumph of political democracy—and the accompanying notion of political equality for free males—heightened the perception that freedom for blacks meant trouble for whites. When Frederick Law Olmsted traveled through the Southern backcountry, he found substantial enmity toward planters—and toward the system of slavery that supported them in haughty idleness—but potential opposition to slavery yielded time and again to the practical reality of white racism. "I reckon the majority would be right glad if we could get rid of the niggers," one poor white told Olmsted. "But it wouldn't never do to free 'em and leave 'em here. I don't know anybody, hardly, in favor of that. Make 'em free and leave 'em here and they'd steal every thing we made. Nobody couldn't live here then."[8]

Reinforcing this racist reluctance to set blacks loose in a "white man's" country was a surge of Southern patriotism. Because the attack on slavery came primarily from outside the South, and was combined with attacks on the decadence of Southern ways, defenders of slavery found it easy to portray themselves as defenders of the South. Southern politics, correspondingly, increasingly came to revolve around the defense of Southern interests—foremost of which was assumed to be slavery—as well as defense of the right of Southerners to shape their own destiny without outside interference. The identification of slavery as central to the preservation of Southern "liberty" marked the intellectual as well as political hegemony of slave owners throughout the antebellum South.

It also marked their power. Numerous latent (and some not so latent) tensions simmered beneath the commitment to slavery that dominated Southern politics. Up-country representatives struggled with those from plantation districts over the location of state capitals, over principles of taxation, and over whether legislative representation should be apportioned according to the total population or the white population (or, as in the United States Congress, a compromise between the two). Many non-slaveholding whites, especially in the hill country, resented the arrogant ways of slave-owning planters, whose "aristocratic" character seemed to threaten the republican equality of the American social and political order.

Occasionally, these tensions surfaced for all to see. In 1831–32, in the wake of Nat Turner's insurrection, representatives from the western part of Virginia mounted a direct challenge to the political ascendancy and economic interests of eastern planters by proposing in the state legislature the gradual abolition of slavery. In 1857, similar anti-planter resentment found clear expression in North Carolinian Hinton Helper's pamphlet *The Impending Crisis of the South*, a broadside that Northern anti-slavery groups hailed for demonstrating the existence of widespread if usually quiescent hostility to slavery in the South. Using familiar free-labor rhetoric, Helper denounced slavery for holding back Southern economic development, degrading Southern labor, and impoverishing the majority of Southerners to feed the greed of a small class of self-satisfied aristocrats. Insisting that "free labor is far more respectable, profitable, and productive, than slave labor," Helper appealed directly to anti-elitist sentiment among common whites: "Non-slaveholders of the South! farmers, mechanics and workingmen, we take this occasion to assure you that the slaveholders, the arrogant demogogues whom you have elected to offices of honor and profit, have hookwinked you, trifled with you, and used you as mere tools for the consummation of their wicked designs."[9]

Strong stuff, such challenges called for and received an equally strong response. The Virginia legislative debate, which culminated in a decisive rebuff to the western insurgents, marked the last public airing of anti-slavery in the South; for the next three decades, Southern politicians recognized that whatever doubts they might privately harbor about the morality or wisdom of owning slaves, any public challenge to the peculiar institution left one open to charges of anti-Southern behavior, and thus constituted political suicide. Increasingly, Southern spokesmen—politicians, editors, clergymen, intellectuals—treated questioning of slavery not only as misguided but as part of a diabolical plot to overthrow Southern institutions and the Southern way of life. In fact, few Southern whites in the late antebellum period were able to judge for themselves the merits of anti-slavery arguments, because such arguments did not circulate freely in the South. Postmasters—acting both on their own and in conformity with hastily passed state laws—routinely refused to deliver "incendiary" publications, and individuals suspected of being abolitionist "agents" were subjected to both verbal and physical harassment. The outcry in response to *The Impending Crisis* was so extreme that Helper prudently fled to the North, where he found a more cordial reception: lionized as a representative of the South's great silent majority, Helper saw his book distributed as a campaign document by Republicans in 1860, and in 1861 he was appointed consul to Buenos Aires by President Lincoln. One reason that it is so difficult to gauge dissent over slavery in the late antebellum South is that such dissent could only be expressed surreptitiously.

More and more, slaveholders—and the defense of slaveholders' interests—dominated Southern politics. This was true despite the increasingly democratic tenor of Southern political life, as state after state joined the national trend in adopting universal white manhood suffrage and saw the triumph of an anti-elitist political ethic in which candidates denounced their enemies as privileged aristocrats and portrayed themselves as men of the people. With the important exception of South Carolina, which continued to invest extraordinary powers in the state legislature rather than in the electorate at large, politics in the South differed little in many respects from that in the North, as Whigs and Democrats boisterously struggled for popular support and political ascendancy. But the democratic *tone* of Southern politics translated only very partially into democratic *content*: most significantly, attacks on "privilege" and "aristocracy" represented rhetorical flourishes that were almost never aimed at the actual source of privilege and aristocracy in the South, slavery.

Reinforcing the hegemonic hold of slaveholding interests over Southern politics was the simple numerical preponderance of slaveholders in Southern governments. As Ralph A. Wooster showed, slaveholders increasingly dominated all levels of government, especially the highest. In Alabama, for example, the proportion of state legislators who owned slaves increased from at least 66.4 percent in 1850 to at least 76.3 percent in 1860. A majority of legislators in every slave state except Missouri, Arkansas, and Delaware were slave owners in 1860; typically, about three-quarters of deep-South legislators and two-thirds of upper-South legislators owned slaves. At the gubernatorial level, slaveholding was virtually universal.

There was nothing unusual, of course, in Southern government officials being wealthier than the citizenry at large; governments are rarely in the hands of society's least affluent. But the slaveholding character of most Southern politicians greatly facilitated the identification of Southern interests with slaveholding interests, both in their own minds and in the minds of others. Southern politics increasingly revolved around the defense of slavery, which was cast as defense of the South itself. As ministers, intellectuals, and editors joined politicians in rallying around the flag, gradually a divided and ambivalent section became a seemingly united nation.

V

A PERVASIVE CONSERVATISM accompanied the growing identification of slavery as central to Southern life. During the Revolutionary era, liberal Southern statesmen had been at the forefront of "enlightened" thought, questioning the morality of slavery, enunciating doctrines of equal rights, and challenging the traditional Puritanism of New England with liberal religious views that ranged from insistence on strict separation of church and state to a widespread agnosticism (that usually took the politically safer guise of "Deism"). During the antebellum decades, however, even as the Northern states abolished the last remnants of slavery, turned from rigid Calvinism, and saw the proliferation of a huge variety of reform movements that transformed the social climate, the South became the home of religious and social orthodoxy. To both Southerners and Northerners, slavery and conservatism appeared inextricably linked. Challenged by reformers who would remake society, slavery was, its defenders insisted, the bedrock of the true social order.

The decline of moderate anti-slavery sentiment that was noticeable in the upper South as early as the 1790s accelerated in the 1820s and 1830s. The notion that slavery was an unfortunate legacy of a less enlightened age and would gradually wither away in the era of equal rights ran headlong into the reality of the cotton kingdom and gradually withered away itself. Ambivalence over slavery persisted, especially in the upper South, in the hill country, and in cities; so, too, did a qualified, Jeffersonian opposition to slavery that William W. Freehling has recently dubbed "Conditional Termination."[10] During the 1810s and 1820s, the idea of "colonizing" blacks out of the United States drew support from many Southern as well as Northern whites, an idea whose time seemed to have come with the founding of the American Colonization Society in 1817. But colonization hardly provided a solution for Southerners squeamish over slavery. The movement foundered on the hard realities of shaky finances, a hostile response from many blacks (few of whom embraced the idea of being sent "back" to Africa), and factional disputes among its supporters. Indeed, many Southern colonizationists, unlike their Northern counterparts, were actually *proponents* of slavery who believed that they could strengthen the peculiar institution by expelling those Southerners who were most subversive: free blacks. Between 1817 and 1867, the ACA helped send about six thousand blacks to Liberia (the numerical equivalent of about two months' natural increase of the slave population in the 1820s), and support for some form of colonization resurfaced sporadically throughout the antebellum years and even during the Civil War, but by the late 1820s, it was clear to most Americans that colonization represented a dead end.

The decline of anti-slavery sentiment was part of a broad conservative reaction that pervaded the South during the half century preceding the Civil War and sharply intensified after 1830. This reaction is elusive, because in some ways Southern intellectual and political trends seemed to parallel those in the North. Not only did democratic politics and exaltation of the "common man" sweep

South as well as North, but so also did the religious revivalism of the Second Great Awakening, with the concomitant spread of evangelical Protestantism, especially Baptism and Methodism. Accompanying these political and religious transformations went a variety of movements to reform society, movements that encompassed a broad range of efforts, including those to alleviate suffering through charitable and benevolent work, to instill knowledge and values compatible with the needs of the emerging social order through newly formed Sunday schools and public schools, and to induce correct behavior—for example, temperance—through moral suasion and, if necessary, legal compulsion.

Just as the common democratic style of Southern and Northern politics masked important differences in their content, so, too, did apparent similarities in social trends belie a fundamental societal divergence between North and South. The "perfectionist" spirit that undergirded so much of the Northern reform effort in antebellum years, the drive continually to improve both social organization and the very human character itself, was largely absent in the South. Far more than their Northern counterparts, Southern evangelical Protestants stressed the importance of individual piety rather than social regeneration. Equally important, as representatives and exponents of a slave-based social order, Southern political, religious, and intellectual leaders had precious little room for social experimentation. Acutely conscious of the dangers to their world implicit in questioning established human relations, these leaders instinctively shied away from efforts to tinker with existing institutions, and increasingly came to see reform of any but the tamest sort as heresy that threatened time-tested traditions.

It is hardly surprising, then, that the antebellum years did not constitute an "era of reform" in the South, as it did in the North. Even moderate reform movements that posed little or no threat to the social order often made only a feeble showing in the South. Advocates of public education, for example, made little headway in their drive to persuade Southern state legislatures to emulate their Northern counterparts and establish statewide public schooling; although several states—mostly in the upper South—passed measures that on paper set up school systems, those systems remained either drastically underfunded or totally unfunded, and it was only after the Civil War that public education became widely available in the South. The temperance movement, while embraced by numerous individuals, met similar rebuff at the legislative level. Among slave states, only Delaware and Tennessee joined the thirteen Northern states that passed acts modeled on Maine's 1846 prohibition law, and in both states the acts were largely unenforced and quickly repealed.

More radical reform movements—such as utopian socialism, trade unionism, feminism, pacifism, and of course abolitionism—movements that although never actively supported by the majority of Northerners were important features of antebellum Northern life, were almost totally absent from the South. Indeed, Southern publicists routinely ridiculed such "isms" as absurd curiosities that both typified the excesses of "Yankee" culture and revealed the superiority of the conservative, slave-based Southern order. Southern polemicists typically saw the various "isms" as integrally linked with opposition to slavery and as functions of the excessive freedom and individualism prevalent in the North. As George Frederick Holmes put it in an 1857 essay titled "Theory of Political Individualism," it was no accident that "Fourierism, and Proudhonism, Free Love, and Total Abstinence, and all the other modern forms of philanthropic innovation have found numerous and enthusiastic votaries" in the North, precisely where "an exaggerated and distorted idea of the nature and functions of liberty has inspired the multitudinous heresy of Abolitionism." D. R. Hundley expressed the linkage more succinctly: "as every well-informed person knows, the fact is indisputable, and has often been boasted of by the infidel [i.e., abolitionist] press, that antislavery sentiments were first propagated by the ultra socialists and communists."[11]

As such statements suggest, antebellum Southern sociopolitical thought harbored profoundly anti-democratic currents. These currents never prevailed, for the virtues of the common (white) man and the contrast between a vibrant American democracy and a hidebound European aristocracy had become part of the conventional wisdom in the South as well as in the North, and even among those who did not share this outlook, the necessity of appealing to the votes of non-slaveholding whites limited the public circulation of frankly anti-democratic rhetoric. More common than outright attacks on democracy were denunciations of fanatical reformism and appeals to conservatism, order, and tradition. "We are losing our veneration fast," warned novelist William Gilmore Simms. "We are overthrowing all sacred and hallowing associations and authorities. Marriage is now a bond which we may rend at pleasure. The Sabbath is a wrong and a superstition. Such is the progress of opinion and doctrine among those very classes which show themselves hostile to Southern slavery. The cry is 'On!' and we do not see the beginning of the end."[12]

But there was a thin line between a conservative suspicion of harebrained reformism and an anti-democratic hostility to "too much" liberty. Increasingly, many of the most prominent spokesmen for the South coupled their defense of traditional ways with attacks on the radical spirit of nineteenth-century egalitarianism, whose origins they usually traced to the French Revolution. Deploring revolutionary pandering to "the MOB—THE SANS-CULOTTES, . . . the ignorant uneducated, semi-barbarous mass which swarms and starves upon the face of Europe," South Carolina's planter-statesman James H. Hammond bluntly declared, "I repudiate, as ridiculously absurd, that much lauded but nowhere accredited dogma of Mr. JEFFERSON, 'that all men are born equal.' " Noting that "conservatism in any form is scoffed at," he asked rhetorically, "where will all this end?"[13]

Hostility to reform reflected widespread concern about what its consequences might be for the South's social order. Hammond's question "where will all this end?" clearly implied that slavery was at risk, an implication echoed in the frequent linkage made in pro-slavery rhetoric between abolitionism and other, seemingly distinct, reform movements. Hostility to reform also indicated the degree to which understanding of human capability—and human nature itself—divided along sectional lines. As Eugene D. Genovese has recently shown, antebellum Southern intellectuals were ambivalent over the very idea of progress; they embraced material and scientific improvements, but they were profoundly alarmed by many of the changes they saw around them in a modernizing world, especially in the North and in England. Lauding the Southern *"spirit of conservatism,"* which he attributed to slavery, South Carolina planter Henry W. Ravenel boasted that the South was "the conservator of law and order—the enemy of innovation and change—the breakwater which is to stay that furious tide of social and political heresies now setting towards us from the shores of the old world."[14]

The perfectionist belief that society and humanity could be made (and indeed were being made) better and better, widespread in the antebellum North, found little currency in the slave South. Southerners, who came into daily contact with the harsh reality of human cruelty and suffering, knew better than to believe in such fairy tales. "Believe us Sir, the fault is not in cities, nor yet in slavery, nor in marriage, nor religion," D. R. Hundley lectured would-be reformers; "it is in MAN . . . Although you were to abolish every institution under the sun, so long as the human race continues mortal and frail as at present there will be no lack of sin and shame, sorrow and suffering." The corollary was clear: those who sought to use religion to improve the human condition were on the wrong track, for "the true and only mission of Christianity is, not to abolish institutions or to set up dynasties, but to make every *individual man*, whether bond or free, rich or poor, high or low, *a new creature in Christ Jesus.*"[15]

VI

THE CENTRAL MANIFESTATION of Southern conservatism was the crusade to defend slavery. This movement was conservative in a very literal sense, an effort to preserve an institution, social relationship, and way of life that were under massive, multifaceted attack. By the 1850s, the pro-slavery crusade had come to dominate intellectual life in the South, serving as a rallying flag for white Southerners. Defense of slavery became tantamount to defense of the South.

It had not always been thus. So long as slavery was not under serious attack, there was little need to rush to its defense, and during most of the colonial period pro-slavery polemics were both infrequent and undeveloped. Arguments on behalf of slavery became more evident during the Revolutionary and post-Revolutionary years, when slavery faced its first, restrained challenge; given that this challenge was most successful in the Northern states, it is not surprising that, as Larry Tise has pointed out, some of the most carefully articulated early defenses of slavery emanated from the North rather than from the South. Even in the early years of the nineteenth century, however, nothing approaching a pro-slavery "crusade" existed. If pressed on the issue, most slave owners undoubtedly would have defended their ownership of slaves. In the first quarter of the nineteenth century, however, travelers to the South typically found a hesitant, cautious attitude on the part of whites, many of whom willingly conceded that slavery was undesirable and must eventually be abolished. Even more prevalent was silence on a subject that still was more taken for granted than vigorously debated.

The situation changed dramatically during the 1820s and 1830s, and especially during the 1840s and 1850s, as Southern slavery was subjected to withering attack from without and white Southerners increasingly came to identify their section with the peculiar institution. The attack was by no means limited to abolitionists. Indeed, although abolitionist invective was highly irritating to slave owners—who bitterly resented the new rhetorical absolutism under which slave owners became alien criminals and sinners rather than misguided compatriots—it is unlikely that such invective alone could have provoked the ensuing avalanche of pro-slavery polemics, because the abolitionists were (at least during the 1830s and early 1840s) so lacking in influence that they posed little substantive threat to Southern interests. It was primarily because they operated in the context of powerful additional challenges to slave-owner interests, and thus appeared the tip of the anti-slavery iceberg, that abolitionists were so alarming to Southern whites.

These challenges were in part economic, as the growing developmental gap between North and South became clear to informed observers; in part political, as supporters of "free soil" principles urged the containment of slavery within its existing boundaries so that the West could become the home of free white settlers rather than of masters and slaves; and in part ideological, as "free labor" advocates developed the practical argument that slavery prevented the South from achieving its true potential. In addition, Southerners were faced with growing geographic isolation, as slavery became a aberrant rather than a routine feature of social relations in the Americas. At the time of the American Revolution, slavery could be found almost everywhere in the New World; on the eve of the Civil War, far more slaves resided in the Southern states than in all the other remaining slave societies combined (Brazil, Cuba, Puerto Rico) and—together with Russian serfdom—Southern slavery had come to symbolize for much of the Western world a retrograde system resistant to change. It is no wonder that many white Southerners, feeling bypassed by the modern world, identified more with the past than with the future.

Beginning in the 1820s, Southern spokesmen elaborated with increasing volume, detail, and sophistication a series of arguments in defense of the peculiar institution. Designed to appeal to a diverse audience, these justifications of slavery contained a wide variety of themes, some of which were overlapping and mutually reinforcing and some of which worked at cross-purposes with each other. Less a unified pro-slavery "argument" than a hodgepodge of pro-slavery arguments, the defense of slavery grew less hesitant, tentative, and apologetic over the course of the late antebellum period, more insistent on the positive virtues of slavery and the society it fostered.

Among the earliest and most persistent arguments in behalf of slavery were those that spoke to its "practical" necessity or advantages. Emancipation was impossible, insisted Thomas R. Dew in an influential essay that appeared in the wake of the Virginia legislative debate of 1831–32, because it was not feasible either to send all two million slaves back to Africa or to free them in a "white man's" country where they would refuse to work and cause social disorder that would lead to race war and eventual extinction of the black race in America. Numerous pro-slavery spokesmen insisted that slavery was essential for Southern prosperity (and ultimately, therefore, that of the entire United States), because it made possible the massive cotton cultivation that propelled American economic growth. The sharp decline in sugar production that occurred after emancipation in most of the British West Indies supposedly proved the economic folly of hasty philanthropy, just as the massive Haitian slave revolt of the 1790s demonstrated the danger of social catastrophe that faced every slave society when authorities failed to maintain proper vigilance. (The obvious rejoinder that freeing slaves would *preclude* slave rebellion was left to abolitionist voices.) One of the biggest advantages of these and other practical arguments was that they did not rest on assertion that slavery was good in and of itself so much as on denial that realistic alternatives to it existed (at least in the immediate future); as a result, these arguments could appeal to those who harbored real Jeffersonian doubts about the theoretical morality of slaveholding. The most moderate weapon in the pro-slavery arsenal, practical justifications were especially popular in the upper South, where doubts about slavery's ethical implications were more persistent than in the cotton states, and continued to receive wide circulation until emancipation rendered them superfluous.

Religious arguments provided a kind of bridge between practical justifications based on slavery's necessity and more far-reaching theories predicated on its desirability. Religious idioms pervaded the pro-slavery literature, in part because Protestant ministers played a leading role in the defense of slavery and in part because such language was well calculated to appeal to antebellum Southerners. Indeed, historian Drew Gilpin Faust suggested that "the Bible served as the core" of the "proslavery mainstream."[16]

Three kinds of religious arguments in behalf of slavery were most common. To Southerners steeped in the Bible and predisposed to look to precedent for guidance, the facts that the ancient Hebrews (God's chosen people) owned slaves and that Jesus, who was not hesitant to condemn behavior that he considered immoral, never criticized slavery or reproached anyone for owning slaves seemed to provide clear divine sanction for the peculiar institution. So, too, did the specific biblical precedent provided by Noah's curse of his son Ham, and through him his grandson Canaan, for Ham's indiscreet gaze upon his father as he lay drunk and naked in his tent ("Cursed be Canaan; a slave of slaves shall he be to his brothers"), a story that white Southerners frequently cited to indicate God's condemnation of the black (or Hamitic) peoples to eternal slavery. But probably the most widespread and effective religious argument was the simple suggestion that slavery was part of God's plan to expose a hitherto heathen people to the blessings of Christianity. Like the "practical" arguments discussed above, this message left room for ambiguity over whether slavery need be a permanent feature of the black condition.

This was not true of racial arguments in behalf of slavery, since those arguments were predicated on the supposedly permanent and immutable inferiority of blacks to whites. Racist sentiment, widespread among antebellum white Americans, was pervasive in pro-slavery writings and speeches; it was rare for any pro-slavery polemic, no matter what its focus, to omit at least passing reference to racial characteristics. Racially based pro-slavery thought received its fullest, most extreme elaboration in the 1840s and 1850s, when "scientific" racists such as Dr. Samuel Cartwright and Dr. Josiah Nott popularized ethnological research that "proved" blacks were physiologically different from—and inferior to—whites. Blacks had distinctive nervous, circulatory, and pulmonary systems, Cartwright insisted, but more important still was the deficient character of their "head and face," which were "anatomically constructed more after the fashion of the simiadiae and the brute creation" than of the

Caucasian. "Thus, in the typical negro, a perpendicular line, let fall from the forehead, cuts off a large portion of the face," he asserted, "throwing the mouth, the thick lips, and the projecting teeth anterior to the cranium, but not the entire face, as in the lower animals and monkey tribes." Smaller brains supposedly limited blacks' intellectual capacity.[17]

Although such pseudo-scientific efforts to defend slavery represented the logical extension of a common racist mind-set, their influence was severely limited. Suggestions that blacks represented a distinct species of human beings (or, in the reformulation of some pro-slavery proponents, that they were the product of a separate creation) violated the Christian sensibilities of most white Southerners, and the ridicule to which some "scientific" racists subjected the biblical story of creation raised serious questions about their credentials. Far more widespread within pro-slavery propaganda than detailed ethnological analyses were brief, unscientific, and vaguely supported assertions that blacks were by nature different, inferior, and thereby unsuited for freedom. Hardworking, loyal, and productive under loving but firm direction (i.e., slavery), they lacked the temperament and intellectual capacity for independent existence, and in freedom would quickly degenerate, falling into ignorance, superstition, and perhaps even extinction. The "savagery" of Africa, whose natives over the millennia had supposedly failed to develop civilized society, clinched the point.

Even such a general, low-level form of racism provided an intellectually risky foundation on which to rest the defense of slavery. It hardly followed as a matter of course that black inferiority necessitated black enslavement; after all, most Northern whites took the first for granted without accepting the second. Furthermore, the suggestion that inferiority, whether mental or physical, required enslavement held potentially disturbing implications, since capabilities obviously varied widely within the white population. Racist arguments, therefore, were most useful—and most in evidence— not in isolation but in conjunction with arguments that stressed the positive virtues of slavery.

Among such arguments, an increasing number took the moral high ground by insisting that slavery provided unmatched benefits to everyone involved—masters, slaves, and society at large. Proponents of this social justification of slavery almost always accepted— and usually expressed in passing—the conventional wisdom about black inferiority, but racial arguments constituted supplementary ammunition, not their main weapon in behalf of slavery. The key point was rather the general superiority of slavery to the free-labor system. Developed in highly abstract, sociological form by Virginian George Fitzhugh and Mississippian Henry Hughes, this theme occupied a central place in the thought of leading pro-slavery propagandists such as South Carolinians James Henry Hammond and William Harper, and could be found in watered-down form in a vast number of writings, speeches, and conversational comments by Southern whites. Indeed, by the 1840s and 1850s, few Southerners attempted to defend slavery without including at least brief reference to the systemic preferability of slave over free labor.

Two principal components made up the heart of this broadly comparative defense of slavery. One was the proposition that far from being oppressed under slavery, Southern slaves received unparalleled care and protection and were in fact better off than most supposedly free workers in Britain and the Northern United States. Flowing naturally from the slave owner's self-image as a loving, paternalistic master who provided for his people, this proposition drew additional strength from the widespread attention given during the 1830s and 1840s to the plight of industrial workers in the North and especially in England. Southern blacks, pro-slavery spokesmen maintained, lived far better than these supposedly free "wage slaves," not to mention the impoverished peasants of Ireland or Italy. Unlike freely hired workers, whose employers took no interest in them except as instruments for their own aggrandizement, slaves received free food, housing, clothing, and medical care and did not face the threat of being laid off if their services were no longer needed. "Their condition . . . is now better than that of any equal number of laborers on earth," boasted Virginia's Baptist minister Thornton Stringfellow in a typical statement, "and is daily improving."[18]

Linked to this assertion of the slaves' superior material condition was a more general systemic comparison of slavery with free labor. This comparison invariably concluded that slavery produced a humane, orderly, and conservative social order, one far superior to that based on the dangerous experiment in free labor under way in the North and in England, an experiment that inevitably led to class warfare, social disintegration, radicalism, a spirit of selfish individualism, and a reckless enthusiasm for one new faddish idea after another. In language that shared much with that of early socialist theorists writing at the same time, Southern publicists denounced the cruelties inherent in wage labor—unlike most pro-slavery writers, Fitzhugh actually used the word "exploitation"—and mocked the supposed "freedom" of free labor as a chimera. "The present condition of the laboring classes in Great Britain differs from personal bondage chiefly in the name," legal scholar Thomas R. R. Cobb of Georgia asserted, in a statement that typified the efforts of many pro-slavery spokesmen to recast what seemed the unfavorable language of the debate over slavery. "Necessity and hunger are more relentless masters than the old Saxon lords."[19]

Unlike the socialists, however, defenders of slavery did not propose to replace free labor with a more egalitarian productive system but, rather, to hold the line against the creeping spread of egalitarianism. Linking the exploitation of wage labor with a host of other social ills that stemmed from excessive infatuation with liberty and equality, they insisted that only the South's tried and true system —slavery—could provide a cure for these ills. Time after time, pro-slavery spokesmen directly tied the proliferation of the "isms" that they saw plaguing the North with a mindless rush to promote ever more democracy, and explained both as functions of the free-labor experiment. The bolder and franker of these spokesmen explicitly embraced order, hierarchy, and inequality as the building blocks of all true civilizations, and put forth slavery as the only alternative to a revolutionary leveling trend that would eventually result in the nightmare of socialism. "Inequality is the fundamental law of nature, and hence alone the harmony of the universe," proclaimed Hammond. Noting that radical abolitionists denounced slave society as aristocratic, he responded, "I accept the terms . . . Slavery does indeed create an aristocracy—an aristocracy of talents, of virtue, of generosity and courage. In a slave country every *freeman* is an aristocrat." Labeling the freeing of Western Europe's serfs a "cruel failure," Fitzhugh urged Southerners to abandon the attempt to justify slavery on the basis of race, an attempt saddled with "a thousand absurdities and contradictions," in favor of a more abstract defense of slavery as "a normal, natural, and, *in general*, necessitous element of civilized society, without regard to race or color."[20]

Fitzhugh was not an entirely typical defender of slavery. In specifically asserting that slavery was a desirable condition for white as well as black laborers, he took a position that was at the very least politically untenable in the South, where the majority of voters were non-slaveholders who must inevitably wonder about their proper place in a society where slavery was based on criteria other than race. But he was not, as some have suggested, entirely aberrant. He expressed in extreme version, and gave order to, arguments that were widely circulating, and his effort to play down the racial component of pro-slavery thought was part of a general trend to broaden the defense of slavery by phrasing it in disinterested terms: slavery was good, not because it served the selfish interest of a slaveholding minority, but because it served the general interest of society. Representing one end of a pro-slavery spectrum, Fitzhugh's ideas had considerable appeal to wealthy slave owners who considered themselves natural leaders. Ridiculing the biblical argument that "either the Africans generally, or the negroes particularly, are descended from Ham," Alabama's Edmund Ruffin praised Fitzhugh as "a profound thinker, though a careless writer," confiding to his diary that "nearly all that he says of slavery, & of what I have called class-slavery, & which he terms slavery of labor to capital, is true & forcible."[21]

Arguments in favor of slavery were historically conditioned by the felt need to defend the peculiar institution; they arose opportunistically and they evolved over time. For decades, slaveholders supported slavery with a minimum of rationalization, accepting it as natural without bothering to construct carefully articulated arguments in its behalf; many—probably most—masters continued to do so down to the Civil War. Southern leaders could hardly afford this luxury; forced to respond to attack, they grasped at every potentially useful argument within sight—even when they were mutually exclusive—and used them all, in the process producing essays and speeches that often lacked intellectual consistency. Thus it is not at all uncommon to find pro-slavery tracts in which racial arguments were juxtaposed with appeals to the precedent of the non-racial slavery of Greece and Rome, or in which attacks on the excessive egalitarianism of Northern society were followed by assertions that slavery was a great leveler that rendered all Southern white men equal. In short, most defenses of slavery cannot be categorized as based on appeals to race *or* class *or* religion *or* practicality; rather, they combined these in a jumble of repetitive arguments with differing relative emphases. Despite this heterogeneity, the defense of slaveholding society as a whole became increasingly central to pro-slavery rhetoric during the 1840s and 1850s. In part, this trend reflected the desire of Southern spokesmen to take the moral high ground, to express their commitment to slavery in terms of principle rather than of interest. (Their interests conditioned their principles, of course, but in this they were hardly alone.) But it also represented a very specific response—and the mirror image—to free-labor critiques of slavery that proliferated in the North during these years, critiques that stressed the way in which slavery retarded the South's economic development, degraded its labor, and corrupted the very fiber of its being. In their insistence that it was the *North* that suffered from untold social ills and that it was *slavery* that produced a superior social order, pro-slavery polemicists joined the battle and raised the stakes. After all, their society was indeed under attack, and its very survival was at issue.

VII

THE PRO-SLAVERY CRUSADE set the South off from other slave societies. Elsewhere, too, of course, elites defended threatened prerogatives; nowhere did entrenched privilege abdicate gracefully under pressure. In the Caribbean and Brazil, slave owners insisted that slavery underpinned economic prosperity and social order, and warned that abolition would constitute a gross violation of established "rights"; Russian noblemen made similar arguments in defense of serfdom. But spokesmen for the Old South developed these arguments with unique volume, frequency, and sophistication. Nowhere else did the defense of slavery turn into a veritable pro-slavery crusade, as it did in the United States; nowhere else did slave owners refuse to accept emancipation and go to war to preserve their interests. In their hour of crisis, masters elsewhere grumbled, groused, and dragged their heels, but ultimately they reluctantly went along with decisions taken by central governments to convert to free labor. In the Southern United States, slaveholders determined that they would rather fight than switch.

The unique militancy of the Southern defense of slavery was in part a function of the unique American political system, which was both federal and democratic. Because antebellum politics was democratic, Southern slaveholders were able to listen to and vote for men who expressed their interests; because politics was federal, with power concentrated at the state rather than at the central level, those slaveholders were able to elect candidates who expressed their interests. Indeed, as William J. Cooper, Jr., and other historians have shown, Southern politics during the antebellum period often revolved around who could prove himself to be a better defender of Southern interests—by being more pro-slavery than his opponent. Because slavery was by now confined to the Southern states and the attack on slavery came almost entirely from without, the defense of slavery became, as we have seen, tantamount to the defense of the South. In short, the decentralized and democratic nature of the American political system provided an ideal forum for the defense of interests that were entrenched at the state or local level, while the sectional nature of Southern slavery encouraged slaveholders to take advantage of that forum to the fullest.

But on a broader level, the militance of Southern pro-slavery reflected the unusual commitment of Southern slaveholders to the peculiar institution itself. As we have seen, Southern slaveholders were far more often than those in most other countries resident masters with a strong paternalistic self-image. Slavery to them represented not just an economic interest but also a way of life; abolition threatened not just the loss of money but also the loss of a world. Elsewhere—for example, in the British colonies and in Russia—governments made provisions for the economic security of the masters, providing various forms of compensation for the loss of their human property; such provisions eased the shock of emancipation for masters who seemed more concerned with the threatened pecuniary loss than with any other consequence of abolition. Southern slaveholders time after time spurned opportunities for compensated emancipation, even when it was clear, during the Civil War, that the only alternative they faced was the strong likelihood of an enforced, *uncompensated* emancipation. In doing so, they expressed a great deal about their peculiar commitment to slavery, and about Southern slavery itself. As historian C. Vann Woodward has suggested, "the end of slavery in the South can be described as the death of a society, though elsewhere it could more easily be characterized as the liquidation of an investment."[22]

By the 1850s, the white South had taken on a siege mentality. More and more, Southern politics came down to defending slavery from alien attack. Determined to maintain what they now identified as their interests and their way of life, Southern politicians threatened to withdraw from the United States and form their own country should any government come to power in Washington that put those interests and that way of life at risk. When Abraham Lincoln was elected President, they made good on that threat, plunging the United States into a secession crisis and then into civil war. Ironically, by going to war for the preservation of slavery, they took the only action that could foreseeably have led to its speedy and complete abolition.

7

The End of Slavery

I

THE NINETEENTH CENTURY was a century of emancipation. Beginning with the Northern United States in the years following the American Revolution and ending with Brazil in 1888, forced labor gave way to free throughout the Western world. The end of Southern slavery, like Southern slavery itself, was thus part of a general process, and emancipation in the South shared basic characteristics with emancipation elsewhere. With the important exception of Haiti, freedom came from above, the result of decisions taken by central or metropolitan governments over the protests of reluctant—in some cases more than reluctant—local elites. In varying degrees, however, the actions of the slaves themselves helped bring about those decisions, as bondspeople took advantage of weakened authority to sabotage the old order through flight and unruly behavior.

Once freed from the shackles of bondage, the freedpeople everywhere struggled to maximize their social autonomy and to avoid falling into a dependency reminiscent of the old days. The dawning of a new order generated enormous excitement, hopes, and expectations, not all of which could be fulfilled. The post-emancipation world brought significant changes to the lives of the freedpeople—as well as to society at large—but it also brought continued hardship, exploitation, and oppression. As a result, within a generation, hope largely gave way to disappointment, and enthusiasm yielded to sullen resentment and sometimes to despair. Was this really the freedom for which they had longed?

Just as Southern slavery was in some ways distinctive, however, so, too, was Southern emancipation. The unusual vehicle for emancipation in the Southern states—civil war—accentuated many of the features associated with the transition from slavery to freedom. The war provided Southern slaves with unprecedented opportunities to resist authority, opportunities they seized upon to engage in acts of "self-liberation" that prodded the federal government to turn a war for union into a war for freedom. The war also drastically reduced the influence of the former slave owners. Elsewhere, former masters maintained enormous economic and political power, typically received financial compensation for the losses they suffered in emancipation, and played a major role in drawing up the ground rules for the new order. As traitors to the United States, however, Southern masters forfeited both any claims to compensation and any role in framing the emancipation settlement. Reconstruction consequently represented an unusually far-reaching effort to remake the slave South into a free-labor South, and raised exceptional expectations on the part of the freedpeople and their allies. The eventual dashing of many of those expectations was correspondingly pronounced and set the tone of Southern history for many years to come.

II

THE CIVIL WAR began as a war for—and against—Southern independence. Although slavery was the issue that both underlay and precipitated the conflict between North and South, the initial war goals of both sides were simple, and only indirectly linked to the peculiar institution: Confederates fought for the right to secede and form their own country; federal forces fought to prevent them from doing so. During the secession crisis preceding the start of hostilities, Abraham Lincoln had promised that the new Republican Administration, although opposed to the *expansion* of slavery, would pose no threat to slavery in the states where it already existed, and in the early months of the war he took pains to reemphasize his government's limited war goal: preservation of the Union. As late as

August 1862, Lincoln insisted that abolition was not on the horizon: "My paramount object in this struggle is to save the Union," he lectured anti-slavery editor Horace Greeley, "and is not either to save or to destroy slavery."[1]

Lincoln's caution stemmed not from moral equivocation—he consistently reiterated his belief that slavery was wrong and ought to be abolished—but from potent practical considerations. Four slave states—Maryland, Delaware, Missouri, and Kentucky—remained in the Union, and a fifth, West Virginia, was in the process of breaking away from its Confederate parent; defining the war as a struggle over slavery threatened to push these states into the Confederate column. The loyalty of Maryland, which harbored considerable pro-Confederate sentiment, was especially critical, for the state's secession would leave Washington, D.C., surrounded by enemy territory. Equally troubling were the political risks associated with too hasty a commitment to abolition. Most Northern Democrats strongly supported the war effort so long as the war remained one to preserve the status quo; a war to overturn slavery, however, was an altogether different matter, and leading Democrats made it clear that the President could not count on their support in such a contest. Concerned to maximize Northern support for the war effort and to minimize the ability of Democrats to exploit the racist fears of voters, Lincoln bided his time.

As the war dragged on, however, the President also faced mounting pressures to seize the moment and embrace a new war aim: freedom for the slaves. Such a move appeared increasingly desirable to American diplomats striving to prevent foreign powers—most important, Great Britain—from extending recognition (and assistance) to the Confederacy; so long as the Confederates could portray their rebellion as an exercise in national self-determination, their cause aroused considerable sympathy abroad, but much of this sympathy would be likely to dissipate if the war could be redefined as a struggle over slavery. Military needs also seemed to suggest the desirability of broadening Union war aims. Recruiting Union soldiers became steadily more difficult during 1862 as patriotic enthusiasm for what many at first believed would be a quick, glorious victory evaporated in the face of the grim reality of protracted war. Embracing emancipation as a war goal—or, better yet, as the central war goal—would help rekindle enthusiasm for the war effort and, by hitting at the underpinning of the Southern economy, undermine the ability of the Confederates to wage war. It would also make it possible for the army to make use of tens of thousands of potential black recruits eager to strike a blow for freedom. One did not have to be a fervent advocate of black equality to favor the recruitment of black soldiers. Many Northerners shared the hope of Iowa Senator James W. Grimes that employment of black troops would reduce deaths among whites; as Grimes told an audience in Dubuque, he would prefer to "see a negro shot down in battle rather than the son of a Dubuquer."[2]

The longer the war continued, the more inexorably a conservative effort to preserve the status quo evolved into a revolutionary effort to remake the South. Two interrelated catalysts of this transformation were especially significant. The first was the behavior of Southern blacks, who by refusing to act like slaves hastened slavery's internal collapse and forced Northerners to come to grips with the war's revolutionary potential. The second was the behavior of Northern whites, an increasing number of whom came to see the war as an unprecedented opportunity to remake the South.

The wartime behavior of Southern slaves has been a source of continuing controversy and myth. Noting the absence of major slave rebellions in the Confederate South, former masters reminisced about stereotypical "faithful darkies" and historians pointed to the slaves' ingrained—or in some cases inherent—docility. This theme received almost universal currency by the early twentieth century, challenged only by a small number of contrary reminiscenses and scholarly essays whose authors were usually black; the most sweeping early repudiation of the notion that slave docility characterized the wartime South was offered by the famous black scholar and activist W.E.B. Du Bois, who in his 1935 volume *Black Reconstruction in America* put forth the thesis that during the Civil War the slaves engaged in a massive "general strike" that tipped the tide of battle in favor of the North. More recently, many historians have built upon Du Bois's basic insight to argue that the slaves played a major role in bringing on the downfall of slavery. The most forceful support for the position that the slaves were "the prime movers in securing their own liberty" has come from the editors of the Freedmen and Southern Society Project, a massive ongoing effort to collect and publish documentary material relating to the emancipation of the Southern slaves.[3]

Despite the fears of Southern whites, slaves did not seize upon the wartime disruption to engage in a Haitian-style uprising; the absence of such insurrection points to basic differences between Southern and Caribbean slavery both in demographic conditions and in master–slave relations. But if slaves did not rise in massive rebellion, they did take advantage of weakened authority resulting from the war to engage in acts that undermined the ability of masters to govern and that persuaded federal officials the time had come to bury the peculiar institution. Although Du Bois's language suggests a greater degree of organization than was usually present, the term "general strike" comes as close as any to catching the enormous significance of what occurred: by refusing to cooperate with the slave regime—in other words, by refusing to act like slaves—blacks throughout the South struck a mortal blow to slavery.

Slaves learned far more than they let on about the course and character of the war. Their information was not always accurate in detail; rumors spread quickly in the slave quarters and at times endured with a stubborn resilience unrelated to reality. Years later, for example, several former slaves recalled a personal showdown between Abraham Lincoln and Jefferson Davis. In one version, Lincoln met Davis in South Carolina before the start of hostilities and ordered him to free the slaves, but Davis responded, "You can't make us give up our property," and the war began; in another, which explained the origins of the popular Yankee song "Hang Jeff Davis to a Sour Apple Tree," the two Presidents met toward the end of the war "under de ole apple tree" and "Lincoln stuck a shot gun in Jeff Davis' face an' yelled, 'Better surrender, else I shoot you an' hang you,' " whereupon Davis responded, " 'Yessir, Marse Lincoln, I surrender.' "[4] But by listening and observing carefully, slaves acquired a broad general understanding of the war, which they correctly perceived to revolve around slavery. There could be no doubt about where their loyalties lay in such an encounter.

Masters who thought they knew their "people" well reported troubling signs, both subtle and dramatic, that all was not well. Slaves took advantage of their masters' absence at war to drag their feet, chip away at rules and regulations, and break down traditional discipline. Many were less deferential—or did they just seem that way in the slaveholder's panicky imagination?—less willing to fulfill orders quickly and cheerfully; they smirked, whispered, and watched. The difficulty many plantation mistresses had in maintaining slave discipline with their husbands gone seemed to underline the patriarchal character of slavery. Not all slaves gave offense; some stood loyally by masters and mistresses through thick and thin, and even those who did not rarely engaged in (or even threatened) acts of violence against them. But clearly, as both slaves and owners realized, the war had changed the ground rules under which they operated. The changes produced anxiety and anticipation.

Wherever Union troops approached, the transformation of master–slave relations became unmistakable as slaves sensed their impending liberation. They became unruly and "demoralized"; they defiantly refused to obey orders and talked back to masters; and they ran away, at first one by one, then in droves. Flocking to Union lines, they offered their services to the military and crowded into hastily set-up refugee camps, forcing the issue of what to do with the fugitives—and ultimately the issue of slavery itself—upon often reluctant federal officials. Slavery ended for hundreds of thousands of slaves well before the war was over, as Union troops occupied larger and larger areas of the Confederacy and increasing numbers of blacks fled from their owners in areas still under Confederate control.

Conditions changed for those who stayed behind, too. In much of the South, slavery collapsed as the war's resolution became clear. "The people are all idle on the plantations, most of them seeking their own pleasure," confided Georgia plantation mistress Mary Jones to her diary in January 1865, as federal troops approached. The arrival of those troops proved traumatic. "Their condition is one of perfect anarchy and rebellion," Jones wrote of the slaves two weeks later. "They have placed themselves in perfect antagonism to their owners and to all government and control." Most distressing of all was the news that "nearly all the house servants have left their homes"; to Mrs. Jones, as to countless other slave owners across the South, the "ingratitude" and "disloyalty" of trusted servants raised, if only for a fleeting moment, troubling questions about their entire past relationship. The slaves—we must now call them freedpeople—felt a very different emotion: "free at last."[5]

At the same time that Southern blacks were demonstrating their determination to be free, public opinion within the North was warming to the idea. The status quo never constituted a very exciting war goal, and as the war progressed, an increasing number of Northerners endorsed the notion that the war must destroy slavery as well as preserve the Union. The logic of fighting against a slaveholders' rebellion dictated making slavery a target of the Northern war effort, and the widely shared belief in progress—manifested in its most extreme form as perfectionism—militated in favor of *improving* Southern conditions rather than simply restoring them. In short, the war provided an ideal opportunity to remake the South.

A significant share of Republicans had held this view from the start. Dubbed radicals because of their advocacy of extreme or far-reaching measures, they were a diverse lot with divergent, overlapping goals. Some radical Republicans were principled abolitionists who sought to create a racially egalitarian society, whereas others cared little about Southern blacks but hated the haughty, "unrepublican" behavior of Southern aristocrats. Many shared prevailing prejudices against blacks at the same time that they detested slavery as an affront to human dignity. On issues unrelated to the South and slavery they differed widely among themselves, some favoring and others opposing high protective tariffs, for example; some espousing and others deploring the organization of workers into labor unions; some championing and others ridiculing the movement to give greater rights to women. What they agreed upon was that the war provided the ideal opportunity to abolish slavery and create a better, more just social order in the South.

The ranks of these radicals grew rapidly, both among Republican Party officials and among the population at large. The longer the war lasted, the more many Northerners seemed willing to embrace radical measures; indeed, the war produced a kind of revolutionary momentum propelling public opinion forward to an extent that few could have imagined before the outbreak of hostilities. For this reason, what it meant to be a radical Republican was continually in flux: in 1861, it was radical to demand the immediate abolition of slavery, but by 1865, many radicals were proposing to extend equal voting rights to blacks. Radicals remained on the cutting edge, however, determined to take advantage of an unprecedented opportunity to bring sweeping changes to the South.

Operating in a uniquely favorable political environment—in no other period of American history except that of the Civil War and Reconstruction has the term "radical" carried generally positive connotations to the majority of Americans—radical Republicans firmly believed that they represented forces of progress, democracy, and decency. As Senator Benjamin F. Wade of Ohio put it, "The radical men are the men of principle; they are the men who feel what they contend for. They are not your slippery politicians who can jigger this way or that, or construe a thing any way to suit the present occasion."[6] Reviled by their Democratic opponents as dangerous revolutionaries and "nigger lovers" and long dismissed by historians as opportunists, fanatics, or representatives of business interests, radical Republicans have in recent years aroused renewed interest and respect from scholars impressed by their real if often flawed commitment to social change.

Faced with a protracted military stalemate, a restive slave population in the South, and a radicalized public opinion in the North, President Lincoln determined by the fall of 1862 to move against slavery. By that time, the political risks of inactivity equaled or exceeded those of appearing rash and desperate and freed the President to act on his anti-slavery principles. On September 22, 1862, he warned the Confederates that unless they ended their rebellion he would move against slavery on January 1, 1863, and with the onset of the new year he made good his promise, declaring that "all persons held as slaves" in rebel areas "are, and henceforward shall be, free"; he added that "such persons of suitable condition will be received into the armed service of the United States."[7] Drawing its legal justification from the President's power as commander in chief of the armed forces to take whatever action he deemed necessary to win the war, the Emancipation Proclamation did not immediately end slavery: the proclamation applied only to rebel territory—where the federal government lacked the ability to enforce the law—and left untouched slaves held in loyal states. Nevertheless, the decree had enormous symbolic significance, transforming a conservative war to restore the Union into a revolutionary war to reconstruct it. Northerners and Southerners, white and black, now knew that a Union victory meant the end of slavery. The Thirteenth Amendment to the Constitution, passed by Congress in January 1865 and ratified by the states in December, fulfilled this promise, barring slavery anywhere in the United States.

The war against slavery proceeded with accelerating momentum. In areas of the South occupied by federal forces—at first the Sea Islands off the coast of South Carolina and Georgia, southern Louisiana, northern Virginia, western Tennessee; then ever-expanding territory wrested from the shrinking Confederacy—Southern blacks eagerly sought both to enjoy the fruits of liberty and to help its cause. During the war, Reconstruction had already begun for hundreds of thousands of blacks living under federal protection. Continuing to flee from their masters, they experienced a variety of free and semi-free conditions as slavery gave way to free labor. Many labored under contract for planters, Northern speculators, and federal agencies. Others worked for the Union Army, either as soldiers—of some 180,000 blacks who served in the Union forces, close to half came from the Southern states—or as civilian employees. Others still crowded into Union-run refugee camps, seeking security and food and straining the administrative abilities (and often the tempers) of Union officers.

Even in the chaos engendered by war and social revolution, the determination of Southern blacks to grasp the opportunities at hand helped put to rest the doubts some Northerners continued to harbor about their capacity for freedom and served to radicalize further the Northern public. The eagerness with which young black men sought to join the military, followed by reports of responsible and at times heroic service under adverse circumstances, surprised and delighted those who, even in the North, had grown up believing that "Sambo" lacked the "manly courage" to stand up for his rights. Nothing else confirmed Northern whites in their judgment that blacks deserved to be free quite so much as their willingness to fight and die for that freedom—and for the Union cause.

Almost as persuasive was their passion for education. Many Northern whites, without thinking much about it, subscribed to the prevailing stereotypical view that blacks had limited intellectual abilities and lacked the capacity for rational thought. Reports sent back by hundreds of Northern missionary teachers who followed Union armies south told a different story. These teachers found blacks eager and able to learn—as quickly as whites, some noted with delight—and determined to make something of themselves. "The children . . . hurry to school as soon as their work is over," reported an American Missionary Association teacher from Norfolk, Virginia, in 1864. "The plowmen hurry from the field at night to get their hour of study. Old men and women strain their dim sight with the book two and a half feet distant from the eye, to catch the shape of the letter. I call this heaven-inspired interest."[8] To a nation in the midst of a struggle for freedom, the image of an oppressed people grasping for learning was as inspiring as it was comforting. Surely they deserved a little help from their friends.

III

THE END OF THE WAR left the slaves freed but their status otherwise undetermined. Precisely where and how they were to fit into a supposedly egalitarian system was the most pressing question to be resolved in the postwar "Reconstruction" of American—and especially Southern—society. This question, together with that of the relationship between the former Confederate states and the federal Union, seemed especially intractable because no precedent existed to guide policymakers as they struggled with it. Never before having fought a civil war or turned a slave into a free-labor society, Americans vigorously debated how to proceed. Sharp differences of opinion concerned not only what should be done but also how to go about doing it. Perhaps it is not altogether surprising that members of Congress assumed that Reconstruction would proceed through congressional legislation, while Lincoln's successor, Andrew Johnson, defended Presidential prerogative and most Southern whites argued that the individual states should be allowed substantial leeway to shape their own destiny. For two years, national politics centered on the formulation of an appropriate Reconstruction program.

During this period, congressional opinion (and that within the country at large) grew progressively more radical as Americans reacted with anger to what they saw as the efforts of former slaveholders, abetted by President Johnson, to steal victory from the jaws of defeat and deny true freedom to the former slaves. Well into 1865, some Southern whites continued to deny the reality of emancipation. Noting in her journal entry of April 1, 1865, that "the negroes' freedom was brought to a close today," a member of a prominent South Carolina planting family related how local whites "requested the negroes be called up, and told them they were not free, but slaves, and would be until they died . . . Poor deluded creatures!" she concluded. "Their friends the Yankees have done them more harm than good."[9]

Although the delusion that slavery would remain untouched soon faded, the notion that blacks would remain less than free did not. Northerners reacted with dismay and disbelief as Southern state legislatures—containing large numbers of former Confederates—passed "black codes" that relegated blacks to a status somewhere between slave and free; these codes typically restricted blacks' occupations, ownership of property, and access to the judicial system and contained provisions that enabled officials to impose forced labor on "vagrants" who "loitered" or lacked employment as well as on children whose parents were unable to support them. Meanwhile, Northern journalists and political figures who toured the Southern states in 1865 and early 1866 brought back reports of widespread hostility to Northerners and violence against "loyal" Southerners. Abolitionist General Carl Schurz, for example, found that most Southern whites refused to believe blacks would work except under compulsion; he generalized that "although the freedman is no longer considered the property of the individual master, he is considered the slave of society," and concluded that "it will hardly be possible to secure the freedman against oppressive class legislation and private persecution, unless he be endowed with a certain measure of political power."[10] Such reports had a powerful impact on the Northerners—and on the Republicans who represented most of them.

The Reconstruction program eventually enacted was consequently substantially more far-reaching than at first appeared likely, and included guarantees of both civil rights and voting rights to the former slaves. A chronological listing of some of the most important Reconstruction legislation reveals its increasingly radical tenor:

- The Thirteenth Amendment to the Constitution (passed January 1865, ratified December 1865) abolished slavery in the United States.
- The Civil Rights Act (passed over President Johnson's veto, March 1866) defined all persons born in the United States as American citizens, with equal rights "to make and enforce contracts, to sue, be parties, and give evidence, to inherit, purchase, lease, sell, hold, and convey real and personal property, and to full and equal benefit of all laws and proceedings for the security of person and property."[11]
- The Fourteenth Amendment to the Constitution (passed June 1866, ratified 1868) incorporated the Civil Rights Act's definition of citizenship into the Constitution; prohibited any state from abridging "the privileges or immunities of citizens" or depriving "any person of life, liberty or property, without due process of law"; encouraged the Southern states to enfranchise black men by providing for proportional reduction in congressional representation for states denying the vote to any male citizens "except for participation in rebellion or other crime"; disqualified from holding federal or state office all those who rebelled against the

United States after swearing as government officials to support the Constitution; and declared void all Confederate war debts and claims to compensation for emancipated slaves.[12]

- The Reconstruction Acts of 1867 divided the ex-Confederate states (except for Tennessee, which alone among the rebel states had ratified the Fourteenth Amendment and been readmitted to congressional representation) into five military districts, each under the control of a military commander who was to oversee the process of political normalization. Only when a state had "formed a constitution of government in conformity with the Constitution of the United States in all respects," adopting and ratifying a new state constitution providing for full manhood suffrage, and when that state had ratified the Fourteenth Amendment to the U.S. Constitution, would it be restored to full self-rule and admitted to congressional representation.[13]

- The Fifteenth Amendment to the Constitution (passed 1869, ratified 1870) completed the work of enfranchisement begun in the Fourteenth Amendment, by declaring simply: "The right of the citizens of the United States to vote shall not be denied or abridged by the United States or by any State on account of race, color, or previous condition of servitude."[14]

Despite the protracted debate over the proper course of action, the Reconstruction settlement was conceptually quite simple—and prototypically American. Congress rejected the most extreme proposals put forth by radicals—proposals for massive land confiscation and redistribution and for an extended period of federal rule over the ex-Confederate states—and instead based its program on the principle of equal civil and political rights. Blacks would enjoy all the rights of United States citizens, now expanded for the first time to include suffrage for males, and would be free to sink or swim on their own; political power would revert to the states—although this power was circumscribed by the Fourteenth and Fifteenth Amendments as well as by the threat of federal intervention in case of noncompliance with the terms of Reconstruction legislation—and there would be no massive federal "welfare" program. Even strong proponents of black rights often shared this basic understanding of the sequel to slavery. "Let them alone," declared Frederick Douglass in 1862 in response to the question of what should be done with the ex-slaves; "our duty is done better by not hindering than by helping our fellow-men," he explained, and "the best way to help them is just to let them help themselves."[15]

Two exceptions illustrate the prevalence of this basic laissez-faire policy. The most ambitious government effort, at the time totally without precedent in American history and suggestive of much larger twentieth-century programs, was provided by the Freedmen's Bureau (officially the Bureau of Refugees, Freedmen, and Abandoned Lands), a War Department agency that grew out of wartime relief work. Established in May of 1865 to oversee the transition from slavery to freedom, the bureau was headed by General O. O. Howard and staffed largely by Union Army officers; during its brief existence it distributed food to destitute blacks and whites, supervised the establishment of free-labor agriculture, and furnished much-needed financial assistance to set up schools for the ex-slaves. Bureau operations varied, depending to a considerable extent on the character of individual agents. Some freedpeople complained that agents cooperated with planters to enforce repressive regulations or to ignore blatant cheating of blacks by whites; far more bitterly and consistently, Southern whites denounced the bureau as part of a revolutionary plan to overthrow established relations and rile blacks up against those who had their true interests at heart. In fact, both freedpeople and planters turned to the bureau for help, and the agency provided assistance to both in adjusting to new and often perplexing circumstances.

But the scope of this assistance was limited. Even at its peak, in 1866, the bureau employed only twenty agents in Alabama and twelve in Mississippi, far too few to monitor closely either the freedpeople's affairs or their relations with planters. The bureau's entire budget for the year ending June 30, 1867, was $6,940,450, most of which went for relief and hospitals. Always viewed as a temporary agency designed to meet a specific crisis, the bureau began phasing out all but its educational functions in early 1868 and ceased most of its activities by the end of the year, although it was not officially abolished until 1872.

Even more limited was federal assistance to former slaves who sought to acquire land. Some radical congressmen—most notably Thaddeus Stevens of Pennsylvania and George W. Julian of Indiana—favored massive land redistribution, both to help the former slaves make their way in a largely agricultural society and to foster a more "republican" South by breaking the economic power of its landed aristocracy. "Instead of large estates, widely scattered settlements, wasteful agriculture, popular ignorance, social degradation, the decline of manufactures, contempt for honest labor, and a pampered oligarchy," declared Julian in 1865 as he propounded the advantages of land redistribution, "you want small farms, thrifty tillage, free schools, social independence, flourishing manufactures and the arts, respect for honest labor, and equality of political rights."[16] But such proposals, although not without support in Congress, met defeat at the hands of those who feared that massive confiscation of private property would set a dangerous and uncontrollable precedent.

The defeat of proposals for general land confiscation did not totally scuttle federal efforts to help freedpeople acquire land, but such efforts were halfhearted, sporadic, and ineffective. General W. T. Sherman's order reserving thousands of acres of abandoned lands in the Sea Islands and low country of South Carolina and Georgia to the freedpeople for homesteading, issued in January 1865 to disperse the throngs of refugees following his army, aroused enormous enthusiasm and enabled perhaps forty thousand blacks to become temporary settlers. President Johnson reversed this policy in the fall of 1865, however, and—over the opposition of Freedmen's Bureau Commissioner Howard—restored most of the holdings to their former owners. In 1866, Congress passed the Southern Homestead Act, which provided for homesteading on public lands in five deep-South states, limited for the first year to citizens who had been loyal during the war. Complications and hidden expenses, however, prevented freedpeople from taking advantage of the new measure. A prospective homesteader had to go to a federal land office—often a considerable distance—file a claim, hire a surveyor, and pay a series of fees in order to acquire forty acres of federal land; equally problematical, with the partial exception of Florida, land remaining in the public domain was of marginal quality. As a result, between 1866 and 1869, only about four thousand blacks—most of whom resided in Florida—filed homesteading claims. With postwar land prices depressed and homesteading so difficult, it is not surprising that far more freedpeople acquired land through outright purchase than through homesteading. Equal legal rights and competition in the marketplace, not affirmative-action programs to redress the wrongs suffered under slavery, defined the basic contours of the emancipation settlement.

For many years criticized as vindictive and cruel to Southern whites, the Reconstruction effort has in more recent years often been dismissed as insufficiently supportive of Southern blacks. Some scholars have derided Republicans for lacking political nerve, noting that almost everywhere in the South, rather than confronting prevailing racial prejudices head on, they adjusted to them by establishing segregated facilities for blacks, facilities that inevitably received inferior funding and provided inferior quality. Others have lamented the failure of Republicans to redistribute land, arguing that only by providing the freedpeople with a firm economic foundation could Reconstruction have been salvaged. The essence of these complaints is that the Republicans were too timid, that in being insufficiently radical they missed a golden opportunity to bring true revolution to the South and guaranteed the eventual failure of Reconstruction.

Although from the vantage point of the late twentieth century the limitations of Reconstruction are notable, it must be judged within the context of the times rather than against a generalized ideal. As Howard N. Rabinowitz has perceptively pointed out, the alternative to segregation that blacks faced throughout the South was not integration but exclusion; segregated schools, for example, replaced not integrated schools but no schools at all. From this vantage point, segregation, which appears retrograde in the late twentieth century, represented a significant advance in the middle of the nineteenth. Similarly, the failure to confiscate and redistribute Southern plantations can legitimately be criticized from a moral standpoint, but it must be remembered that in freeing the slaves the Republicans *had* just engaged in a massive confiscation and redistribution of private property—the only one of such proportions in American history. Nor is it clear that giving small plots of land to the freedpeople would by itself have provided the panacea that some have imagined: the condition of peasant proprietors in post-emancipation Russia, Haiti, and Jamaica should at least cause one to question the degree to which small-scale landownership, without a fundamental redistribution of political power, could serve as a basis for social regeneration.

For its time, the Reconstruction settlement represented an unprecedented effort to guide the South through a transition from slave to free labor. Republicans embarked upon this effort with high excitement and expectation. Here was the chance of a lifetime: the hated "slave power" was crushed, and a new, more virtuous social order was waiting to be born. Republicans differed on numerous specifics of what should be done, but they shared a broad conviction that slavery had stifled Southern development, and that with slavery removed, free labor would usher in a bright future for a formerly benighted region. As one congressman predicted grandly, "the wilderness shall vanish, the church and school house will appear; . . . the whole land will revive under the magic touch of free labor."[17]

Of course, other countries, too, faced the transition from slave to free labor, but nowhere else (except in Haiti) was the political context within which emancipation took place so promising for the freedpeople as it was in the United States. For this reason, Reconstruction was not only without precedent in the United States; it was also without true parallel abroad. Elsewhere, former masters (and their allies) played decisive roles in shaping the terms of the emancipation settlement, guaranteeing protection of their own interests through financial compensation (as in Russia and the British colonies), a protracted period of apprenticeship or gradual abolition (as in Russia, Brazil, Cuba, and the Northern United States in an earlier age), and elaborate legislation designed to define the position of the former bondspeople in the new social order. In Brazil, even abolitionists quickly lost interest in the plight of the former slaves, who faced the "benign neglect" of society—and the rivalry of cheap European immigrant labor hired by planters tired of dealing with "troublesome" blacks. In much of the West Indies, planters imported East Asian contract laborers to replace the former slaves, who showed an annoying tendency to prefer cultivating their own holdings to those of their former masters.

Southern blacks faced enormous hardships, but they were the beneficiaries of an unusual political configuration in which their cause was identified with that of the Union, while their former masters were viewed as traitors and stripped of much of their political power. As a result, proponents of black equality—a tiny abolitionist minority before the war—enjoyed undreamed-of political respectability that enabled them to enact many although not all of their legislative goals. In accordance with the Reconstruction Acts of 1867, the ex-Confederate states held constitutional conventions and established new state governments based on universal manhood suffrage. These Reconstruction governments varied widely in character and endurance. In South Carolina and Florida, Reconstruction regimes survived a decade, whereas in Virginia and North Carolina, they lasted only a couple of years. In general, Reconstruction was more radical and persistent in the deep South, where blacks constituted about half the electorate, than in the upper South, where a substantial white majority constrained radical behavior. But throughout the South, Republican-dominated governments passed civil rights acts, established public school systems, and sought to promote the emergence of a free-labor economy. In much of the deep South, black men exercised considerable political power on the local level, and elected black politicians sat in the legislatures of every Southern state. Historians continue to debate how radical "Radical Reconstruction" really was, but from the vantage point of Southern blacks, the vast majority of whom had been slaves until 1865, there can be no doubt that Reconstruction represented an extraordinary departure.

IV

SOUTHERN BLACKS did not wait for handouts from above. As soon as they were able, they acted to augment their autonomy and to reject the dependent status that slavery had forced upon them. The first moment of freedom—which came at different times throughout the South—was typically marked by a "jubilee," as freedpeople laid down their tools and engaged in a festive celebration of the long-sought deliverance from bondage; some crowded into nearby cities that had previously been off limits, others sassed their owners, slept late, visited neighbors without securing passes, or simply exulted in the amazing reality that they were free at last. " 'Member de fust Sunday of freedom," recalled Charlotte Brown.

We was all sittin' roun' restin' an' tryin' to think what freedom meant an' ev'ybody was quiet an' peaceful. All at once ole Sister Carrie who was near 'bout a hundred started in to talkin':

> Tain't no mo' sellin' today,
> Tain't no mo' hirin' today,
> Tain't no pullin' off shirts today,
> Its stomp down freedom today.
> Stomp it down!

An when she says, "Stomp it down," all de slaves commence to shoutin' wid her . . . Wasn't no mo' peace dat Sunday . . . Chile, dat was one glorious time![18]

Despite the alarm of many whites, who expressed fears that this unrestrained behavior confirmed their belief that blacks would not work without the compulsion of slavery, the jubilee was a fleeting occurrence, a brief but symbolic marking of the passing of the old order. More significant in the long run was the continued determination of the freedpeople to make sure that they were *really* free, not just free in name. Taking advantage of the favorable political climate, they were able to secure substantial, if sometimes contradictory, changes both in their relations with whites and in their relations with one another. Many but not all of these changes outlived the relatively brief period of political Reconstruction.

The unifying feature of the freedpeople's behavior during the postwar years was their determination to get as far as possible from slave dependence, to demonstrate to themselves and others that they were really free. They showed a powerful urge to reject old and to test new relationships. Thus, they refused to work under the authority of hated overseers, showed a frequent preference for contracting with planters other than their former owners, engaged in widespread local migration, abandoned white churches for churches of their own, and generally sought to avoid placing themselves in situations where they would be pushed around or told what to do. When Northern newspaper reporter Whitelaw Reid asked a black man living in a tent outside Selma why he did not go "home," he replied, "I's want to be free man, cum when I please, and nobody say nuffin to me, nor order me roun'."[19]

In the countryside, where the vast majority of freedpeople remained, blacks struggled to square "free labor" with their own ideas of freedom. Faced with a variety of possible agricultural relationships, they repeatedly opted for those that afforded the greatest autonomy and resisted those that smacked of slave-like subservience. Seeking most of all to acquire land of their own, they generally favored rental and sharecropping arrangements over dependent wage labor, and vigorously resisted remnants of the old order such as gang labor under the supervision of overseers. The freedpeople were not able to achieve all their goals; landownership remained an unrealized dream for most, and in parts of the South—for example, the sugar fields of southern Louisiana—gang labor continued to prevail. Throughout most of the cotton and tobacco South, however, blacks forced a fundamental change in agricultural relations, change that brought them a substantial increase in social autonomy.

The most autonomous were those who acquired their own land. The failure of various proposals to distribute land to the freedpeople did not completely shut the door on black landownership; depressed prices facilitated purchase of land on the open market, and during the postwar years tens of thousands of families scrimped and saved in order to buy their own holdings. Black landowning continued to expand, not only during Reconstruction years but also in the less salubrious political climate that ensued. As historians Claude F. Oubre and Loren Schweninger have demonstrated, the proportion of Southern black agricultural families that owned their own farms increased from about 2 percent in 1870 to 21 percent in 1890 to 24 percent in 1910, even as the rate of landownership among white Southerners declined. (The proportion of black farm owners in 1910 averaged 19 percent in the deep South and 44 percent in the upper South.) The great majority of these black farm-owning families eked out a relatively modest existence on small holdings, but the sense of accomplishment and independence that landownership gave to former slaves was immeasurable.

Increased independence was also the goal of the rural majority that did *not* acquire land. Taking advantage of an intense shortage of labor that—together with the favorable political climate—gave them considerable bargaining power, blacks wasted little time in struggling for improved terms of agricultural labor. The process began immediately after emancipation, when freedpeople began refusing to work under the control of overseers. It accelerated in the fall of 1865 when across much of the South blacks refused until the last minute to agree to new yearly contracts promoted by the Freedmen's Bureau to take effect with the new year, thus forcing concessions from desperate planters panicked by rumors of an impending mass uprising. And it continued in succeeding years, as the freedpeople gained new sophistication in bargaining on the basis of practical experience and left (or threatened to leave) uncooperative employers for those willing to offer more generous terms.

The result over the next few years was something of a stalemate, but one that contained substantial (if not always recognized) victories for the freedpeople. Black agricultural laborers, unable to achieve the total independence they sought, successfully resisted being turned into "free" but dependent plantation hands, whose lives were directed as they had been under slavery by planters and their subordinate administrators. A variety of working relationships ensued, including several kinds of sharecropping arrangements, in which transactions between those who owned the land and those who worked it involved a portion of the crop instead of cash. Under the share *wage* system, planters paid laborers an agreed-upon share of the crop—often as little as one-sixth or one-eighth in 1865, typically one-quarter in 1866 and 1867, by which time the freedpeople had learned to drive a harder bargain—and provided them with food, shelter, livestock, and agricultural implements. Under the share *rental* system, which began to replace share wages in the late 1860s and became prevalent in the 1870s, croppers paid landowners a share of the crop for the right to work the land, fed themselves, and often provided their own tools and animals as well; typical terms allotted one half the crop to the landowner and one half to the renter (or, in a more complex version, one-third of the crop for each of land, labor, and livestock).

Sharecroppers lacked the independence of farmers. In the post-Reconstruction years, with the changed balance of political power, they often became financially (and at times physically) dependent on merchants and planters who supplied them with credit at usurious rates. But sharecropping did provide the freedpeople with substantially more control over their lives than did wage labor. Because croppers had an economic stake in working hard, they did not require the same kind of supervision that hired employees (or slaves) did, and were free to work at their own pace; no one told sharecroppers when to rise or retire, when to eat, when to begin and break from work. If planters liked the incentive to diligent work that sharecropping provided, the freedpeople welcomed the increased autonomy that it allowed, and usually considered it far preferable to wage labor, which somehow seemed less free. Unlike wage laborers, who were clearly in a subordinate position, sharecroppers saw themselves more as partners than as employees of landowners. Insisting that he had the right to leave work at will to attend political rallies, Alabama freedman Bernard Houston explained to his employer the prerogatives of a sharecropper. "I am not working for wages," he declared proudly, "but am part owner of the crop and as I have all the rights that you or any other man has I shall not suffer them abridged."[20]

The rise of sharecropping, together with continued resistance on the part of the freedpeople to dependent social relations, transformed the lives of rural blacks. Throughout most of the South, gang labor under the supervision of planters or overseers quickly became a thing of the past. So, too, did the slave quarters, as scattered cabins, each surrounded by the land cultivated by its family inhabitants, replaced collective living and working arrangements designed to facilitate supervision of slaves. Most freedpeople in the cotton and tobacco South lived and worked on land owned by white landlords (although an increasing proportion, especially in the tobacco region, were landowners themselves), but they neither lived nor worked under the direction of those landlords. Contact between those who owned the land and those who worked it declined precipitously; indeed, many planters who had formerly prided themselves on their paternalistic management of their farming and their "people" now paid little attention to either so long as they received their rent. In short, although plantations often survived as units of landownership, the old plantation system of agricultural production quickly perished.

Other changes in black life accompanied this basic transformation of agricultural relations, as the freedpeople strove to maximize their social autonomy. The family was a major beneficiary of emancipation as well as a major focus of the freedpeople's drive for independence. Free from forced separation through sale, black families faced a new threat in much of the deep South in efforts by planters to secure the labor of children whose parents were "unable" to care for them by having such children apprenticed to a suitable "master" or "mistress"; in 1865 and 1866, several states passed laws giving former owners first claim on such children. Blacks vigorously resisted—sometimes physically—the stealing of their children, flooding Freedmen's Bureau offices with heartrending complaints; "General, I dont know the way to apply to you in because I dont know your rules," declared one desperate Alabama woman seeking the return of her grandchild in 1867. "I have got a white friend to write this for me."[21] Such complaints became so numerous—and so troubling to Freedmen's Bureau agents and other authorities—that eventually they could no longer be ignored. The wholesale apprenticing of black children came to an end in 1867, as bureau officials began issuing orders revoking acts of indenture, military commanders disallowed the most oppressive segments of the black codes, and the states prepared to elect new constitutional conventions in conformity with the Reconstruction Acts. The changed political climate of 1867–68 enabled freed blacks to withstand a major assault on the integrity of their families.

Secure from forcible separation, freedpeople acted both substantively and symbolically to promote the welfare of their families. Separated husbands and wives, as well as parents and children, sought each other out. Many joyfully celebrated the restoration of severed relationships, although the discovery of a long-lost spouse could create renewed pain and suffering for someone who had happily remarried after years of separation. Some couples who had lived together for years as man and wife underwent legal marriage ceremonies, to formalize existing relationships. And throughout the South, in a move that infuriated planters ridiculed as "playing the lady," rural black women marked their free status by abandoning field work for housework, in the process demonstrating the degree to which emancipation freed blacks to adhere to prevailing conventions of proper gender relations.

One of the most tangible signs of the freedpeople's concern for their families was in their eager embracing of education. Denied schooling as slaves, freed blacks associated it with freedom and enthusiastically sought access to education. They begged Freedmen's Bureau officials and representatives of Northern benevolent groups for assistance in setting up schools, and shouldered tuition fees that reached as high as a dollar per month (a very substantial fee when monthly wages for agricultural labor rarely exceeded twelve dollars). Adults as well as children—sometimes whole families together—went to school; the opening of night schools and Sunday schools attracted those who worked during the day. Everywhere, to the delight of Northern reformers and the bemused puzzlement of Southern whites, the freedpeople clamored for more schools, more teachers, more books.

Quasi-private schools sponsored during and immediately after the war by benevolent societies and the Freedmen's Bureau merged in the late 1860s and early 1870s with the new public school systems established by the Reconstruction governments in every Southern state. The schools faced enormous problems. These included a shortened school year geared to both the growing season and the reluctance of many Northern teachers to remain in the South during the "unhealthful" summer season; severe shortages of funds (although only after the overthrow of Reconstruction governments did funding for black schools begin to lag dramatically behind that for white); and student bodies whose diligence, regularity of attendance, and perseverance did not always match their enthusiasm. Still, given the magnitude of the task, the results were impressive as all over the South hundreds of thousands of black children began attending school. Recent research has revealed the extent to which the freedpeople themselves contributed to the rise of the schools, not just by supporting them enthusiastically but also by volunteering their labor to put up school buildings, pooling scarce resources to hire teachers, and serving as teachers themselves. Although most of the early teachers were Northern missionaries (usually white but occasionally black), Southern black instructors were increasingly numerous. At first most black teachers came from the ranks of slaves or free blacks who had enjoyed exceptional opportunities before the war or of "advanced" students who after a year or two of training in the freedpeople's schools were themselves ready to begin teaching, but in the 1870s their numbers were swelled by thousands of graduates of newly established normal schools for blacks—there were already twenty such institutions in existence by 1870—that proliferated throughout the Reconstruction South under both public and private funding. Within a few years, such graduates would represent the great majority of teachers in black schools.

Black churches, like black schools, served as focal points of the freedpeople's lives. Unlike the schools, however, the churches did not represent a new departure so much as a coming out into the open—and a strengthening—of already existing bodies. Throughout the South, emancipated blacks wasted little time in seceding from the churches of their masters and forming their own churches with their own ministers. The process occurred with a lightning-like speed that amazed most white observers, and was possible only because of the prior existence of the "invisible church": by the late 1860s, the separation of black from white religious bodies was largely complete. The movement was largely spontaneous—although not without help from without, especially among the Methodists, who enjoyed substantial organizational strength in the North in the African Methodist Episcopal and African Methodist Episcopal Zion churches—and indicated as clearly as anything else the desire of blacks to manage their own affairs free of white control. With black preachers catering to all-black congregations, the black church became an important symbol of independence to the freedpeople, one that grew in importance after Reconstruction, when that independence appeared increasingly tenuous.

In much of the South, blacks worked toward their goals—and expressed their desire for independence—through active political struggle. Of course, withholding labor to secure better working conditions, refusing to allow children to be indentured, and withdrawing from white churches were all inherently "political" acts in that they involved relations of power, but the Reconstruction Acts inaugurated a period of black participation in politics narrowly defined as well: that is, voting and governing. Historians have long since refuted the old myth of "Black Reconstruction," or Reconstruction governments in which blacks dominated the political process. In fact, blacks were almost everywhere underrepresented (in terms of their proportion of the population) in Reconstruction governments, especially at the highest levels: between 1868 and 1877, blacks provided only two United States senators (both from Mississippi), sixteen United States representatives (seven from South Carolina), and no elected governors. (In Louisiana, Pinckney Benton Stewart Pinchback served as governor for six weeks after the state legislature suspended Henry C. Warmoth from the office during an impeachment proceeding.) But throughout the deep South, where blacks constituted about half the population at the statewide level and a substantial majority of the population in many areas, black men served in large numbers as state legislators and local officials such as sheriffs and city councilmen. During the Reconstruction decade, more than six hundred blacks sat in state legislatures, the great majority former slaves from plantation districts of South Carolina, Mississippi, Louisiana, Alabama, Virginia, Georgia, and Florida. In South Carolina (but nowhere else), blacks constituted a majority in the House of Representatives (and briefly in the Senate).

Blacks in politics progressed rapidly from caution and moderation to increasingly radical assertion of rights. Whereas the Alabama Colored Convention of 1865 reassured whites that "it will continue to be our purpose to work industriously and honestly," that of 1867 proclaimed bluntly that "it is our undeniable right to hold office, sit on juries, to ride on all public conveyances, to sit at public tables, and in public places of amusement."[22] During the 1870s, black politicians demanded—and received—an increasing share of nominations for high political office; the number of blacks sitting in the

United States Congress, for example, increased from three in 1869–71 to five in 1871–73 to seven in both 1873–75 and 1875–77, even as the number of states that continued to elect black congressmen plummeted with the overthrow of Reconstruction governments. But it was not just black politicians whose political behavior was impressive. The mass of black voters demonstrated perspicacity, discipline, and often real courage in continuing to vote Republican in overwhelming numbers despite obfuscation, bribes, threats, and violence directed at them. These voters not only provided the basis of Republican rule in the South; they also confounded many white observers who had predicted that they would quickly become political pawns of their former masters.

V

HISTORIANS HAVE LONG DEBATED, and continue to debate, the degree to which emancipation transformed Southern—and black—life. Those impressed most by continuity between the Old and the New South—like economist Jay Mandle—have stressed that the South continued to lag behind the North in industrialization and urbanization and remained far poorer as well. Despite slavery's demise, white racism limited the opportunities of blacks for economic advancement. The overwhelming majority of blacks continued to work for whites as agricultural laborers, and a substantial degree of coercion continued to characterize relations between planters and laborers; indeed, scholars such as Jonathan Wiener have maintained that planter dominance of society remained so great that the South should be seen as deviating from the mainstream of American development and following a distinctive "Prussian road" to capitalism instead. And as we shall see, some of Reconstruction's benefits proved to be temporary gains that disappeared with Reconstruction itself.

But although there was much that did not change, in many ways the abolition of slavery enabled the South to move toward the American mainstream. Intense class struggle marked the spread of capitalist relations through the rural South, as freedpeople strove to secure what they considered their rightful fruits of freedom and planters endeavored to maintain as much control as possible over their "free" laborers. Exploitation, poverty, and hardship remained prominent features of Southern life, and new social relationships and attitudes struggled with old and sometimes yielded hybrid patterns—such as sharecropping—that marked the New South as different both from the Old and from the free-labor ideal. Emancipation did not produce the almost instantaneous regeneration of the South expected by many abolitionists. But the non-arrival of the predicted utopia should not blind us to the many changes that did occur during the postwar decades.

These changes, which can receive only brief mention here, produced a significant, if incomplete, transformation of the South during the generation following emancipation. Sharp increases in urbanization and industrialization affected where Southerners lived and how they worked; from 1869 to 1899, the real value added by manufacturing grew at an annual rate of 7.8 percent in the eleven ex-Confederate states versus 5.8 percent in the United States as a whole. Public schooling, almost totally absent before the Civil War, spread throughout the South, and literacy rates increased among both whites and blacks; in five deep-South cotton states, the proportion of fifteen-to-twenty-year-olds unable to write declined from 24.2 to 14.3 percent among whites and from 85.3 percent to 54.1 percent among blacks between 1870 and 1890. Southern life became increasingly commercial, as both freedpeople and up-country farmers were drawn into the market economy. At the other end of the social spectrum, entrenched privilege gave way to uneasy competition as slave owners became businessmen and capitalist landlords and as "New South" boosters rejoiced that the South had finally abandoned its "peculiar" past and was now poised to compete with the North on its own terms. Encompassing all these developments—and the changes in the lives of the former slaves—was the halting yet momentous shift to a social order based on free labor rather than on slavery. "Like a massive earthquake," concluded Eric Foner in his aptly titled recent synthesis, *Reconstruction: America's Unfinished Revolution*, "the Civil War and the destruction of slavery permanently altered the landscape of Southern life."[23]

Among black Southerners, the new order at times seemed suspiciously like the old. This was true not just because of the persistent efforts of planters to secure cheap labor and the continued racism that permeated society at large but also because blacks themselves often seemed ambivalent about many of the changes sweeping the South. Certainly, the post-emancipation drive for independence did not instantaneously wipe away all vestiges of the past. Many years later, Nate Shaw, a black cotton farmer born in 1885, deplored those vestiges. "My daddy was a free man but in his acts he was a slave," Shaw told an interviewer. "Didn't look ahead to profit hisself in nothing that he done. Is it or not a old slave act? Anything a man do in a slum way and don't care way, I just lap it right back on slavery time days." The elder Shaw was born a slave, but Nate considered his own children—third-generation freedpeople—slavish in character as well, and bitterly bemoaned their failure to appreciate his work on behalf of a sharecroppers' union in the 1930s. "I don't want no chicken-hearted boys," he declared sadly.[24]

Shaw's comments illustrate the difficulty of generalizing about the impact of emancipation. Even as blacks seized upon the opportunity to remake their lives, they sometimes confounded their free-labor supporters by seeming to cling to old ways rather than embrace the new. They firmly resisted, for example, the "conversion" efforts pushed on them by Northern white missionaries, and their Christianity remained largely that of the slave community. Similarly, the attempt of Northern teachers to instill a wide range of bourgeois cultural traits—punctuality, frugality, restraint, Victorian sexual morality—was at best only very partially successful. Freedpeople were often grateful to Northern missionaries, both religious and secular, but when the advice that those missionaries offered assumed too coercive a tone, it usually fell on deaf ears. Autonomy was autonomy; the freedpeople were not about to trade dependence on slave owners for dependence on "new masters," no matter how well-meaning they might be.

The drive for independence underlay other contradictory features of black behavior after emancipation. On one hand, the self-assertion evident in labor relations, defense of families, establishment of schools, secession from white churches, and active participation in politics fostered a growing sense of community among blacks. Together with this often went an increasing separation from white society. Some of this separation, such as the creation of dual public school systems for the two races, was clearly the result of white acts and presaged the Jim Crow system that would make its appearance a generation later. Much of the separation, however, stemmed from a tendency of blacks to pull apart from whites and rely on themselves: they seceded from white churches, showed a marked preference for black teachers, demanded the nomination of more black politicians, and drifted away from overwhelmingly white areas where they often felt unsafe. In a variety of ways, emancipation facilitated the communal activities of African-Americans and strengthened their recognition of themselves as a common people, with shared interests and values.

Black society faced centrifugal as well as centripetal tendencies, however, that have so far received relatively little attention from scholars. The restraints provided by slavery had provided the environment—the slave quarters—for the flourishing of a vital sub-culture; the removal of those restraints dramatically altered that environment, and therefore that subculture as well. When freed-people took advantage of the new freedom to leave their plantations and seek employment elsewhere, they also left friends and relatives and fragmented existing slave communities. The breakup of the old slave quarters and the decline of gang labor that accompanied the rise of sharecropping had a similar impact; as Gerald D. Jaynes has suggested, "in accepting family-based farming, the workers relinquished much of the social cohesiveness that had been supported by the collective work group."[25]

Another potentially disruptive force was the increase in black social stratification that followed emancipation. Freedom created new opportunities for individuals to distinguish themselves, and consequently permitted the rise of new divisions among a population whose slave dependence had previously created a broadly shared social outlook. Teachers, ministers, and politicians catered to black constituents, but they also saw themselves as different from the black masses; so, too, did the far more numerous landowners, small businessmen, and successful artisans who formed the basis of a new economic elite. Scholars have not yet given this new stratification the serious study it deserves, although some have suggested that it produced competing interests and values among African-Americans. Historian Leon F. Litwack, for example, chided black politicians for ignoring the economic aspirations of the mass of freedpeople while concentrating instead on middle-class concerns such as political and civil rights; "black spokesmen," he argued, "did not wish to undermine their own position by appearing to advocate confiscation."[26] One must not exaggerate the clashes of interest among blacks; political rights were important for the well-being of all blacks in the tumultuous years following emancipation, the degree of social and economic stratification was still relatively slight, and common racial identity in a racist society served as a strong source of black unity. Still, the overthrow of slavery fostered new sources of division among blacks as well as new opportunities for the defense of common interests.

The unifying theme underlying the diverse efforts of the freedpeople remained the drive for autonomy and independence. That drive expressed itself both at the collective level, in the struggle to achieve rights for blacks in general, and at the individual and family level, as particular blacks sought to take advantage of new opportunities. In this sense, the behavior of elite blacks who sought to promote their own interests did not so much contradict that of the freedpeople at large as constitute a different manifestation of a common pattern. Freed from a broad variety of constraints they had suffered under as slaves, blacks now struggled, both as a people and as individuals, against new forms of social, economic, and political dependence. What they wanted most of all as free men and women was the opportunity to live their own lives without being ordered around; this, to the ex-slaves, was the very essence of freedom.

The efforts of Southern blacks to maximize their autonomy conformed to general patterns of behavior among freedpeople in other post-emancipation societies. Although the precise manner varied, depending on concrete circumstances, former slaves and serfs everywhere resisted dependent relations that reminded them of their previous bondage, and sought to put as much distance as they could between themselves and that bondage. Thus, in the West Indies, freedpeople fled from the plantations on which they had toiled as slaves and set themselves up wherever possible as independent peasant proprietors. In Russia, peasants resisted the influence not only of the noble landholders who formerly owned them but also of well-meaning reformers who sought to modernize "backward" village ways, insisting that real freedom meant the right to do things their own way, without outside interference. But because the autonomy of American slaves had been constrained to an unusual degree by the particular conditions they faced, their post-emancipation quest for autonomy was especially pronounced and produced results that were especially far-reaching.

In prizing independence above all else, the freedpeople revealed the degree to which their worldview was shaped by their former bondage, for what they were seeking was to get as far from that bondage as possible, and many of their aspirations were defined by what had formerly been forbidden. Not everyone, however, shared the freedpeople's understanding of freedom as consisting above all in the right not to be ordered around. Different understandings of freedom would soon cause major problems.

VI

GIVEN THE REVOLUTIONARY DYNAMIC of events associated with emancipation, it is not surprising that those events engendered their own counterrevolutionary phase. By this I refer not just to the assault on and overthrow of the Southern states' Reconstruction governments but also to the overwhelming sense of disappointment and disillusionment that had set in by the 1870s and that deepened in succeeding years. Almost everyone—freedpeople, former slave owners, poor whites, Yankee reformers—seemed to feel (although from diverse perspectives) that things were going terribly wrong. The myth of Reconstruction as a "tragic era" was born in this pervasive disillusionment with the aftermath of emancipation.

The unhappiness of the former slaveholders is of course hardly surprising. Emancipation totally transformed the world of the slaveholders, who were turned almost overnight, in the felicitous phrase of historian Gavin Wright, "from laborlords to landlords"; as historian James Roark has observed, "from the planters' perspective, the postbellum plantation was almost unrecognizable."[27] Although some planters professed to welcome emancipation because it freed *them* from having to care for their troublesome slaves, such sour-grapes protestations only thinly masked the intense feelings of outrage, humiliation, and anxiety that they felt at the twin losses of their war and their slaves. Under the circumstances, virtually any postwar settlement was likely to have appeared tragic to the former masters.

What is more remarkable is the pervasive discontent that came to grip the Civil War's winners. Their sense of failure and disillusionment must be understood in the context of the revolutionary hopes, fears, and predictions that accompanied emancipation. The overthrow of slavery aroused expectations among blacks, poor whites, abolitionists, and free-labor reformers that were not only grandiose but also diverse and at times contradictory. If former slaves and poor whites most of all sought increased autonomy, many Republican reformers were more likely to look for increased efficiency as the chief benefit of emancipation. Critics of slavery had portrayed the peculiar institution as an incubus that kept the South degraded and backward in every way; with abolition, they believed, the stultifying effects of slavery would vanish and the region would be transformed virtually overnight into an orderly, prosperous, and virtuous society—a kind of idealized Southern New England.

Despite the momentous changes that came to the South, expectations were so elevated and so diverse that they could not possibly be fulfilled. Emancipation may have changed the Southern landscape, but despite all hopes, free labor did not produce anyone's version of utopia. Life remained hard, and the legacy of slavery— whether racism, economic backwardness, or pre-modern work habits—proved stubbornly ingrained. Under the circumstances, it was easier to see the problems that remained than the transformation that had occurred.

By the 1870s, perception of tragedy, failure, and missed opportunity was ubiquitous. When free-labor advocates looked south, instead of a flourishing economy, cheerful and efficient laborers, and a political system that was the model of disinterested republican virtue, they saw greed, corruption, ignorance, crudeness, and lethargy; surely this was not the goal for which they had worked so hard. An increasing number of Northern reformers—including some with good abolitionist and radical Republican credentials—came to question whether they had not made a terrible mistake and whether blacks were in fact "ready" for equality. The "excesses" of Reconstruction now appeared more evident, the desirability of devoting national resources to promoting the Reconstruction "experiment" more and more dubious. Former anti-slavery advocate James S. Pike's broadside *The Prostrate State* (1874), which purported to reveal the thieving, corruption, and debauchery that accompanied "negro government" in South Carolina, was typical of the new trend toward blaming the ills of the Reconstruction South on ignorant blacks and venal carpetbaggers, but even those who abjured Pike's racism frequently concluded sadly that the effort to "force" equality on the South was misguided. As early as 1870, for example, radical Republican Senator Carl Schurz denounced the "tendency . . . to thrust the hand of the National Government into local affairs on every possible occasion" as "false radicalism in the highest degree" and defended "State-rights as the embodiment of true and general self-government."[28]

Southern white proponents of emancipation and Reconstruction—"scalawags," in the parlance of the period—grew equally disillusioned. Non-slaveholding whites who expected to benefit from the destruction of slavery found themselves drawn into new market relations that put them increasingly at the mercy of impersonal outside forces, including low prices for cotton and tobacco and usurious interest rates set by planters and merchants, and dreamed of the sturdy independence they had supposedly enjoyed before the war; instead of gaining more control over their lives, they now seemed to have less. Hard pressed to pay the sharply higher taxes needed to fund schools and railroad construction, they were highly susceptible to Democratic suggestions that Republican governments took too much of their hard-earned money and squandered it in corruption and excessive benefits for blacks. Planters who had cast their lot with the Republicans in the belief that by doing so they would be able to "lead"—or control—the freedpeople were dismayed at the stubborn independence they displayed. Blacks rarely looked to their former masters for political leadership and increasingly sought to reap the rewards of office themselves rather than support their white Republicans allies. To both planters and poorer white scalawags, it seemed as if blacks were garnering most of Reconstruction's goodies, and during the 1870s, most of these white Republicans abandoned the cause and threw in their lot with the Democrats.

But it was among black Southerners that the sense of disillusionment was most intense. The freedpeople had expected much from emancipation, and the gains they received were inevitably too little to satisfy those expectations. Hopes for land distribution, widespread in the immediate postwar months, faded by 1868, but the freedpeople continued to look for a "real" freedom that would enable them to maximize their independence and provide them with equal rights, if not equal conditions. Beginning in the 1870s and accelerating in succeeding decades, blacks experienced a growing sense of despair as that freedom appeared ever more remote; in state after state, Reconstruction governments were replaced with conservative administrations that sharply curtailed spending on education, rolled back civil and political rights, and created a new political climate in which violence against "uppity" blacks flourished. The most savage assault on black rights did not occur until the 1890s and early years of the twentieth century, but by the 1880s, widespread disappointment had replaced the excitement and optimism that had suffused the freedpeople in the immediate postwar period.

One sign of this disappointment was a renewed interest among blacks in leaving the South. In the years immediately following emancipation, few freedpeople had moved North; indeed, some Northern blacks (and former fugitive slaves) had moved South to take part in the great Reconstruction experiment. Beginning in the late 1870s, however, black migration out of the South slowly accelerated; the most notable early manifestation of this trend occurred in 1879–80, when, prompted by rumors of cheap and plentiful land, tens of thousands of Southern black "Exodusters" relocated to Kansas. Still in the future was the "Great Migration" of the first half of the twentieth century, when millions of blacks would flee the South in search of employment and refuge in the cities of the North.

The post-emancipation disillusionment that gripped the South was not unusual; elsewhere, too, the results of abolition proved disappointing. Following emancipation in the British Caribbean in the 1830s, free-labor advocates were dismayed by the freedpeople's persistent efforts to become independent landholders and their reluctance to work cheerfully and efficiently—at low wages—for their former masters; to the former slaves, however, the new freedom seemed insufficiently free. A similar situation prevailed in post-emancipation Russia in the 1870s and 1880s, where reformers and government bureaucrats lamented the persistence of "backward" ways among the freed peasants, and those peasants, struggling to defend their autonomy against outside interference, questioned whether they had actually received the true freedom they had been promised. In Brazil, where establishment of a republic in 1889 followed by one year the final abolition of slavery, the freedpeople revealed their discontent by expressing widespread pro-monarchist sentiment, much to the surprise of observers who felt that former slaves should be good republicans.

But if a sense of things gone wrong was evident in numerous post-emancipation societies, nowhere except in Russia, where emancipation was accompanied by an effort to reconstitute the social order similar in some respects to Reconstruction, was that sense as pervasive—as characteristic of an entire era—as it was in the United

States South. That this was so suggests the extent to which the "great disappointment" was a function not only of harsh conditions but also of dashed expectations. Because emancipation in the Southern United States, like emancipation in Russia, produced an unusually sweeping effort to remake society, hopes were raised to an exceptionally high level and the disappointment at the failure completely to fulfill those hopes was correspondingly pronounced. "The shadow of a deep disappointment rests upon the Negro people," wrote W.E.B. Du Bois in his poetic essay *The Souls of Black Folk* (1903), "—a disappointment all the more bitter because the unattained ideal was unbounded save by the simple ignorance of a lowly people."[29]

Three specific developments exacerbated the Southern freedpeople's general disillusionment and rendered the initial decades of freedom especially trying. Perhaps the most all-encompassing—and least noticed—of these was agricultural depression. In assessing the economic hardships that faced the Southern freedpeople (and the South in general), scholars have paid insufficient attention to a cruelly ironic historical accident: emancipation in the United States coincided with the onset of an unusually sharp agricultural depression that lasted some three decades. Most prices fell during the last third of the nineteenth century, but agricultural prices (especially cotton) fell faster and further than non-agricultural prices; among the results—in both South and West, among both blacks and whites—were material suffering, dispossession of farms, a sharp rise in rural debt and tenancy, and a concomitant growth of agricultural protest movements that culminated in the Populist crusade of the 1890s. Depression provided a poor environment in which to undertake the transformation of a society, aggravated tensions and animosities, and contributed significantly to the widespread sense of social malaise that gripped the South in the post-emancipation decades.

A second element was the political retrenchment stemming from the collapse of the Reconstruction regimes. In state after state, conservatives, taking advantage of the declining Northern interest in the freedpeople, launched what amounted to a counterrevolutionary effort to topple the Republican-dominated governments. The tactics varied somewhat, depending on local conditions. In most of the upper South, where blacks constituted less than 40 percent of the electorate, appeals to white unity against "carpetbaggers,"

"Yankee rule," and "negro domination" were enough to bring about what was euphemistically known as "home rule" or "redemption"; in the deep South, by contrast, where blacks formed about half the population, only massive fraud, violence, and intimidation of voters did the trick. Although the Ku Klux Klan was largely suppressed in the early 1870s by federal force and publicity, other terroristic groups—with equally poetic names such as the Red Shirts and the Knights of the White Camelia—slashed, burned, and shot their way across the deep South, with devastating effect.

Under the onslaught, most white Republicans—reviled by their enemies as "nigger-lovers" and "scalawags"—broke ranks and defected to the Democrats, who portrayed themselves proudly as the "white man's party." Although few blacks followed them, some stayed home on election day and others were prevented from voting Republican by subterfuge, fraud, and outright theft. In state after state, new, Democratic administrations came to power: joining Georgia and the upper-South states, all of which were "redeemed" by 1871, were Texas, Arkansas, and Alabama in 1874, Mississippi and South Carolina in 1876, Florida and Louisiana in 1877. Despite the promises they sometimes made to allay black fears, these new governments slashed spending on education, overturned civil rights laws, promoted policies favorable to planters rather than laborers, and discouraged (without yet actually forbidding) black voting. By the 1880s, few blacks felt, as they had in the heady early days of Reconstruction, like citizens whose government represented them; political discouragement—and often apathy and indifference as well—replaced the sense of excitement and commitment that had seemed to signal the dawning of a new age.

Finally, pervasive white racism reminded blacks that that new age remained a distant hope rather than a current reality. Racism was a feature of the antebellum as well as of the postbellum South, of course, but with emancipation it became far more virulent. Slavery had, ironically, shielded its victims from the most extreme consequences of racism: with enslaved blacks apparently safely under control, masters commonly stressed their paternalistic duty to protect their dependent human property. Emancipation not only freed the slaves from direct slave-owner control; it also freed the masters from their protective role—and attitude. The changed ground rules of the postbellum South fostered intensely competitive social relations as planters and freedpeople struggled over terms of labor, poor whites who previously prided themselves on having special privileges by virtue of their color now faced the shock of competing with black citizens, and all three groups jockeyed for political power. In short, free blacks, especially those who asserted their equal rights, proved far more threatening than slaves to whites who took racial inferiority for granted. Here, too, developments in the United States South were not entirely typical of those elsewhere: although blacks suffered racial discrimination in other post-emancipation societies, the unusually vigorous effort to give blacks citizenship rights in what had previously been seen as a "white man's country" lent Southern white racism an exceptional virulence.

Throughout the South, racially inspired violence erupted, directed especially at independent blacks whose behavior seemed insufficiently deferential. Teachers, ministers, landowners, and politicians were special targets of abuse; burnings, whippings, and lynchings supplemented the far more frequent warnings and threats directed at "uppity niggers." Both rich and poor whites participated in the orgy of hate: although it became fashionable for respectable citizens to blame the worst excesses on white "riffraff," planters played an important role in organizing—and sometimes in committing—much of the violence, especially that directed at maintaining the subservience of black laborers. Not all whites supported the racist attacks, and some actively opposed them, but those attacks set the tone for political discourse and social relations in the post-Reconstruction South. All too often, when whites spoke about blacks, their words (and the thoughts behind them) turned nasty: the "my people" of slavery days yielded to the taunt of "nigger" and to grim warnings of "mongrelization" that awaited those too timid to protect their racial purity.

The ease with which many paternalists adopted the tactics of thugs reveals the thin line that had always separated paternalism from thuggery (a point missed by those who see depiction of slave-owner paternalism as an effort to whitewash slavery). Defeat knocked a master class that had seemed larger than life down to size and revealed the seamy reality that lurked behind its thin veneer of gentility: after the Civil War, high-minded statesmen seemed remarkably like whiny complainers, courteous planters like sharp-edged businessmen, and benevolent masters like small-time bullies.

The racist reaction did not reach its culmination until a generation after Reconstruction. At the end of the nineteenth and beginning of the twentieth centuries, state after state passed new restrictive legislation designed to put blacks "in their place." Complex voting laws that included literacy tests, poll taxes, and all-white primaries achieved the de facto disfranchisement of almost all black—and some white—voters; during the first half of the twentieth century, Southern politics was a sordid if farcical game, one for whites only. Less complex laws provided for racial segregation of virtually every aspect of public life, from schools and transportation facilities to theaters, restaurants, hotels, parks, beaches, hospitals, cemeteries, waiting rooms, and drinking fountains. Facilities open to blacks usually received sharply limited funding and provided distinctly inferior services. Meanwhile, white scholars, politicians, and publicists celebrated the virtues of a Southern civilization now "gone with the wind" and sang the glories of the "lost cause." An uninformed observer of the South in 1910 might well be pardoned if he or she concluded that the Confederates had won the Civil War.

VII

SUCH AN OBSERVER would have been mistaken, not just in the narrow sense that the Union armies prevailed over those of the Confederacy, but also in the more important sense that the old regime had perished. Although the postwar South was a product of its past, and many elements of the New South were strongly reminiscent of the Old, with the overthrow of slavery Southern social relations underwent a fundamental transformation. The market, with liberal assistance from the law, replaced the lash as the arbiter of labor relations. Changes came to the lives of both blacks and whites, to relations between blacks and whites, and to relations among blacks and among whites. Even as blacks became the objects of intensified racial oppression, they struggled to remake their lives as free men and women, and succeeded to a remarkable degree in their efforts to secure greater independence for themselves. In assessing these developments, the question of perspective remains critical: the South of 1910 was hardly the South they would have chosen had they been given carte blanche, but it was far removed from the South of 1860.

The effort to secure true freedom did not end with the overthrow of Reconstruction. During subsequent decades, even as blacks bore the brunt of racial proscription, they went to school and acquired land in increasing numbers, looked to their families and churches for support, entered into new businesses, and formed benevolent societies to look after each other in times of hardship. And in the years after World War II, again with the help of white allies, they spearheaded a "second Reconstruction"—grounded on the legal foundation provided by the first—with the goal of creating an interracial society that would finally overcome the persistent legacy of slavery.

Appendix
Statistical Tables

TABLE 1

ESTIMATES OF BLACKS AS A PERCENTAGE OF THE POPULATION, BY COLONY, 1680–1770

Colony	1680	1700	1720	1750	1770
NORTH					
New Hampshire	3.7	2.6	1.8	2.0	1.0
Massachusetts	0.4	1.5	2.4	2.2	1.8
Rhode Island	5.8	5.1	4.6	10.1	6.5
Connecticut	0.3	1.7	1.9	2.7	3.1
New York	12.2	11.8	15.5	14.3	11.7
New Jersey	5.9	6.0	7.7	7.5	7.0
Pennsylvania	3.7	2.4	6.5	2.4	2.4
SOUTH					
Delaware	5.5	5.5	13.2	5.2	5.2
Maryland	9.0	10.9	18.9	30.8	31.5
Virginia	6.9	28.0	30.3	43.9	42.0
North Carolina	3.9	3.9	14.1	25.7	35.3
South Carolina	16.7	42.8	70.4	60.9	60.5
Georgia	——	——	——	19.2	45.2
Totals					
North	2.3	3.6	5.2	4.8	4.4
South	5.7	21.1	27.7	38.0	39.7
Thirteen Colonies	4.6	11.1	14.8	20.2	21.4

Source: Computed from *Historical Statistics of the United States: Colonial Times to 1957* (Washington, 1960).

TABLE 2

FREE BLACK POPULATION, IN ABSOLUTE NUMBERS AND AS A PERCENTAGE OF TOTAL BLACK POPULATION, 1790–1860

	1790	*1810*	*1840*	*1860*
United States	59,466 (7.9%)	186,446 (13.5%)	386,303 (13.4%)	488,070 (11.0%)
North	27,109 (40.2%)	78,181 (74.0%)	170,728 (99.3%)	226,152 (100%)
South	32,357 (4.7%)	108,265 (8.5%)	215,575 (8.0%)	261,918 (6.2%)
Upper South	30,158 (5.5%)	94,085 (10.4%)	174,357 (12.5%)	224,963 (12.8%)
Deep South	2,199 (1.6%)	14,188 (3.9%)	41,218 (3.1%)	36,955 (1.5%)
UPPER SOUTH				
Delaware	30.5%	75.9%	86.7%	91.7%
Maryland	7.2%	23.3%	40.9%	49.1%
D.C.	——	32.1%	64.0%	77.8%
Virginia	4.2%	7.2%	10.0%	10.6%
North Carolina	4.7%	5.7%	8.5%	8.4%
Kentucky	1.0%	2.1%	3.9%	4.5%
Missouri	——	16.8%	2.6%	3.0%
Tennessee	9.6%	2.9%	2.9%	2.6%
DEEP SOUTH				
South Carolina	1.7%	2.3%	2.5%	2.4%
Georgia	1.3%	1.7%	1.0%	0.8%
Florida	——	——	3.1%	1.5%
Arkansas	——	——	2.3%	0.1%
Alabama	——	——	0.8%	0.6%
Louisiana	7.3%*	18.0%	13.1%	5.3%
Mississippi	——	——	0.7%	0.2%
Texas	——	——	——	0.2%

* In 1785.

Source: Ira Berlin, *Slaves Without Masters: The Free Negro in the Antebellum South* (New York, 1974), 46–47, 136–37.

TABLE 3

SLAVE POPULATION AND DISTRIBUTION, 1790 and 1860

	1790		*1860*	
United States	697,897	(17.8%)	3,953,760	(12.6%)
North	40,370	(2.1%)	64†	(0.0%)
regional share	5.8%		0.0%	
South	657,527	(33.5%)	3,953,696	(32.1%)
regional share	94.2%		100.0%	
Upper South	521,169	(32.0%)	1,530,229	(22.1%)
regional share	74.7%		38.7%	
Deep South	136,358	(41.1%)	2,423,467	(44.8%)
regional share	19.5%		61.3%	
UPPER SOUTH				
Delaware	8,887	(15.0%)	1,798	(1.6%)
Maryland	103,036	(32.2%)	87,189	(12.7%)
D.C.	——		3,185	(4.2%)
Virginia	293,427	(39.2%)	490,865	(30.7%)
North Carolina	100,572	(25.5%)	331,059	(33.4%)
Kentucky	11,830	(16.2%)	225,483	(19.5%)
Missouri	——		114,931	(9.7%)
Tennessee	3,417	(9.5%)	275,719	(24.8%)
DEEP SOUTH				
South Carolina	107,094	(43.0%)	402,406	(57.2%)
Georgia	29,264	(35.5%)	462,198	(43.7%)
Florida	——		61,745	(44.0%)
Arkansas	——		111,115	(25.5%)
Alabama	——		435,080	(45.1%)
Louisiana	16,544*	(51.6%)	331,726	(46.9%)
Mississippi	——		436,631	(55.2%)
Texas	——		182,566	(30.2%)

* In 1785; not included in regional or national totals.
† Includes 18 lifetime "apprentices" in New Jersey.

Sources: computed from *Return of the Whole Number of Persons within the Several Districts of the United States* (1790 Census: Philadelphia, 1791); *Population of the United States in 1860: Compiled from the Original Returns of the Eighth Census* (1860 Census: Washington, 1864); Ira Berlin, *Slaves Without Masters: The Free Negro in the Antebellum South* (New York, 1974), 396–97.

TABLE 4

DISTRIBUTION OF SLAVES BY SIZE OF HOLDING,
1860

Percentage of Slaves Held in Units of

	1–9	10–49	50–199	>199
South	25.6	49.5	22.5	2.4
Upper South	35.4	52.7	11.2	0.6
Deep South	19.4	47.4	29.6	3.6
Jamaica*	8.7	15.8	39.6	35.9

* Jamaican figures, included for purposes of comparison, are for 1832, just before emancipation; Jamaican slaveholding units are 1–10, 11–50, 51–200, and >200.

Sources: Lewis C. Gray, *History of Agriculture in the Southern United States to 1860* (2 vols., Washington, D.C., 1933), I, 530; B. W. Higman, *Slave Population of the British Caribbean, 1807–1834* (Baltimore, 1984), 105.

Appendix

TABLE 5

MEDIAN HOLDINGS* OF SLAVES, BY STATE,
1790, 1850, AND 1860

	1790	*1850*	*1860*
Louisiana		38.9	49.3
South Carolina	36.2	38.2	38.9
Mississippi		33.0	35.0
Alabama		29.9	33.4
Florida		28.5	28.4
Georgia		26.0	26.4
Arkansas		18.4	23.4
North Carolina	13.3	18.6	19.3
Virginia	17.4	18.1	18.8
Texas		14.9	17.6
Tennessee		15.2	15.1
Maryland	15.5	12.2	14.0
Kentucky		10.3	10.4
Missouri		8.6	8.3
Delaware		5.7	6.3
Total Deep South		30.9	32.5
Total Upper South		15.3	15.6
Total South		20.6	23.0

* Equal numbers of slaves were held in units larger than and smaller than the median figure.

Source: Lewis C. Gray, *History of Agriculture in the Southern United States to 1860*, I, 530–31.

TABLE 6

SLAVES IN THE EIGHT LARGEST SOUTHERN CITIES,
1840 AND 1860

		Total Population	*Slave Population*	*Slaves as Percentage of Total Population*
Baltimore	1840	102,313	3,199	3.1%
	1860	212,418	2,218	1.0%
New Orleans	1840	102,193	23,448	22.9%
	1860	168,675	13,385	7.9%
St. Louis	1840	16,469	1,531	9.3%
	1860	160,773	1,542	1.0%
Louisville	1840	21,210	3,430	16.2%
	1860	68,033	4,903	7.2%
Washington*	1840	23,364	1,713	7.3%
	1860	61,122	1,774	2.9%
Charleston	1840	29,261	14,673	50.1%
	1860	40,522	13,909	34.3%
Richmond	1840	20,153	7,509	37.3%
	1860	37,910	11,699	30.9%
Mobile	1840	12,672	3,869	30.5%
	1860	29,258	7,587	25.9%
8 Cities	1840	327,635	59,372	18.1%
	1860	778,711	57,017	7.3%

* Figures are for "Washington City," and exclude Georgetown and rural portions of the District of Columbia.

Source: Richard C. Wade, *Slavery in the Cities: The South, 1820–1860* (New York, 1964), 325–27.

Notes

1: ORIGINS AND CONSOLIDATION

1. Lawrence Stone, *The Crisis of the Aristocracy, 1558–1641* (abridged ed., London, 1967), 20.
2. Quoted in Elizabeth Donnan, ed., *Documents Illustrative of the History of the Slave Trade to America* (4 vols., New York, 1969; orig. pub. 1930–35), IV:131–32.
3. William Nelson, ed., "Extracts from American Newspapers Relating to New Jersey: Vol. III, 1751–1755," in *Documents Relating to the Colonial History of the State of New Jersey*, XIX (Paterson, N.J., 1897), 101.
4. "An act declaring that baptisme of slaves doth not exempt them from bondage" (Virginia, 1667), in Willie Lee Rose, ed., *A Documentary History of Slavery in North America* (New York, 1976), 19.
5. Quoted in Nicholas P. Canny, "The Ideology of English Colonization: From Ireland to America," *William and Mary Quarterly*, XXX (October 1973), 588.
6. Peter H. Wood, *Black Majority: Negroes in Colonial South Carolina from 1670 through the Stono Rebellion* (New York, 1974), 96.
7. T. H. Breen and Stephen Innes, *"Myne Owne Ground": Race and Freedom on Virginia's Eastern Shore, 1640–1676* (New York, 1980), 5.
8. *The Diary of Colonel Landon Carter of Sabine Hall, 1752–1778*, ed. Jack P. Greene (2 vols. in 1, Charlottesville, Va., 1965), 429–30.
9. Daniel C. Littlefield, *Rice and Slaves: Ethnicity and the Slave Trade in Colonial South Carolina* (Baton Rouge, La., 1981), 13.
10. *Equiano's Travels: His Autobiography; The Interesting Narrative of the Life*

of Olaudah Equiano or Gustavus Vassa the African (1789), abridged and ed. by Paul Edwards (London, 1967), 25.

11. Quoted in Daniel P. Mannix with Malcolm Cowley, *Black Cargoes: A History of the Atlantic Slave Trade, 1518–1865* (New York, 1962), 117.

2: THE COLONIAL ERA

1. Philip D. Morgan, "Work and Culture: The Task System and the World of Lowcountry Blacks, 1700 to 1880," *William and Mary Quarterly*, XXXIX (October 1982), 597.

2. Richard S. Dunn, *Sugar and Slaves: The Rise of the Planter Class in the English West Indies, 1624–1713* (New York, 1973), 237; Daniel Field, *The End of Serfdom: Nobility and Bureaucracy in Russia, 1855–1861* (Cambridge, Mass., 1976), 22.

3. *The Secret Diary of William Byrd of Westover, 1709–1712*, ed. Louis B. Wright and Marion Tinling (Richmond, Va., 1941), 89; *The Diary of Colonel Landon Carter of Sabine Hall, 1752–1778*, ed. Jack P. Greene (2 vols. in 1, Charlottesville, Va., 1965), 140.

4. *The Diary of Colonel Landon Carter*, 301, 303.

5. E. Franklin Frazier, *The Negro Family in the United States*, rev. and abridged (Chicago, 1966; orig. pub. 1939), 15; Sterling Stuckey, *Slave Culture: Nationalist Theory and the Foundations of Black America* (New York, 1987), 37.

6. Charles Ball, *Slavery in the United States: A Narrative of the Life and Adventures of Charles Ball, a Black Man* (New York, 1837), 219.

7. Albert J. Raboteau, *Slave Religion: The "Invisible Institution" in the Antebellum South* (New York, 1978), 86.

8. Quoted in Roger D. Abrams and John F. Szwed, eds., *After Africa* (New Haven, Conn., 1983), 388.

9. Beverley quoted in Willie Lee Rose, ed., *A Documentary History of Slavery in North America* (New York, 1976), 26.

10. Alexander Hewatt, *An Historical Account of the Rise and Progress of the Colonies of South Carolina and Georgia* (2 vols., London, 1779), II:97.

11. *The Secret Diary of William Byrd*, 85, 84, 112.

12. Ball, *Slavery in the United States*, 22, 164–65.

13. Quoted in Michael Mullin, ed., *American Negro Slavery: A Documentary History* (Columbia, S.C., 1976), 53.

14. Hewatt, *An Historical Account of the Rise and Progress of the Colonies*, 102–3; John B. Boles, ed., *Masters & Slaves in the House of the Lord: Race and Religion in the American South, 1740–1870* (Lexington, Ky., 1988), 5.

15. *The Secret Diary of William Byrd*, 202; *The Diary of Colonel Landon Carter*, 925, 1056–57.

16. *The Secret Diary of William Byrd*, 205; *The Journal of the Rev. Charles Wesley, M.A.*, ed. Thomas Jackson (2 vols., London, 1849), 36; *Journal*

& *Letters of Philip Vickers Fithian, 1773–1774: A Plantation Tutor of the Old Dominion*, ed. Hunter Dickinson Farish (Charlottesville, Va., 1968), 38; Helen Tunnicliff Catterall, ed., *Judicial Cases Concerning American Slavery and the Negro* (5 vols., New York, 1968; orig. pub. 1926–37), III:443.

17. *Another Secret Diary of William Byrd of Westover, 1739–1741, with Letters & Literary Exercises, 1696–1726*, ed. Maude H. Woodfin (Richmond, Va., 1942), 110; *The Diary of Colonel Landon Carter*, 691; *The Diaries of George Washington, 1748–1799*, ed. John C. Fitzpatrick (4 vols., Boston and New York, 1925), III:124.

18. Mechal Sobel, *The World They Made Together: Black and White Values in Eighteenth-Century Virginia* (Princeton, N.J., 1987), 233.

19. Catterall, ed., *Judicial Cases*, III: 6.

3: THE AMERICAN REVOLUTION

1. William Byrd II to the Earl of Egmont, 1736, in Elizabeth Donnan, ed., *Documents Illustrative of the History of the Slave Trade to America* (4 vols., New York, 1969; orig. pub. 1930–35), IV:131–32.

2. Laurens letters, January 7, 1757, February 15, 1763, and March 19, 1763, in *The Papers of Henry Laurens*, ed. Philip M. Hamer (3 vols., Columbia, S.C., 1968–72), II:402; III:259–60; III:373–74.

3. Jefferson to Condorcet, August 30, 1791, in *Thomas Jefferson's Farm Book with Commentary and Relevant Extracts from Other Writings*, ed. Edwin Morris Betts (Princeton, N.J., 1953), 11.

4. David Brion Davis, *The Problem of Slavery in the Age of Revolution, 1770–1823* (Ithaca, N.Y., 1975), 237–38; John Woolman, *The Journal with Other Writings of John Woolman* (London, 1910), 54.

5. *Journal & Letters of Philip Vickers Fithian, 1773–1774: A Plantation Tutor of the Old Dominion*, ed. Hunter Dickinson Farish (Charlottesville, Va., 1968), 92.

6. Quoted in Gerald W. Mullin, *Flight and Rebellion: Slave Resistance in Eighteenth-Century Virginia* (New York, 1972), 132.

7. *The Diary of Colonel Landon Carter of Sabine Hall, 1752–1778*, ed. Jack P. Greene (2 vols. in 1, Charlottesville, Va., 1965), 1051, 1052; *Thomas Jefferson's Farm Book*, 29.

8. Helen Tunnicliff Catterall, ed., *Judicial Cases Concerning American Slavery and the Negro* (5 vols., New York, 1968; orig. pub. 1926–37), II:290–91.

9. Lorena S. Walsh, "Rural African Americans in the Constitutional Era in Maryland, 1776–1810," *Maryland Historical Magazine*, LXXXIV (Winter 1989), 336, 337.

10. Both quotations are from Mullin, *Flight and Rebellion*, 145, 158.

11. Philip D. Morgan, "Black Society in the Lowcountry, 1760–1810," in Ira Berlin and Ronald Hoffman, eds., *Slavery and Freedom in the Age of the American Revolution* (Charlottesville, Va., 1983), 110.

12. Quoted in Davis, *The Problem of Slavery in the Age of Revolution*, 275.

13. Quoted in Edgar J. McManus, *Black Bondage in the North* (Syracuse, N.Y., 1973), 165.

14. Catterall, ed., *Judicial Cases*, III:601.

15. Quotations are from John Chester Miller, *The Wolf by the Ears: Thomas Jefferson and Slavery* (New York, 1977), 8; Thomas Jefferson, *Notes on the State of Virginia* (New York, 1964), 133, 134; Jefferson to William A. Burwell, January 28, 1805, in *Thomas Jefferson's Farm Book*, 20; Jefferson to Edward Coles, August 25, 1814, ibid., 39; Miller, *The Wolf by the Ears*, 241.

16. Fredrika Teute Schmidt and Barbara Ripel Wilhelm, eds., "Early Proslavery Petitions in Virginia," *William and Mary Quarterly*, XXX (January 1973), 139–40.

4: ANTEBELLUM SLAVERY:
ORGANIZATION, CONTROL, PATERNALISM

1. Robert William Fogel and Stanley L. Engerman, *Time on the Cross: The Economics of American Negro Slavery* (Boston, 1974), 48; Michael Tadman, *Speculators and Slaves: Masters, Traders, and Slaves in the Old South* (Madison, Wis., 1989), 45.

2. Clark and Maddox testimony in George P. Rawick, ed., *The American Slave: A Composite Autobiography* (19 vols., Westport, Conn., 1972), VI:72, 272; Randall testimony in Charles L. Perdue et al., eds., *Weevils in the Wheat: Interviews with Virginia Ex-Slaves* (Charlottesville, Va., 1976), 236.

3. Bennet H. Barrow, "Rules of Highland Plantation" (1838), in Edwin Adams Davis, ed., *Plantation Life in the Florida Parishes of Louisiana, 1836–1846, as Reflected in the Diary of Bennet H. Barrow* (New York, 1943), 409–10.

4. "Overseers at the South," *DeBow's Review*, XXI (August 1856), 148.

5. Haller Nutt Journal of Araby Plantation, November 1, November 2, November 4, 1843, in Haller Nutt Papers, microfilm copy of original in Duke University Library.

6. Dr. R. W. Gibbes to Governor R.F.W. Allston, March 6, 1858, in *DeBow's Review*, XXIV (April 1858), 321.

7. Frances Anne Kemble, *Journal of a Residence on a Georgian Plantation in 1838–1839* (Chicago, 1969), 25, 45.

8. Henry Bibb, *Narrative of the Life and Adventures of Henry Bibb, an American Slave* (New York, 1849), 136; Austin Steward, *Twenty-Two Years a Slave, and Forty Years a Freeman* (Rochester, N.Y., 1859), 32; Mollie Tillman in Rawick, ed., *The American Slave*, VI:381.

9. Frederick Douglass, *Narrative of the Life of Frederick Douglass, an American*

Slave, Written by Himself (New York, 1968; orig. pub. 1845), 34; Frederick Law Olmsted, *The Cotton Kingdom: A Traveller's Observations on Cotton and Slavery in the American Slave States* (2 vols., New York, 1861), I:236.

10. Charles C. Jones, *The Religious Instruction of the Negroes. In the United States* (New York, 1969; orig. pub. 1842), 159, 165; "Rules on the Rice Estate of P. C. Weston" (1856), in Ulrich B. Phillips, ed., *Plantation and Frontier*, Vol. I of John R. Commons et al., eds., *A Documentary History of American Industrial Society* (Cleveland, 1910), 116.

11. Douglass, *Narrative*, 65.

12. Ulrich B. Phillips and James David Glunt, eds., *Florida Plantation Records from the Papers of George Noble Jones* (St. Louis, 1927), 539, 91.

13. April 18, 1857, Diary of Leonidas Pendleton Spyker, 62, microfiche copy of original in Louisiana State University Archives.

14. Eliza L. Magruder Diary, January 31, February 5, 1846, microfiche copy of original in Louisiana State University Archives; Douglass, *Narrative*, 84.

15. Solomon Northup, *Twelve Years a Slave* (New York, 1855), 97.

16. Olmsted, *The Cotton Kingdom*, 39–40.

17. *DeBow's Review*, XI (October 1851), 371.

18. Barrow, "Rules of Highland Plantation," 407. The concept of the "design for mastery" is persuasively developed by Drew Gilpin Faust in *James Henry Hammond and the Old South: A Design for Mastery* (Baton Rouge, La., 1982).

19. Barrow, "Rules of Highland Plantation," 409; Ralph Butterfield, "The Health of Negroes," *DeBow's Review*, XXV (November 1858), 571.

20. Faust, *James Henry Hammond and the Old South*, 104; "Governor Hammond's Instructions to His Overseer," in Willie Lee Rose, ed., *A Documentary History of Slavery in North America* (New York, 1976), 345–54.

21. Helen Tunnicliff Catterall, ed., *Judicial Cases Concerning American Slavery and the Negro* (5 vols., New York, 1968; orig. pub. 1926–37), II:85–86.

22. "Governor Hammond's Instructions to His Overseer," 347.

23. "The Plantation Diary of Bennet H. Barrow," in Davis, ed., *Plantation Life in the Florida Parishes of Louisiana*, 174, 175; Perdue et al., eds., *Weevils in the Wheat*, 215.

24. A Mississippi Planter, "Management of Negroes Upon Southern Estates," *DeBow's Review*, X (June 1851), 623.

25. Barrow, "Rules of Highland Plantation," 408–9.

26. C. Vann Woodward, ed., *Mary Chesnut's Civil War* (New Haven, 1981), 29; Harriet A. Jacobs, *Incidents in the Life of a Slave Girl, Written by Herself*, ed. Jean Fagin Yellin (Cambridge, Mass., 1987), 27.

27. Faust, *James Henry Hammond and the Old South*, 87.

28. Jacobs, *Incidents in the Life of a Slave Girl*, 28.
29. Perdue et al., eds., *Weevils in the Wheat*, 128.
30. Catterall, ed., *Judicial Cases*, III:143.
31. Janet Duitsman Cornelius, *"When I Can Read My Title Clear": Literacy, Slavery, and Religion in the Antebellum South* (Columbia, S.C., 1991), 35.
32. Rose, ed., *A Documentary History of Slavery*, 187, 189, 192.
33. Edward L. Ayers, *Vengeance and Justice: Crime and Punishment in the 19th-Century American South* (New York, 1984), 134; Catterall, ed., *Judicial Cases*, III:637.
34. Rose, ed., *A Documentary History of Slavery*, 205, 203, 204.

5: ANTEBELLUM SLAVERY: SLAVE LIFE

1. Ulrich B. Phillips, *American Negro Slavery* (Baton Rouge, La., 1966; orig. pub. 1918), 291, 342.
2. Kenneth M. Stampp, *The Peculiar Institution: Slavery in the Ante-Bellum South* (New York, 1956), 364.
3. Stanley M. Elkins, *Slavery: A Problem in American Institutional and Intellectual Life* (Chicago, 1959), 128–29.
4. Frederick Douglass, *Narrative of the Life of Frederick Douglass, an American Slave, Written by Himself* (New York, 1968; orig. pub. 1845), 22.
5. John W. Blassingame, ed., *Slave Testimony: Two Centuries of Letters, Speeches, Interviews, and Autobiographies* (Baton Rouge, La., 1977), 374.
6. Ann Patton Malone, *Sweet Chariot: Slave Family and Household Structure in Nineteenth-Century Louisiana* (Chapel Hill, N.C., 1992), 258.
7. Frederick Douglass, *My Bondage and My Freedom* (New York, 1969; orig. pub. 1855), 40–42.
8. Malone, *Sweet Chariot*, 257, 255.
9. Erskine Clarke, *Wrestlin' Jacob: A Portrait of Religion in the Old South* (Atlanta, 1979), 40; Harriet A. Jacobs, *Incidents in the Life of a Slave Girl, Written by Herself*, ed. Jean Fagin Yellin (Cambridge, Mass., 1987), 68–69; Charles L. Perdue et al., eds., *Weevils in the Wheat: Interviews with Virginia Ex-Slaves* (Charlottesville, Va., 1976), 100.
10. R. Q. Mallard to his wife, Mary, in Robert Manson Myers, ed., *The Children of Pride: A True Story of Georgia and the Civil War* (New Haven, Conn., 1972), 483; Perdue et al., eds., *Weevils in the Wheat*, 100.
11. John B. Boles, ed., *Masters & Slaves in the House of the Lord: Race and Religion in the American South, 1740–1870* (Lexington, Ky., 1988), 10, 2.
12. "The Plantation Diary of Bennet H. Barrow," in Edwin Adams Davis, ed., *Plantation Life in the Florida Parishes of Louisiana, 1836–1846, as Reflected in the Diary of Bennet H. Barrow* (New York, 1943), 323–24; Henry Bibb, *Narrative of the Life and Adventures of Henry Bibb, an American Slave* (New York, 1849), 22–23.

13. George P. Rawick, ed., *The American Slave: A Composite Autobiography* (19 vols., Westport, Conn., 1972), VI:256.

14. Jacob Stroyer, *Sketches of My Life in the South* (Salem, 1879), 47–50; George White in Perdue et al., eds., *Weevils in the Wheat*, 310.

15. Clarence E. Walker, *Deromanticizing Black History: Critical Essays and Reappraisals* (Knoxville, Tenn., 1991), xv.

16. George P. Rawick, ed., *The American Slave: A Composite Autobiography. Supplement, Series 1* (12 vols., Westport, Conn., 1977), I:87.

17. Charles Joyner, *Down by the Riverside: A South Carolina Slave Community* (Urbana, Ill., 1984), 223–24.

18. Thomas L. Webber, *Deep Like the Rivers: Education in the Slave Quarter Community, 1831–1865* (New York, 1978), 261–62.

19. Victor V. Magagna, *Communities of Grain: Rural Rebellion in Comparative Perspective* (Ithaca, N.Y., 1991), 14.

20. James Oakes, *Slavery and Freedom: An Interpretation of the Old South* (New York, 1990), 8.

21. Michael Flusche, "Joel Chandler Harris and the Folklore of Slavery," *Journal of American Studies*, IX (December 1975), 349.

22. Frederick Law Olmsted, *The Cotton Kingdom: A Traveller's Observations on Cotton and Slavery in the American Slave States* (2 vols., New York, 1861), I:106; Charles Ball, *Slavery in the United States: A Narrative of the Life and Adventures of Charles Ball, a Black Man* (New York, 1837), 298–99.

23. *The Narrative of William W. Brown, a Fugitive Slave* (Reading, Mass., 1969; orig. pub. 1847), 42.

24. G. E. Manigault to Louis Manigault, January 21, 1861, Louis Manigault Papers, microfilm copy of original in Duke University Library.

25. *State v. Abram* (*a slave*), 10 Ala. 928 (January 1847), in Helen Tunnicliff Catterall, ed., *Judicial Cases Concerning American Slavery and the Negro* (5 vols., New York, 1968; orig. pub. 1926–37), III:162; Perdue et al., eds., *Weevils in the Wheat*, 194; Douglass, *My Bondage and My Freedom*, 246.

26. Bibb, *Narrative*, 17, 16; Blassingame, ed., *Slave Testimony*, 434.

27. Douglass, *My Bondage and My Freedom*, 95.

28. Paul D. Escott, *Slavery Remembered: A Record of Twentieth-Century Slave Narratives* (Chapel Hill, N.C., 1979), 95.

29. Rawick, ed., *The American Slave*, VI:60, 129.

30. *An Autobiography of the Reverend Josiah Henson* (Reading, Mass., 1969; orig. pub. 1849), 20–21; Charles Ball, *Slavery in the United States*, 52–53, 385, 387.

31. Rawick, ed., *The American Slave*, VI:90; Perdue et al., eds., *Weevils in the Wheat*, 72.

32. Douglass, *Narrative*, 37.

6: THE WHITE SOUTH:
SOCIETY, ECONOMY, IDEOLOGY

1. Charles Grier Sellers, Jr., ed., *The Southerner as American* (New York, 1966; orig. pub. 1960), vi–vii.

2. James Oakes, *Slavery and Freedom: An Interpretation of the Old South* (New York, 1990), 54.

3. Elizabeth Fox-Genovese and Eugene D. Genovese, *Fruits of Merchant Capital: Slavery and Bourgeois Property in the Rise and Expansion of Capitalism* (New York, 1983), 5.

4. Robert William Fogel, *Without Consent or Contract: The Rise and Fall of American Slavery* (New York, 1989), 87.

5. Seward, quoted in Eric Foner, *Free Soil, Free Labor, Free Men: The Ideology of the Republican Party Before the Civil War* (New York, 1970), 41.

6. Charles C. Jones, Jr., to Rev. C. C. Jones, in Robert Manson Myers, ed., *The Children of Pride: A True Story of Georgia and the Civil War* (New Haven, Conn., 1972), 241–42.

7. Frederick Douglass, *Narrative of the Life of Frederick Douglass, an American Slave, Written by Himself* (New York, 1968; orig. pub. 1845), 50.

8. Frederick Law Olmsted, *A Journey in the Back Country* (New York, 1970; orig. pub. 1860), 203.

9. Harvey Wish, ed., *Ante-Bellum: Writings of George Fitzhugh and Hinton Rowan Helper on Slavery* (New York, 1960), 175, 195.

10. William W. Freehling, *The Road to Disunion: Secessionists at Bay, 1776–1854* (New York, 1990), esp. 119–210.

11. Holmes, "Theory of Political Individualism," *DeBow's Review*, XXII (February 1857), 134; Hundley, *Social Relations in Our Southern States* (New York, 1860), 16–17.

12. Simms, "The Morals of Slavery," in *The Pro-Slavery Argument; as Maintained by the Most Distinguished Writers of the Southern States* (Charleston, S.C., 1852), 264.

13. *Selections from the Letters and Speeches of the Hon. James H. Hammond, of South Carolina* (New York, 1866), 43–44; *DeBow's Review*, VII (October 1849), 295; ibid., VIII (February 1850), 132–33.

14. H. W. Ravenel, *Anniversary Address, Delivered Before the Black Oak Agricultural Society, April, 1852* (Charleston, S.C., 1852), 5–6, in Thomas Porcher Ravenel Papers, microfilm copy of original in South Carolina Historical Society.

15. Hundley, *Social Relations*, 149–50.

16. Drew Gilpin Faust, ed., *The Ideology of Slavery: Proslavery Thought in the Antebellum South, 1830–1860* (Baton Rouge, La., 1981), 10.

17. S. A. Cartwright, "Slavery in the Light of Ethnology," in E. N. Elliott, ed., *Cotton Is King, and Pro-Slavery Arguments* (New York, 1968; orig. pub. 1860), 707, 709.

18. Thornton Stringfellow, "The Bible Argument: Or, Slavery in the Light of Divine Revelation," in Elliott, ed., *Cotton Is King*, 491.

19. Thomas R. R. Cobb, *An Inquiry into the Law of Negro Slavery in the United States of America* (Philadelphia, 1858), cxxxi.

20. Hammond, *Selections from the Letters and Speeches*, 281, 44–45; Fitzhugh, "Southern Thought," *DeBow's Review*, XXIII (October 1857), 338, 348, 347.

21. *The Diary of Edmund Ruffin*, I, ed. William Kauffman Scarborough (Baton Rouge, La., 1972), 308, 215, 240.

22. C. Vann Woodward, "The Price of Freedom," in *What Was Freedom's Price?*, ed. David G. Sansing (Jackson, Miss., 1978), 97.

7: THE END OF SLAVERY

1. Abraham Lincoln to Horace Greeley, August 22, 1862, *Selected Writings and Speeches of Abraham Lincoln*, ed. T. Harry Williams (n.p., 1980; orig. pub. 1943), 174.

2. V. Jacque Voegeli, *Free But Not Equal: The Midwest and the Negro During the Civil War* (Chicago, 1967), 102.

3. Ira Berlin et al., eds., *Freedom: A Documentary History of Emancipation, 1861–1867. Series I, Volume I: The Destruction of Slavery* (Cambridge, England, 1985), 3.

4. Norman R. Yetman, ed., *Life Under the "Peculiar Institution": Selections from the Slave Narrative Collection* (New York, 1970), 296; Charles L. Perdue, Jr., et al., eds., *Weevils in the Wheat: Interviews with Virginia Ex-Slaves* (Charlottesville, Va., 1976), 127.

5. Robert Manson Myers, ed., *The Children of Pride: A True Story of Georgia and the Civil War* (New Haven, Conn., 1972), 1241, 1247, 1248.

6. Harold M. Hyman, ed., *The Radical Republicans and Reconstruction, 1861–1870* (Indianapolis, 1967), 160–61.

7. *Selected Writings and Speeches of Abraham Lincoln*, 201.

8. Quoted in Joe M. Richardson, *Christian Reconstruction: The American Missionary Association and Southern Blacks, 1861–1890* (Athens, Ga., 1986), 13.

9. Journal Letter Kept by Miss Charlotte St. J. Ravenel, 41, in Thomas Porcher Ravenel Papers, microfilm copy of original in South Carolina Historical Society.

10. Carl Schurz, *Report on the Condition of the South* (New York, 1969; orig. pub. as Senate Exec. Doc. No. 2, 39th Congress, 1st Session, 1865), 45–46.

11. Michael Les Benedict, *The Fruits of Victory: Alternatives in Restoring the Union, 1865–1877*, rev. ed (New York, 1986), 105.

12. Benedict, *Fruits of Victory*, 112–13.

13. Benedict, *Fruits of Victory*, 114.

14. Benedict, *Fruits of Victory*, 118.

15. *Douglass' Monthly*, January 1862, reprinted in Michael Meyer, ed., *Frederick Douglass: The Narrative and Selected Writings* (New York, 1984), 374, 376.

16. Benedict, *Fruits of Victory*, 97–98.

17. Eric Foner, *Reconstruction: America's Unfinished Revolution, 1863–1877* (New York, 1988), 235.

18. Perdue et al., eds., *Weevils in the Wheat*, 58–59.

19. Whitelaw Reid, *After the War: A Tour of the Southern States, 1865–1866* (New York, 1965), 389.

20. Bernard Houston to George S. Houston, Athens, Ala., August 3, 1867, George S. Houston Papers, Duke University Library.

21. Peter Kolchin, *First Freedom: The Responses of Alabama's Blacks to Emancipation and Reconstruction* (Westport, Conn., 1972), 64.

22. Kolchin, *First Freedom*, 153, 158.

23. Foner, *Reconstruction*, 11.

24. Theodore Rosengarten, *All God's Dangers: The Life of Nate Shaw* (New York, 1974), 26–27, 547.

25. Gerald David Jaynes, *Branches Without Roots: Genesis of the Black Working Class in the American South, 1862–1882* (New York, 1986), 222.

26. Leon F. Litwack, *Been in the Storm So Long: The Aftermath of Slavery* (New York, 1979), 521.

27. Gavin Wright, *Old South, New South: Revolutions in the Southern Economy since the Civil War* (New York, 1986), 17; James L. Roark, *Masters Without Slaves: Southern Planters in the Civil War and Reconstruction* (New York, 1977), 196.

28. Hyman, ed., *The Radical Republicans*, 506, 507.

29. Du Bois, *The Souls of Black Folk*, reprinted in John Hope Franklin, ed., *Three Negro Classics* (New York, 1965), 217.

Bibliographical Essay

THIS ESSAY IS intended as a guide for those who would read more about American slavery. The existing literature on slavery is so extensive that even a fairly lengthy bibliography can mention only a small fraction of published works. I have therefore found it necessary to exclude many books—including good books—and most articles; each item is listed only once, even if it could appropriately appear under more than one heading. For help in locating material not included in this essay, see the works listed immediately below, under "Guides to Further Reading."

GUIDES TO FURTHER READING

THE MOST COMPLETE, broad-ranging, and up-to-date bibliography is Joseph Miller, *Slavery: A Worldwide Bibliography* (White Plains, N.Y., 1985), supplemented annually in the journal *Slavery and Abolition*; as the title indicates, this work covers slavery throughout the world, not just America. For useful historiographical surveys that focus on *American* slavery, see Peter J. Parish, *Slavery: History and Historians* (New York, 1989); Peter Kolchin, "American Historians and Antebellum Southern Slavery, 1959–1984," in William J. Cooper, Jr., et al., eds., *A Master's Due: Essays in Honor of David*

Herbert Donald (Baton Rouge, La., 1985), 87–111; and Charles B. Dew, "The Slavery Experience," in John B. Boles and Evelyn Thomas Nolen, eds., *Interpreting Southern History: Historiographical Essays in Honor of Sanford W. Higginbotham* (Baton Rouge, La., 1987), 120–61. The last-mentioned volume also contains other pertinent historiographical essays. For a useful encyclopedia containing alphabetically arranged entries together with brief bibliographies, see Randall M. Miller and John D. Smith, eds., *Dictionary of Afro-American Slavery* (New York, 1988).

ACCESSIBLE PRIMARY SOURCES

FOR AN EXCELLENT DOCUMENTARY overview of American slavery, see Willie Lee Rose, ed., *A Documentary History of Slavery in North America* (New York, 1976). Michael Mullin, ed., *American Negro Slavery* (New York, 1976), is best on the colonial period.

Readers with access to a good library can explore an abundance of additional primary source material on American slavery. Despite the long-prevalent view that slavery had to be studied primarily on the basis of what whites said about it because the slaves themselves were "inarticulate," blacks in fact left a surprising quantity of records documenting their perspective on the peculiar institution. The two most important categories of these records, to which recent historians have paid great attention in their continuing reinterpretation of slavery, are autobiographies by and interviews of former slaves. Most of the autobiographies were written either during the antebellum period, by fugitives who escaped to the North, or after the Civil War, by freedmen and -women; by far the largest collection of interviews was conducted during the 1930s, under the auspices of the Federal Writers' Project. These sources are most revealing, therefore, of conditions during the last years of slavery. For varying evaluations of their utility, see John W. Blassingame, "Using the Testimony of Ex-Slaves: Approaches and Problems," *Journal of Southern History*, XLI (November 1975), 473–92; David Thomas Bailey, "A Divided Prism: Two Sources of Black Testimony on Slavery," *Journal of Southern History*, XLVI (August 1980), 381–404; Norman R. Yetman, "Ex-Slave Interviews and the Historiography of Slavery," *American Quarterly*, XXXVI (Summer 1984), 181–210;

and William L. Andrews, *To Tell a Free Story: The First Century of Afro-American Autobiography, 1760–1865* (Urbana, Ill., 1986).

Among the most compelling of the numerous autobiographies are Olaudah Equiano, *The Interesting Narrative of the Life of Olaudah Equiano, or Gustavus Vassa, the African, Written by Himself* (London, 1789, and numerous subsequent editions), one of the very few eighteenth-century narratives; Harriet A. Jacobs, *Incidents in the Life of a Slave Girl, Written by Herself*, ed. Jean Fagan Yellin (Cambridge, Mass., 1987), for many years after its appearance in 1861 discounted as ghost-written but recently authenticated by literary scholar Jean Fagan Yellin; and three successively more detailed versions of Frederick Douglass's story, originally published in 1845, 1855, and 1881: *Narrative of the Life of Frederick Douglass, an American Slave, Written by Himself* (New York, 1968); *My Bondage and My Freedom* (New York, 1969); and *Life and Times of Frederick Douglass* (New York, 1962).

Other useful autobiographies include Charles Ball, *Slavery in the United States: A Narrative of the Life and Adventures of Charles Ball, a Black Man* (New York, 1837); Henry Bibb, *Narrative of the Life and Adventures of Henry Bibb, an American Slave* (New York, 1849); William W. Brown, *The Narrative of William W. Brown, a Fugitive Slave* (Reading, Mass., 1969; orig. pub. 1847); Elizabeth Keckley, *Behind the Scenes. Or, Thirty Years a Slave, and Four Years in the White House* (New York, 1868); Solomon Northup, *Twelve Years a Slave* (New York, 1855); and Austin Steward, *Twenty-Two Years a Slave, and Forty Years a Freeman* (Rochester, N.Y., 1859).

The Federal Writers' Project interviews can be sampled in Norman R. Yetman, ed., *Life under the "Peculiar Institution": Selections from the Slave Narrative Collection* (New York, 1970); and Charles L. Perdue, Jr., et al., eds., *Weevils in the Wheat: Interviews with Virginia Ex-Slaves* (Charlottesville, Va., 1976). They can also be read in their entirety in 39 volumes, in George P. Rawick, ed., *The American Slave: A Composite Autobiography* (Westport, Conn., 1972–1979).

Other useful collections of slave and ex-slave testimony include Benjamin Drew, ed., *The Refugee: A North-Side View of Slavery* (Reading, Mass., 1969), a compilation of interviews with fugitives living in Canada originally published in 1855; John W. Blassingame, ed., *Slave Testimony: Two Centuries of Letters, Speeches, Interviews, and Autobiographies* (Baton Rouge, La., 1977); and Robert S. Starobin, *Blacks in Bondage: Letters of American Slaves* (New York, 1974). For a good collection of African-American folklore, see Richard M. Dorson, ed., *American Negro Folktales* (Greenwich, Conn., 1967).

Documentary evidence on slavery left by whites is even more extensive. A vast collection of plantation records, drawn from diverse Southern archives and edited by Kenneth M. Stampp, is now available on microfilm from University Publications of America, under the title "Records of Ante-Bellum Southern Plantations from the Revolution through the Civil War." So far, these records include some 862 reels of microfilm, organized into 10 series (A to J), each comprising material from a different archive.

Numerous diaries, letters, and other records left by slaveholders are also available in published form. For the colonial and Revolutionary periods, see *The Secret Diary of William Byrd of Westover, 1709–1712*, ed. Louis B. Wright and Marion Tinling (Richmond, Va., 1941); *Another Secret Diary of William Byrd of Westover, 1739–1741, with Letters & Literary Exercises, 1696–1726*, ed. Maude H. Woodfin (Richmond, Va., 1942); *The Diary of Colonel Landon Carter of Sabine Hall, 1752–1778*, ed. Jack P. Greene (Charlottesville, Va., 1965); *William Fitzhugh and His Chesapeake World, 1676–1701: The Fitzhugh Letters and Other Documents*, ed. Richard Beale Davis (Chapel Hill, N.C., 1963); *Thomas Jefferson's Farm Book with Commentary and Relevant Extracts from Other Writings*, ed. Edwin Morris Betts (Princeton, N.J., 1953); *The Letterbook of Elisa Lucas Pinckney, 1739–1762*, ed. Elise Pinckney (Chapel Hill, N.C., 1972); and *The Diaries of George Washington, 1748–1799*, 4 vols., ed. John C. Fitzpatrick (Boston and New York, 1925).

For the nineteenth century, see John Spencer Bassett, ed., *The Southern Plantation Overseer as Revealed in His Letters* (Northampton, Mass., 1925) (on James K. Polk's plantations in Tennessee and Mississippi); John Blackford, *Ferry Hill Plantation Journal, January 4, 1838–January 15, 1839*, ed. Fletcher M. Green (Chapel Hill, N.C., 1961); Carol Bleser, ed., *Secret and Sacred: The Diaries of James Henry Hammond, a Southern Slaveholder* (New York, 1988); *Mary Chesnut's Civil War*, ed. C. Vann Woodward (New York, 1981); James M. Clifton, *Life and Labor on Argyle Island: Letters and Documents of a Savannah River Rice Plantation, 1833–1867* (Savannah, 1978); Edwin Adams Davis, ed., *Plantation Life in the Florida Parishes of Louisiana, 1836–1846, as Reflected in the Diary of Bennet H. Barrow* (New York, 1943); J. H. Easterby, ed., *The South Carolina Rice Plantation as Revealed in the Papers of Robert F. W. Allston* (Chicago, 1945);

Albert Virgil House, ed., *Planter Management and Capitalism in Ante-Bellum Georgia: The Journal of Hugh Fraser Grant, Ricegrower* (New York, 1954); Frances Anne Kemble, *Journal of a Residence on a Georgian Plantation in 1838–1839* (Chicago, 1969); Robert Manson Myers, ed., *The Children of Pride: A True Story of Georgia and the Civil War* (New Haven, Conn., 1972); Ulrich B. Philips and James David Glunt, eds., *Florida Plantation Records from the Papers of George Noble Jones* (St. Louis, 1927); *The Diary of Edmund Ruffin*, I, ed. William Kauffman Scarborough (Baton Rouge, La., 1972).

Two major collections of polemical arguments in behalf of slavery are E. N. Elliott, ed., *Cotton Is King, and Pro-Slavery Arguments* (New York, 1968; orig. pub. 1860); and Drew Gilpin Faust, ed., *The Ideology of Slavery: Proslavery Thought in the Antebellum South, 1830–1860* (Baton Rouge, La., 1981). For other examples of pro-slavery argumentation, see Thomas R. R. Cobb, *An Inquiry into the Law of Negro Slavery in the United States of America* (Philadelphia, 1858); J.D.B. DeBow, *The Interest in Slavery of the Southern Non-Slaveholder* (Charleston, S.C., 1860); George Fitzhugh, *Cannibals All! or, Slaves Without Masters* (Richmond, Va., 1857); Richard Furman, *Rev. Dr. Richard Furman's Exposition of the Views of the Baptists, Relative to the Coloured Population of the United States* (Charleston, S.C., 1822); D. R. Hundley, *Social Relations in Our Southern States* (New York, 1860); Thomas P. Kettell, *Southern Wealth and Northern Profits* (New York, 1860); Fredrika Teute Schmidt and Barbara Ripel Wilhelm, "Early Proslavery Petitions in Virginia," *William and Mary Quarterly*, XXX (January 1973), 133–46. *DeBow's Review*, which began publication in 1846, occupied a preeminent position among Southern periodicals and is especially revealing of the concerns, interests, and worldview of literate white Southerners.

Many prominent Southern whites, although fully committed to the peculiar institution, called for measures to humanize it; see, for example, Charles C. Jones, *The Religious Instruction of the Negroes. In the United States* (New York, 1969; orig. pub. 1842). A smaller (and declining) number questioned the established order, sometimes obliquely and sometimes head on. See Thomas Jefferson, *Notes on the State of Virginia* (New York, 1964); and Hinton Rowan Helper, *The Impending Crisis of the South* (New York, 1857).

Travel accounts—by Northerners and foreigners—can provide revealing insights into Southern slavery. Among the most interesting are those of Philip Fithian, a Presbyterian minister-in-the-making from New Jersey who spent a year as a tutor on the Virginia plantation of Robert Carter III, and of Frederick Law Olmsted, a New York landscape architect (responsible, among other things, for designing Central Park) who traveled extensively through the South during the 1850s; see *Journal & Letters of Philip Vickers Fithian, 1773–1774: A Plantation Tutor of the Old Dominion*, ed. Hunter Dickinson Farish (Charlottesville, Va., 1968); and Frederick Law Olmsted, *The Cotton Kingdom: A Traveller's Observations on Cotton and Slavery in the American Slave States*, 2 vols. (New York, 1861). Among the numerous travel accounts dating from the period immediately following the Civil War, the most useful include Carl Schurz, *Report on the Condition of the South* (New York, 1969; orig. pub. Washington, 1865); Whitelaw Reid, *After the War: A Tour of the Southern States, 1865–1866*, ed. C. Vann Woodward (New York, 1965); and Sidney Andrews, *The South Since the War*, intro. David Donald (Boston, 1971).

Specialized documentary collections of importance include James O. Breeden, ed., *Advice Among Masters: The Ideal in Slave Management in the Old South* (Westport, Conn., 1980); Helen Tunnicliff Catterall, ed., *Judicial Cases Concerning American Slavery and the Negro*, 5 vols. (New York, 1968; orig. pub. 1926–37); Elizabeth Donnan, ed., *Documents Illustrative of the History of the Slave Trade to America*, 4 vols. (New York, 1969; orig. pub. 1930–35); Paul Finkelman, ed., *Slavery, Race and the American Legal System, 1700–1872*, 16 vols. (New York, 1988); Ulrich B. Phillips, ed., *Plantation and Frontier*, vols. I and II of John R. Commons et al., eds., *A Documentary History of American Industrial Society* (Cleveland, 1910); Henry Irving Tragle, ed., *The Southampton Slave Revolt of 1831: A Compilation of Source Material* (New York, 1971); Lathan A. Windley, ed., *Runaway Slave Advertisements: A Documentary History from the 1730s to 1790*, 4 vols. (Westport, Conn., 1983); and Billy G. Smith and Richard Wojtowicz, eds., *Blacks Who Stole Themselves: Advertisements for Runaways in the Pennsylvania Gazette, 1728–1790* (Philadelphia, 1989).

On emancipation, see the superb ongoing series compiled by an editorial team headed by Ira Berlin and Leslie S. Rowland, *Freedom: A Documentary History of Emancipation, 1861–1867* (Cambridge, England, and New York, 1983–), which contains extensive selections from material in the National Archives; three volumes have been published to date, with several more on the way. The 13-volume report issued in 1871 by the joint Senate and House Committee that investigated Southern racial and political violence (the so-called Ku-

Klux hearings) contains a wealth of information on social relations in the postwar South; see *Testimony Taken by the Joint Select Committee to Inquire into the Condition of Affairs in the Late Insurrectionary States* (Washington, D.C., 1872). For two memoirs by black politicians, see the 1913 autobiography of Mississippi Congressman John R. Lynch, *The Facts of Reconstruction* (New York, 1969); and the previously unpublished autobiography of Virginia legislator George Teamoh, *God Made the Man, Man Made the Slave: The Autobiography of George Teamoh*, ed. F. N. Boney, Richard L. Hume, and Rafia Zafar (Macon, Ga., 1990). For a very different perspective on "black" Reconstruction, see James S. Pike's 1974 racist broadside, *The Prostrate State: South Carolina under Negro Government* (New York, 1968).

SURVEYS, ANTHOLOGIES, AND COMPARISONS

SEVERAL EXCELLENT SURVEYS of African-American history, and a smaller number of surveys of Southern history, are available; slavery, of necessity, assumes a prominent place in these works. On African-Americans, see John Hope Franklin and Alfred A. Moss, Jr., *From Slavery to Freedom: A History of Negro Americans*, 6th ed. (New York, 1988); August Meier and Elliott M. Rudwick, *From Plantation to Ghetto*, 3rd ed. (New York, 1976); John B. Boles, *Black Southerners: 1619–1869* (Lexington, Ky., 1984); and Philip S. Foner, *History of Black Americans*, vols. I–III (Westport, Conn., 1975–1983). For two impassioned accounts of the black experience under slavery, see Nathan Irvin Huggins, *Black Odyssey: The Afro-American Ordeal in Slavery* (New York, 1977); and Vincent Harding, *There Is a River: The Black Struggle for Freedom in America* (New York, 1981). See also V. P. Franklin, *Black Self-Determination: A Cultural History of the Faith of the Fathers* (Westport, Conn., 1984).

On the South, see Clement Eaton, *A History of the Old South*, 3rd ed. (New York, 1975), which is detailed but old-fashioned; and William J. Cooper, Jr., and Thomas E. Terrill, *The American South: A History*, Vol. I (New York, 1991), which is up-to-date. Paul D. Escott and David R. Goldfield, eds., *Major Problems in the History of the American South: Volume I: The Old South* (Lexington, Mass., 1990) provides a useful combination of historians' essays and primary documents.

For more than half a century, two general surveys of American slavery, both of which focused on large plantations in the antebellum South, dominated the historiography of the peculiar institution; see Ulrich B. Phillips, *American Negro Slavery* (Baton Route, La., 1966; orig. pub. 1918), which emphasizes the benign nature of the planter regime and portrays slavery as a school for civilizing African savages; and Kenneth M. Stampp, *The Peculiar Institution: Slavery in the Ante-Bellum South* (New York, 1956), which counters by stressing slavery's brutally exploitative character. Since Stampp's book, however, historians of American slavery have largely foresaken sweeping comprehensive surveys to focus more intensively on particular topics. For an up-to-date collection of some of the most important historical writing on American slavery, see Lawrence B. Goodheart et al., eds., *Slavery in American Society*, 3rd. ed. (Lexington, Mass., 1993).

An exception to this retreat from broad generalizing works has been the effort of a small but growing number of historians to approach slavery comparatively. With a couple of major exceptions— most notably Eugene D. Genovese—there has been relatively little overlap between these historians and the larger number focusing on slavery within the United States. The comparative approach has had a significant impact, however, on the overall interpretation of American slavery. (Limitation of space precludes listing works that focus primarily on slavery outside the United States, although some of them, too, have had an impact on the writing of American history.)

Modern comparative study of slavery in the Americas dates from a short but influential book by Frank Tannenbaum, *Slave and Citizen: The Negro in the Americas* (New York, 1946), that contrasted the rigidity of race relations in the United States with their fluidity in Latin America. This book strongly influenced Stanley M. Elkins, who developed the twin arguments that slavery in the antebellum South was much harsher than that in Latin America and that because of this unique harshness Southern slaves were "infantilized" and turned into "Sambos"; see *Slavery: A Problem in American Institutional and Intellectual Life* (Chicago, 1959).

During the 1960s and 1970s, much of the comparative work on American slavery was aimed at testing the assertions of Tannenbaum and especially of Elkins. Occasionally, as in Herbert S. Klein, *Slavery in the Americas: A Comparative Study of Virginia and Cuba* (New York, 1967), historians found supporting evidence; far more often, however, they refuted the notion that American slavery was uniquely harsh. See, for example, Carl N. Degler, *Neither Black nor White: Slavery and Race Relations in Brazil and the United States* (New York, 1971); Eugene D. Genovese, *The World the Slaveholders Made: Two Essays in Interpretation* (New York, 1969); C. Vann Woodward, "Southern Slaves in the World of Thomas Malthus," in Woodward, *American Counterpoint: Slavery and Racism in the North-South Dialogue* (Boston, 1971), 78–106; Richard S. Dunn, "A Tale of Two Plantations: Slave Life at Mesopotamia in Jamaica and Mount Airy in Virginia, 1799 to 1828," *William and Mary Quarterly*, XXXIV (January 1977), 32–65; Laura Foner, "The Free People of Color in Louisiana and St. Domingue: A Comparative Portrait of Two Three-Caste Slave Societies," *Journal of Social History*, III (Summer 1970), 406–30; Marvin Harris, *Patterns of Race in the Americas* (New York, 1964), esp. chap. 6; and most of the essays in Laura Foner and Eugene D. Genovese, eds., *Slavery in the New World: A Reader in Comparative History* (Englewood Cliffs, N.J., 1969).

Other scholars compared thought about slavery in the Western world. See three important books by David Brion Davis: *The Problem of Slavery in Western Culture* (Ithaca, N.Y., 1966); *The Problem of Slavery in the Age of Revolution, 1770–1823* (Ithaca, N.Y., 1975); and *Slavery and Human Progress* (New York, 1984). See also William McKee Evans, "From the Land of Canaan to the Land of Guinea: The Strange Odyssey of the Sons of Ham," *American Historical Review*, LXXXV (February 1980), 15–43; and Peter Kolchin, "In Defense of Servitude: American Proslavery and Russian Proserfdom Arguments, 1760–1860," *American Historical Review*, LXXXV (October 1980), 809–27.

Since the late 1970s, scholars have significantly expanded the scope of comparative slavery studies. A few have focused on slave resistance: see Eugene D. Genovese, *From Rebellion to Revolution: Afro-American Slave Revolts in the Making of the New World* (Baton Rouge, La., 1979); and Peter Kolchin, "The Process of Confrontation: Patterns of Resistance to Bondage in Nineteenth-Century Russia and the United States," *Journal of Social History*, XI (Summer 1978), 457–90. More have examined emancipation in comparative perspective: see George M. Fredrickson, "After Emancipation: A Comparative Study of White Responses to the New Order of Race Relations in the American South, Jamaica, & the Cape Colony of South Africa," in David G. Sansing, ed., *What Was Freedom's Price?* (Jackson, Miss., 1978), 71–92; C. Vann Woodward, "The Price of

Freedom," ibid., 93–113; Stanley L. Engerman, "Economic Adjustments to Emancipation in the United States and British West Indies," *Journal of Interdisciplinary History*, XIII (Autumn 1982), 191–220; Rebecca Scott, "Comparing Emancipations: A Review Essay," *Journal of Social History*, XX (Spring 1987), 565–83; Steven Hahn, "Class and State in Postemancipation Societies: Southern Planters in Comparative Perspective," *American Historical Review*, XCV (February 1990), 75–98; Steven Hahn, "Emancipation and the Development of Capitalist Agriculture: The South in Comparative Perspective," in Kees Gispen, ed., *What Made the South Different?* (Jackson, Miss., 1990), 71–88; Peter Kolchin, "Some Thoughts on Emancipation in Comparative Perspective: Russia and the United States South," *Slavery and Abolition*, XI (December 1990), 351–67; and the essays in Frank McGlynn and Seymour Drescher, eds., *The Meaning of Freedom: Economics, Politics, and Culture after Slavery* (Pittsburgh, 1992).

A final trend has been to expand the comparative focus beyond the Americas. For comparisons of American slavery with bondage outside the New World, see George M. Fredrickson, *White Supremacy: A Comparative Study in American and South African History* (New York, 1981); Peter Kolchin, *Unfree Labor: American Slavery and Russian Serfdom* (Cambridge, Mass., 1987); and Shearer Davis Bowman, *Masters and Lords: Mid-Nineteenth Century U.S. Planters and Prussian Junkers* (New York, 1993). For two exceptionally wide-ranging surveys by historical sociologist Orlando Patterson, see *Slavery and Social Death: A Comparative Study* (Cambridge, Mass., 1982); and *Freedom: Freedom in the Making of Western Culture* (New York, 1991).

COLONIAL AND REVOLUTIONARY SLAVERY (CHAPTERS 1–3)

FOR GOOD INTRODUCTIONS to indentured servitude, see two old but still useful surveys: Richard B. Morris, *Government and Labor in Early America* (New York, 1946); and Abbot Emerson Smith, *Colonists in Bondage: White Servitude and Convict Labor in America, 1607–1776* (Chapel Hill, N.C., 1947). More recent works of value include James Horn, "Servant Emigration to the Chesapeake in the Seventeenth Century," in Thad W. Tate and David Ammerman, eds., *The Chesapeake in the Seventeenth Century: Essays on Anglo-American*

Society (Chapel Hill, N.C., 1979), 51–95; David W. Galenson, *White Servitude in Colonial America: An Economic Analysis* (Cambridge, England, 1981); and Sharon V. Salinger, *"To Serve Well and Faithfully": Labor and Indentured Servants in Pennsylvania, 1682–1800* (New York, 1987). In *The Economy of British America, 1607–1789* (Chapel Hill, N.C., 1985), John J. McCusker and Russell R. Menard cover the economic conditions that gave rise to indentured servitude and the subsequent shift to slave labor.

On the African background to American slavery, see John Thornton, *Africa and Africans in the Making of the Atlantic World, 1400–1680* (Cambridge, England, 1992); and Philip D. Curtin and Paul Bohannan, *Africa and Africans*, 3rd ed. (Prospect Heights, Ill., 1988). Igor Kopytoff and Suzanne Miers, "African 'Slavery' as an Institution of Marginality," in Miers and Kopytoff, eds., *Slavery in Africa: Historical and Anthropological Perspectives* (Madison, Wis., 1977), 3–81; and Paul E. Lovejoy, *Transformations in Slavery: A History of Slavery in Africa* (Cambridge, England, 1983) provide very different interpretations of African slavery; see also Patrick Manning, *Slavery and African Life: Occidental, Oriental, and African Slave Trades* (Cambridge, England, 1990).

There has been a good deal of work on the African slave trade. For general descriptions, see Basil Davidson, *The African Slave Trade: Precolonial History, 1450–1850* (Boston, 1961); Daniel P. Mannix with Malcolm Cowley, *Black Cargoes: A History of the Atlantic Slave Trade, 1518–1865* (New York, 1962); and James A. Rawley, *The Transatlantic Slave Trade: A History* (New York, 1981). An early classic is W.E.B. Du Bois, *The Suppression of the African Slave Trade to the United States of America, 1638–1870* (New York, 1969; orig. pub. 1896).

More recently, historians have attempted to measure the dimensions of the transatlantic slave trade, as well as to gauge the impact of that trade on Europe, Africa, and America. For some of the most important of these works, see Philip D. Curtin, *The Atlantic Slave Trade: A Census* (Madison, Wis., 1969); Herbert S. Klein, *The Middle Passage: Comparative Studies in the Atlantic Slave Trade* (Princeton, N.J., 1978); Henry A. Gemery and Jan S. Hogendorn, eds., *The Uncommon Market: Essays in the Economic History of the Atlantic Slave Trade* (New York, 1979); Jay Coughtry, *The Notorious Triangle: Rhode Island and the African Slave Trade, 1700–1807* (Philadelphia, 1981); Paul E. Lovejoy, "The Volume of the Atlantic Slave Trade: A

Synthesis," *Journal of African History*, XXIII, no. 2 (1982), 473–501; David Eltis, "Free and Coerced Transatlantic Migrations: Some Comparisons," *American Historical Review*, LXXXVIII (April 1983), 251–80; David Galenson, *Traders, Planters, and Slaves: Market Behavior in Early America* (New York, 1986); David Eltis, *Economic Growth and the Ending of the Transatlantic Slave Trade* (New York, 1987); Joseph C. Miller, *Way of Death: Merchant Capitalism and the Angolan Slave Trade, 1730–1830* (Madison, Wis., 1988); Paul E. Lovejoy, "The Impact of the Atlantic Slave Trade on Africa: A Review of the Literature," *Journal of African History*, XXX, no. 3 (1989), 365–94; Joseph E. Inikori and Stanley L. Engerman, eds., *The Atlantic Slave Trade: Effects on Economies, Societies, and Peoples in Africa, the Americas, and Europe* (Durham, N.C., 1992); and Janet J. Ewald, "Slavery in Africa and the Slave Trades from Africa," *American Historical Review*, XCVII (April 1992), 465–85.

For overviews of slavery, blacks, and race relations in colonial America, see Ira Berlin, "Time, Space, and the Evolution of Afro-American Society on British Mainland North America," *American Historical Review*, LXXXV (February 1980), 44–78; Donald R. Wright, *African Americans in the Colonial Era: From African Origins Through the American Revolution* (Arlington Heights, Ill., 1990); A. Leon Higginbotham, Jr., *In the Matter of Color: Race and the American Legal Process, the Colonial Period* (New York, 1978); and William M. Wiecek, "The Statutory Law of Slavery and Race in the Thirteen Mainland Colonies of British America," *William and Mary Quarterly*, XXXIV (1977), 258–80. Almon Wheeler Lauber, *Indian Slavery in Colonial Times within the Present Limits of the United States* (New York, 1913), although dated, remains the standard book on the white enslavement of Native Americans.

Much of the historical research on slavery in colonial America has focused on the Chesapeake colonies. For the early debate over the shift from indentured servitude to slavery and the relationship between slavery and race prejudice, see Oscar Handlin and Mary F. Handlin, "Origins of the Southern Labor System," *William and Mary Quarterly*, VII (1950), 199–222, who argue that slavery led to racism; Carl N. Degler, "Slavery and the Genesis of American Race Prejudice," *Comparative Studies in Society and History*, II (October 1959), 49–66, who reverses the relationship; and Winthrop D. Jordan, *White Over Black: American Attitudes Toward the Negro, 1550–1812* (Baltimore, 1968), who emphasizes the primacy of white racism in shaping colonial social relations. For a recent overview of this question, see Alden T. Vaughan, "The Origins Debate: Slavery and Racism in Seventeenth-Century Virginia," *Virginia Magazine of History and Biography*, XCVII (July 1989), 311–54.

During the 1970s and 1980s, scholars refined their arguments and refocused the debate. Important works on the consolidation of slavery in the upper South include Wesley Frank Craven, *White, Red, and Black: The Seventeenth-Century Virginian* (Charlottesville, Va., 1971); T. H. Breen, "A Changing Labor Force and Race Relations in Virginia, 1660–1710," *Journal of Social History*, VII (Fall 1973), 3–25; Edmund S. Morgan, *American Slavery, American Freedom: The Ordeal of Colonial Virginia* (New York, 1975); Russell R. Menard, "The Maryland Slave Population, 1658 to 1730: A Demographic Profile of Blacks in Four Counties," *William and Mary Quarterly*, XXXII (January 1975), 29–54; Menard, "From Servants to Slaves: The Transformation of the Chesapeake Labor System," *Southern Studies*, XVI (Winter 1977), 355–90; T. H. Breen and Stephen Innes, *"Myne Owne Ground": Race and Freedom on Virginia's Eastern Shore, 1640–1676* (New York, 1980); Darrett B. Rutman and Anita H. Rutman, *A Place in Time: Middlesex County, Virginia, 1650–1750* (New York, 1984); and Gloria L. Main, *Tobacco Colony: Life in Early Maryland, 1650–1720* (Princeton, N.J., 1982).

On the eighteenth-century Chesapeake, see Thad W. Tate, *The Negro in Eighteenth-Century Williamsburg* (Charlottesville, Va., 1966); Gerald W. Mullin, *Flight and Rebellion: Slave Resistance in Eighteenth-Century Virginia* (New York, 1972); Carole Shammas, "Black Women's Work and the Evolution of Plantation Society in Virginia," *Labor History*, XXVI (Winter 1985), 5–28; Allan Kulikoff, *Tobacco and Slaves: The Development of Southern Cultures in the Chesapeake, 1680–1800* (Chapel Hill, N.C., 1986); Jean Butenhoff Lee, "The Problem of Slave Community in the Eighteenth-Century Chesapeake," *William and Mary Quarterly*, XLIII (July 1986), 333–61; Joan R. Gundersen, "The Double Bonds of Race and Sex: Black and White Women in a Colonial Virginia Parish," *Journal of Southern History*, LII (August 1986), 351–72; Mechal Sobel, *The World They Made Together: Black and White Values in Eighteenth-Century Virginia* (Princeton, N.J., 1987); and Lorena S. Walsh, "Plantation Management in the Chesapeake, 1620–1820," *Journal of Economic History*, XLIX (June 1989), 393–406.

Although there has been less work on slavery elsewhere in colonial

America than in the upper South, it is receiving increasing attention. For the lower South, see Peter H. Wood, *Black Majority: Negroes in Colonial South Carolina from 1670 through the Stono Rebellion* (New York, 1974); Daniel C. Littlefield, *Rice and Slaves: Ethnicity and the Slave Trade in Colonial South Carolina* (Baton Rouge, La., 1981); Betty Wood, *Slavery in Colonial Georgia, 1730–1775* (Athens, Ga., 1985); Julia Floyd Smith, *Slavery and Rice Culture in Low Country Georgia, 1750–1860* (Knoxville, Tenn., 1985); Gwendolyn Midlo Hall, *Africans in Colonial Louisiana: The Development of Afro-Creole Culture in the Eighteenth Century* (Baton Rouge, La., 1992); and Daniel H. Usner, *Indians, Settlers, & Slaves in a Frontier Exchange Economy: The Lower Mississippi Valley Before 1783* (Chapel Hill, N.C., 1992). On slavery in the North, see Edgar J. McManus, *Black Bondage in the North* (Syracuse, N.Y., 1973); McManus, *A History of Negro Slavery in New York* (Syracuse, N.Y., 1966); Lorenzo Johnston Greene, *The Negro in Colonial New England* (New York, 1968; orig. pub. 1942); Robert P. Twombly and Robert H. Moore, "Black Puritan: The Negro in Seventeenth-Century Massachusetts," *William and Mary Quarterly*, XXIV (April 1967), 224–42; Darold D. Wax, "Negro Imports into Pennsylvania, 1720–1766," *Pennsylvania History*, XXXII (July 1965), 254–87; and Alan Tully, "Patterns of Slaveholding in Colonial Pennsylvania: Chester and Lancaster Counties, 1729–1758," *Journal of Social History*, VI, no. 3 (1973), 284–306.

Many of the above-mentioned works deal, at least in passing, with the question of the cultural adaptation of blacks in America and the transformation of Africans into African-Americans. Few recent historians subscribe to the views of either Melville J. Herskovits, who saw African "survivals" virtually everywhere, or E. Franklin Frazier, who insisted that blacks were more fully "Americanized" than any other Americans; see Melville J. Herskovits, *The Myth of the Negro Past* (Boston, 1958; orig. pub. 1941); and E. Franklin Frazier, *The Negro Family in the United States* (Chicago, 1939). For an influential theoretical essay on this question, see Sidney W. Mintz and Richard Price, *An Anthropological Approach to the Afro-American Past: A Caribbean Perspective* (Philadelphia, 1976). For books that, in diverse ways, stress the persistence of distinctive African traditions, see Sterling Stuckey, *Slave Culture: Nationalist Theory and the Foundations of Black America* (New York, 1987); Margaret Washington Creel, *"A Peculiar People": Slave Religion and Community-Culture among the Gullahs* (New York, 1988); and William D. Piersen, *Black Yankees: The*

Development of an Afro-American Subculture in Eighteenth-Century New England (Amherst, Mass., 1988). See also John K. Thornton, "African Dimensions of the Stono Rebellion," *American Historical Review*, XCVI (October 1991), 1101–13.

On the four examples of transition to African-American culture discussed in chapter 2, see (in addition to works already cited) the following: Herbert S. Klein and Stanley L. Engerman, "Fertility Differentials between Slaves in the United States and the British West Indies: A Note on Lactation Practices and Their Possible Implications," *William and Mary Quarterly*, XXXV (April 1978), 357–74; Daniel E. Meaders, "South Carolina Fugitives as Viewed through Local Colonial Newspapers with Emphasis on Runaway Notices, 1732–1801," *Journal of Negro History*, LX (April 1975), 284–319; Marvin L. Michael Kay and Lorin Lee Cary, "Slave Runaways in Colonial North Carolina, 1748–1775," *North Carolina Historical Review*, LXIII (January 1986), 1–39; Philip D. Morgan, "Colonial South Carolina Runaways: Their Significance for Slave Culture," in Gad Heuman, ed., *Out of the House of Bondage: Runaways, Resistance and Marronage in Africa and the New World* (London, 1986), 57–78; Lathan Algerna Windley, "A Profile of Runaway Slaves in Virginia and South Carolina from 1730 through 1787" (Ph.D. diss.: University of Iowa, 1974); John C. Inscoe, "Carolina Slave Names: An Index to Acculturation," *Journal of Southern History*, XLIX (November 1983), 527–53; Cheryll Ann Cody, "There Was No 'Absalom' on the Ball Plantations: Slave-Naming Practices in the South Carolina Low Country, 1720–1865," *American Historical Review*, XCII (June 1987), 563–96; and Gary A. Donaldson, "A Window on Slave Culture: Dances at Congo Square in New Orleans, 1800–1862," *Journal of Negro History*, LXIX (Spring 1984), 63–72.

Slavery during the Revolutionary era, long virtually ignored, is receiving increased attention from historians. Benjamin Quarles, *The Negro in the American Revolution* (Chapel Hill, N.C., 1961) is now superseded by Sylvia R. Frey, *Water from the Rock: Black Resistance in a Revolutionary Age* (Princeton, N.J., 1991). A useful collection of essays is Ira Berlin and Ronald Hoffman, eds., *Slavery and Freedom in the Age of the American Revolution* (Charlottesville, Va., 1983); see especially the pieces in this volume by Allan Kulikoff, "Uprooted Peoples: Black Migrants in the Age of the American Revolution, 1790–1820," 143–71; and Philip D. Morgan, "Black Society in the Lowcountry, 1760–1810," 83–141. Other works that stress the ways in which the Revolution affected the lives of slaves include Lorena S. Walsh, "Rural African Americans in the Constitutional Era in Maryland, 1776–1810," *Maryland Historical Magazine*, LXXXIV (Winter 1989), 327–41; Sarah S. Hughes, "Slaves for Hire: The Allocation of Black Labor in Elizabeth City County, Virginia, 1782 to 1810," *William and Mary Quarterly*, XXXV (April 1978), 260–86; Alfred N. Hunt, *Haiti's Influence on Antebellum America: Slumbering Volcano in the Caribbean* (Baton Rouge, La., 1988); and Douglas R. Egerton, "Gabriel's Conspiracy and the Election of 1800," *Journal of Southern History*, LVI (May 1990), 191–214. See also James W.St.G. Walker, *The Black Loyalists: The Search for a Promised Land in Nova Scotia and Sierra Leone, 1783–1870* (New York, 1976).

For the contradictory efforts of white Americans to grapple with the slavery question, see, in addition to works already cited, William W. Freehling, "The Founding Fathers and Slavery," *American Historical Review*, LXXVII (February 1972), 81–93; Robert McColley, *Slavery and Jeffersonian Virginia* (Urbana, Ill., 1964); John Chester Miller, *The Wolf by the Ears: Thomas Jefferson and Slavery* (New York, 1977); Jack P. Greene, " 'Slavery or Independence': Some Reflections on the Relationship among Liberty, Black Bondage, and Equality in Revolutionary South Carolina," *South Carolina Historical Magazine*, LXXX (July 1979), 193–214; Donald L. Robinson, *Slavery in the Structure of American Politics, 1765–1820* (New York, 1971); Duncan J. MacLeod, *Slavery, Race, and the American Revolution* (Cambridge, England, 1975); Larry Tise, *Proslavery: A History of the Defense of Slavery in America, 1701–1840* (Athens, Ga., 1988); and Rachel N. Klein, *Unification of a Slave State: The Rise of the Planter Class in the South Carolina Backcountry, 1760–1808* (Chapel Hill, N.C., 1990). F. Nwabueze Okoye, "Chattel Slavery as the Nightmare of the American Revolutionaries," *William and Mary Quarterly*, XXXVII (January 1980), 3–28, criticizes "establishment" historians for ignoring the centrality of slavery to Revolutionary-era thought.

Religious developments affected the way both white and black Americans related to slavery in the Revolutionary era. See Lester B. Scherer, *Slavery and the Churches in Early America, 1619–1819* (Grand Rapids, Mich., 1975); Jon Butler, *Awash in a Sea of Faith: Christianizing the American People* (Cambridge, Mass., 1990); Jean R. Soderlund, *Quakers and Slavery: A Divided Spirit* (Princeton, N.J., 1985); and John B. Boles, *The Great Revival, 1787–1805: The Origins of the Southern Evangelical Mind* (Lexington, Ky., 1972).

On the ending of slavery in the North, see Arthur Zilversmit, *The First Emancipation: The Abolition of Slavery in the North* (Chicago, 1967); Gary B. Nash and Jean R. Soderlund, *Freedom by Degrees: Emancipation and Its Aftermath in Pennsylvania* (New York, 1990); Shane White, *Somewhat More Independent: The End of Slavery in New York City, 1770–1810* (Athens, Ga., 1991); and, for a comparative perspective, Robin Blackburn, *The Overthrow of Colonial Slavery, 1776–1848* (London, 1988). On the growth of black community in the North, see Carol V. R. George, *Segregated Sabbaths: Richard Allen and the Emergence of Independent Black Churches, 1760–1840* (New York, 1973); and Gary B. Nash, *Forging Freedom: The Formation of Philadelphia's Black Community, 1720–1840* (Cambridge, Mass., 1988). The standard general study of free blacks in the North remains Leon F. Litwack, *North of Slavery: The Negro in the Free States, 1790–1860* (Chicago, 1961).

The best survey of free blacks in the South is Ira Berlin, *Slaves Without Masters: The Free Negro in the Antebellum South* (New York, 1974); see also Leonard P. Curry, *The Free Black in Urban America, 1800–1850: The Shadow of a Dream* (Chicago, 1981). State studies include John Hope Franklin, *The Free Negro in North Carolina, 1790–1860* (Chapel Hill, N.C., 1943); Herbert E. Sterkx, *The Free Negro in Ante-Bellum Louisiana* (Rutherford, N.J., 1972); and Marina Wikramanayake, *A World in Shadow: The Free Black in Antebellum South Carolina* (Columbia, S.C., 1973). For studies of elite free blacks, see Loren Schweninger, *Black Property Owners in the South, 1790–1915* (Urbana, Ill., 1990); Michael P. Johnson and James L. Roark, *Black Masters: A Free Family of Color in the Old South* (New York, 1984); Larry Koger, *Black Slaveowners: Free Black Slave Masters in South Carolina, 1790–1860* (Jefferson, N.C., 1985); and Gary B. Mills, *The Forgotten People: Cane River's Creoles of Color* (Baton Rouge, La., 1977). For biographies of two highly unusual slaves who followed very different routes to freedom, see Edwin Adams Davis and William Ransom Hogan, *The Barber of Natchez* (Baton Rouge, La., 1973); and Terry Alford, *Prince Among Slaves* (New York, 1977).

ANTEBELLUM SLAVERY (CHAPTERS 4–6)

ANTEBELLUM SLAVERY has attracted an enormous amount of historical attention in recent years. Spurred by the controversy over

Stanley M. Elkins's "Sambo thesis," much of this attention has focused on the lives of the slaves; for a collection of early responses to Elkins, see Ann J. Lane, ed., *The Debate Over Slavery: Stanley Elkins and his Critics* (Urbana, Ill., 1971). Scholars have also delved into a host of other subjects, however, from slave treatment and plantation organization to the slave economy and the distinctiveness of Southern society.

A number of major books on slave life, culture, and community appeared during the 1970s. The most all-encompassing and important of these books is Eugene D. Genovese's monumental *Roll, Jordan, Roll: The World the Slaves Made* (New York, 1974), a sophisticated Marxist work that stresses the centrality of religion to the antebellum slave experience and examines slave life within the confining context of slave-owner paternalism. Widely recognized as the most influential recent historian of slavery, Genovese has also been the object of considerable criticism by those unhappy with his emphasis on class relationships and slave-owner paternalism; for a critical evaluation, see Clarence E. Walker, "Massa's New Clothes: A Critique of Eugene D. Genovese on Southern Society, Master–Slave Relations, and Slave Behavior," in Walker, *Deromanticizing Black History: Critical Essays and Reappraisals* (Knoxville, Tenn., 1991), 56–72.

For works relying heavily on slave autobiographies and/or interviews and stressing the strength of communal life, see John W. Blassingame, *The Slave Community: Plantation Life in the Antebellum South* (New York, 1972 and rev. ed., 1979); Blassingame, "Status and Social Structure in the Slave Community: Evidence from New Sources," in Harry P. Owens, ed., *Perspectives and Irony in American Slavery* (Jackson, Miss., 1976), 137–51; George P. Rawick, *From Sundown to Sunup: The Making of the Black Community* (Westport, Conn., 1972); Leslie Howard Owens, *This Species of Property: Slave Life and Custom in the Old South* (New York, 1976); Thomas L. Webber, *Deep Like the Rivers: Education in the Slave Quarter Community, 1831–1865* (New York, 1978); and Paul D. Escott, *Slavery Remembered: A Record of Twentieth-Century Slave Narratives* (Chapel Hill, N.C., 1979). Charles Joyner, *Down by the Riverside: A South Carolina Slave Community* (Urbana, Ill., 1984) is a good local study of a low-country parish.

Many works have focused on particular features of slave life, the most significant of which include family, religion, folklore, and resistance. Exploration of these subjects made great strides during the 1970s and has continued—in some cases at a more relaxed pace and in others at an accelerated pace—during the 1980s and early 1990s.

The pioneering work on slave families is Herbert G. Gutman, *The Black Family in Slavery and Freedom, 1750–1925* (New York, 1976). This innovative if rambling book spawned considerable additional research. See Richard H. Steckel, "Slave Marriage and the Family," *Journal of Family History*, V (Winter 1980), 406–21; David K. Wiggins, "The Play of Slave Children in the Plantation Communities of the Old South, 1820–1860," *Journal of Sport History*, VII (Summer 1980), 21–39; Charles Wetherell, "Slave Kinship: A Case Study of the South Carolina Good Hope Plantation, 1835–1856," *Journal of Family History*, VI (1981), 294–308; Cheryll Ann Cody, "Naming, Kinship, and Estate Dispersal: Notes on Slave Family Life on a South Carolina Plantation, 1786 to 1833," *William and Mary Quarterly*, XXXIX (January 1982), 192–211; Willie Lee Rose, "Childhood in Bondage," in Rose, *Slavery and Freedom*, ed. William W. Freehling (New York, 1982), 37–48; and especially Ann Patton Malone, *Sweet Chariot: Slave Family and Household Structure in Nineteenth-Century Louisiana* (Chapel Hill, N.C., 1992).

Attention to slave women dates largely from the 1980s. See especially two books with very different approaches: Deborah Gray White, *Ar'n't I a Woman?: Female Slaves in the Plantation South* (New York, 1985); and Elizabeth Fox-Genovese, *Within the Plantation Household: Black and White Women of the Old South* (Chapel Hill, N.C., 1988), which has aroused considerable controversy among historians of women. See also the first chapter of Jacqueline Jones, *Labor of Love, Labor of Sorrow: Black Women, Work, and the Family from Slavery to the Present* (New York, 1985).

The best general work on slave religion is Albert J. Raboteau, *Slave Religion: The "Invisible Institution" in the Antebellum South* (New York, 1978). See also Milton C. Sernett, *Black Religion and American Evangelicalism: White Protestants, Plantation Missions, and the Flowering of Negro Christianity, 1787–1865* (Metuchen, N.J., 1975); Mechal Sobel, *Trabelin' On: The Slave Journey to an Afro-Baptist Faith* (Westport, Conn., 1979); and John B. Boles, ed., *Masters & Slaves in the House of the Lord: Race and Religion in the American South, 1740–1870* (Lexington, Ky., 1988), a collection of essays most of which follow Boles in stressing the shared religion of white and black Southerners.

Lawrence W. Levine, *Black Culture and Black Consciousness: Afro-*

American Folk Thought from Slavery to Freedom (New York, 1977) contains an impressive exploration of slave music and folktales. Other significant works include Leroi Jones, *Blues People: Negro Music in White America* (New York, 1963); Sterling Stuckey, "Through the Prism of Folklore: The Black Ethos in Slavery," *Massachusetts Review*, IX (Summer 1968), 417–37; Eileen Southern, *The Music of Black Americans: A History* (New York, 1971); Dickson D. Bruce, Jr., "The 'John and Old Master' Stories and the World of Slavery: A Study in Folktales and History," *Phylon*, XXXV (December 1974), 418–29; Michael Flusche, "Joel Chandler Harris and the Folklore of Slavery," *Journal of American Studies*, IX (December 1975), 347–63; Gladys-Marie Fry, *Night Riders in Black Folk History* (Knoxville, Tenn., 1975); Dena S. Epstein, *Sinful Tunes and Spirituals: Black Folk Music to the Civil War* (Urbana, Ill., 1977); David R. Roediger, "And Die in Dixie: Funerals, Death & Heaven in the Slave Community, 1700–1865," *Massachusetts Review*, XXII (Spring 1981), 163–83; and Elliott J. Gorn, "Black Spirits: The Ghostlore of Afro-American Slaves," *American Quarterly*, XXXVI (Fall 1984), 549–65. On slave literacy, see Janet Duitsman Cornelius, *"When I Can Read My Title Clear": Literacy, Slavery, and Religion in the Antebellum South* (Columbia, S.C., 1991).

Only recently have scholars begun studying what material culture can reveal about slave life; see especially John Vlach, *The Afro-American Tradition in Decorative Arts* (Cleveland, 1978); William M. Kelso, *Kingsmill Plantation, 1619–1800: An Archaeology of Country Life in Colonial Virginia* (Orlando, Fla., 1984); John S. Otto, *Cannon's Point Plantation, 1794–1860: Living Conditions and Status Patterns in the Old South* (Orlando, Fla., 1984); and Theresa A. Singleton, "The Archaeology of Slave Life," in Edward D. C. Campbell, Jr., and Kym S. Rice, eds., *Before Freedom Came: African-American Life in the Antebellum South* (Richmond, Va., 1991), 155–75.

We still lack a good overall study of slave resistance. Herbert Aptheker's pioneering volume, *American Negro Slave Revolts* (New York, 1943), contains useful information but exaggerates the extent of slave rebellion. For articles that grapple with the general question of slave rebelliousness, see Raymond A. Bauer and Alice H. Bauer, "Day to Day Resistance to Slavery," *Journal of Negro History*, XXVII (October 1942), 388–419; Marion D. de B. Kilson, "Towards Freedom: An Analysis of Slave Revolts in the United States," *Phylon*, XXV, no. 2 (1964), 175–87; George M. Fredrickson and Christopher

Lasch, "Resistance to Slavery," *Civil War History*, XIII (December 1967), 315–29; Eugene D. Genovese, "Rebelliousness and Docility in the Negro Slave: A Critique of the Elkins Thesis," ibid., 293– 314; and Kenneth M. Stampp, "Rebels and Sambos: The Search for the Negro's Personality in Slavery," *Journal of Southern History*, XXXVII (August 1971), 367–92. For an interesting story of a slave who murdered her abusive master—a crime for which she was tried and eventually hanged—see Melton A. McLaurin, *Celia: A Slave* (Athens, Ga., 1991). Slave flight deserves more attention than it has received; see (in addition to sources already cited) Larry Gara, *The Liberty Line: The Legend of the Underground Railroad* (Lexington, Ky., 1961); Stanley W. Campbell, *The Slave Catchers: Enforcement of the Fugitive Slave Law, 1850–1860* (Chapel Hill, N.C., 1968); and Michael P. Johnson, "Runaway Slaves and the Slave Communities in South Carolina, 1799 to 1830," *William and Mary Quarterly*, XXXVIII (July 1981), 418–41.

Among studies of particular plots and uprisings, see John Lofton, *Denmark Vesey's Revolt: The Slave Plot that Lit a Fuse to Fort Sumter* (Kent, Ohio, 1983); Stephen B. Oates, *The Fires of Jubilee: Nat Turner's Fierce Rebellion* (New York, 1975); and Winthrop D. Jordan, *Tumult and Silence at Second Creek: An Inquiry into a Civil War Slave Conspiracy* (Baton Rouge, La., 1993). William Styron's fictional account of the Turner uprising, *The Confessions of Nat Turner* (New York, 1967) ignited a fierce controversy; see the hostile responses to Styron's novel in John Henrik Clarke, ed., *William Styron's Nat Turner: Ten Black Writers Respond* (Boston, 1968). At times, panicked whites saw conspiracies and incipient insurrections where none existed; see, e.g., Philip D. Morgan and George D. Terry, "Slavery in Microcosm: A Conspiracy Scare in Colonial South Carolina," *Southern Studies*, XXI (Summer 1982), 121–46; and Charles B. Dew, "Black Ironworkers and the Slave Insurrection Panic of 1856," *Journal of Southern History*, XLI (August 1975), 321–38. See also the exchange between Richard C. Wade, "The Vesey Plot: A Reconsideration," *Journal of Southern History*, XXX (May 1964), 143–61, who questions whether a Denmark Vesey conspiracy really existed, and Robert S. Starobin, "Denmark Vesey's Slave Conspiracy of 1822: A Study in Rebellion and Repression," in John H. Bracey et al., eds., *American Slavery: The Question of Resistance* (Belmont, Calif., 1971), 142–57, who insists that it did.

The life and thought of Frederick Douglass—a slave who clearly did challenge white authority and who went on to become the most celebrated black spokesman of the nineteenth century—has generated considerable historical scholarship. See Dickson J. Preston, *Young Frederick Douglass: The Maryland Years* (Baltimore, 1980); Waldo E. Martin, Jr., *The Mind of Frederick Douglass* (Chapel Hill, N.C., 1984); David W. Blight, *Frederick Douglass's Civil War: Keeping Faith in Jubilee* (Baton Rouge, La., 1989); and William S. McFeely, *Frederick Douglass* (New York, 1991). For an earlier biography, see Philip S. Foner, *Frederick Douglass: A Biography* (New York, 1964).

Recently some scholars have issued cautionary statements, warning against exaggerating the strength, cohesiveness, and felicity of the slave community and the constant rebelliousness of the slave population. For examples of such statements, reflecting widely diverse perspectives, see Stanley M. Elkins, "The Two Arguments on Slavery," in the 3rd ed. to his *Slavery: A Problem in American Institutional and Intellectual Life* (Chicago, 1976), 267–302; Peter Kolchin, "Reevaluating the Antebellum Slave Community: A Comparative Perspective," *Journal of American History*, LXX (December 1983), 579–601; Laurence Shore, "The Poverty of Tragedy in Historical Writing on Southern Slavery," *South Atlantic Quarterly*, LXXXV (Spring 1986), 147–64; and Bertram Wyatt-Brown, "The Mask of Obedience: Male Slave Psychology in the Old South," *American Historical Review*, XCIII (1988), 1228–52.

The way slave owners organized their holdings and treated their slaves, although no longer the central preoccupation of historians of slavery, continues to receive scholarly attention. The best brief introduction to this topic can be found in chapters 5 and 6 of Drew Gilpin Faust, *James Henry Hammond and the Old South: A Design for Mastery* (Baton Rouge, La., 1982), a book that also provides important insights into the mentality of a wealthy South Carolina planter-politician.

On the growing paternalism of Southern slaveholders, see Willie Lee Rose's sensitive and sensible essay, "The Domestication of Domestic Slavery," in her *Slavery and Freedom*, ed. William W. Freehling (New York, 1982), 18–36. One element of this paternalism was a "mission to the slaves"; see, in addition to works already cited, Donald G. Mathews, "Charles Colcock Jones and the Southern Evangelical Crusade to Form a Biracial Society," *Journal of Southern History*, XLI (August 1975), 299–320; and Erskine Clarke, *Wrestlin' Jacob: A Portrait of Religion in the Old South* (Atlanta,

1979). See also William K. Scarborough, "Slavery—The White Man's Burden," in Harry P. Owens, ed., *Perspectives and Irony in American Slavery* (Jackson, Miss., 1976), 103–35, which unlike most other recent works argues that paternalism created a mild form of slavery.

A number of studies deal with the slaves' health and medical care; see Todd L. Savitt, *Medicine and Slavery: The Diseases and Health Care of Blacks in Antebellum Virginia* (Urbana, Ill., 1978); Kenneth F. Kiple and Virginia Himmelsteib King, *Another Dimension to the Black Diaspora: Diet, Disease, and Racism* (Cambridge, England, 1981); Robert A. Margo and Richard H. Steckel, "The Heights of American Slaves: New Evidence on Slave Nutrition and Health," *Social Science History*, VI (Fall 1982), 516–38; John Campbell, "Work, Pregnancy, and Infant Mortality among Southern Slaves," *Journal of Interdisciplinary History*, XIV (Spring 1984), 793–812; and Richard H. Steckel, "A Peculiar Population: The Nutrition, Health, and Mortality of American Slaves from Childhood to Maturity," *Journal of Economic History*, XLVI (September 1986), 721–41.

On the supervision of plantation labor, see William K. Scarborough, *The Overseer: Plantation Management in the Old South* (Baton Rouge, La., 1966); and William L. Van Deburg, *The Slave Drivers: Black Agricultural Labor in the Antebellum South* (Westport, Conn., 1979). For the low country, see James Herbert Stone, "Black Leadership in the Old South: The Slave Drivers of the Rice Kingdom" (Ph.D. diss.: Florida State University, 1976); James M. Clifton, "The Rice Driver: His Role in Slave Management," *South Carolina Historical Magazine*, LXXXII (October 1981), 331–53; and Clifton, "Jehossee Island: The Antebellum South's Largest Rice Plantation," *Agricultural History*, LIX (January 1985), 56–65. In "Work, Culture, and the Slave Community: Slave Occupations in the Cotton Belt in 1860," *Labor History*, XXVII (Summer 1986), 325–55, Michael P. Johnson cautions against overemphasizing the number of elite slaves and stresses the centrality of field labor to the slave experience; see also Bayly E. Marks, "Skilled Blacks in Antebellum St. Mary's County, Maryland," *Journal of Southern History*, LIII (November 1987), 537–64.

The "internal economy" in which slaves bought, sold, and bartered their "own" goods has recently attracted attention from scholars. See especially Philip D. Morgan, "The Ownership of Property by Slaves in the Mid-Nineteenth Century Low Country," *Journal of Southern History*, XLIX (August 1983), 399–420; Lawrence T. McDonnell, "Money Knows No Master: Market Relations and the American Slave Community," in Winfred B. Moore, Jr., et al., eds., *Developing Dixie: Modernization in a Traditional Society* (Westport, Conn., 1988), 31–44; and essays in Ira Berlin and Philip D. Morgan, eds., *The Slaves' Economy: Independent Production by Slaves in the Americas*, a special issue of *Slavery and Abolition*, XII (May 1991).

For the pervasive impact of the domestic slave trade on antebellum slaves, see Michael Tadman, *Speculators and Slaves: Masters, Traders, and Slaves in the Old South* (Madison, Wis., 1989). See also Donald M. Sweig, "Reassessing the Human Dimension of the Interstate Slave Trade," *Prologue*, XII (Spring 1980), 5–21; and, for a case study of a prominent slave trader, Wendell Holmes Stephenson, *Isaac Franklin: Slave Trader and Planter of the Old South* (Baton Rouge, La., 1938).

Historians have expended considerable effort characterizing the antebellum slave system and debating the impact of that system on the South. The most influential voice on behalf of the argument that slavery set the Old South off from the rest of the country is that of Eugene D. Genovese; see—in addition to his previously cited works—*The Political Economy of Slavery: Studies in the Economy & Society of the Slave South* (New York, 1965); and *The Slaveholders' Dilemma: Freedom and Progress in Southern Conservative Thought, 1820–1860* (Columbia, S.C., 1992). The opposing view, that antebellum slavery was simply a Southern variant of American capitalism, is boldly argued by James Oakes in *The Ruling Race: A History of American Slaveholders* (New York, 1982), but Oakes retreats from this position in his more recent *Slavery and Freedom: An Interpretation of the Old South* (New York, 1990). For a critique of the notion of Southern distinctiveness, see Edward Pessen, "How Different Were the Antebellum North and South?" *American Historical Review*, LXXXV (December 1980), 1119–49.

One focus of this debate has been the economics of slavery. Since the late 1950s, a number of econometricians have sought to refute the view that slavery retarded Southern economic development and to establish instead that the peculiar institution was a highly profitable and efficient form of capitalism; for the earliest version of this argument, see Alfred H. Conrad and John R. Meyer, "The Economics of Slavery in the Ante Bellum South," *Journal of Political Economy*, LXVI (April 1958), 95–130; and Conrad and Meyer, *The*

Economics of Slavery and Other Studies in Econometric History (Chicago, 1964). For the past two decades, however, the econometric assault on what they term the "traditional interpretation" of slavery has been led by Robert William Fogel and Stanley L. Engerman; see their two-volume book, *Time on the Cross: The Economics of American Negro Slavery* and *Time on the Cross: Evidence and Methods—A Supplement* (Boston, 1974), which aroused considerable controversy; and Fogel's latest salvo, *Without Consent or Contract: The Rise and Fall of American Slavery* (New York, 1989), complete with three "companion volumes." Despite their econometric focus, both *Time on the Cross* and *Without Consent or Contract* range far beyond economic matters to present a broad reinterpretation of slavery.

For perspective on these works, and the controversy over them, see Harold D. Woodman, "The Profitability of Slavery: A Historical Perennial," *Journal of Southern History*, XXIX (August 1963), 303–25; Woodman, "Economic History and Economic Theory: The New Economic History in America," *Journal of Interdisciplinary History*, III (Autumn 1972), 323–50; Herbert G. Gutman, *Slavery and the Numbers Game: A Critique of Time on the Cross* (Urbana, Ill., 1975); Paul A. David et al., *Reckoning with Slavery: A Critical Study in the Quantitative History of American Negro Slavery* (New York, 1976); Peter Kolchin, "Toward a Reinterpretation of Slavery," *Journal of Social History*, IX (Fall 1975), 99–113; and Kolchin, "More *Time on the Cross*? An Evaluation of Robert William Fogel's *Without Consent or Contract*," *Journal of Southern History*, LVIII (August 1992), 491–502.

In *The Political Economy of the Cotton South: Households, Markets and Wealth in the Nineteenth Century* (New York, 1978), Gavin Wright presents a portrait of the slave economy very different from Fogel and Engerman's. For varying views on slavery's compatibility with industrialization and urbanization, see Robert S. Starobin, *Industrial Slavery in the Old South* (New York, 1970); Charles B. Dew, "Disciplining Slave Ironworkers in the Antebellum South: Coercion, Conciliation, and Accommodation," *American Historical Review*, LXXIX (April 1974), 393–418; Ronald L. Lewis, *Coal, Iron, and Slaves: Industrial Slavery in Maryland and Virginia, 1715–1865* (Westport, Conn., 1979); Fred Bateman and Thomas Weiss, *A Deplorable Scarcity: The Failure of Industrialization in the Slave Economy* (Chapel Hill, N.C., 1981); Laurence Shore, *Southern Capitalists: The Ideological Leadership of an Elite, 1832–1885* (Chapel Hill, N.C., 1986);

Frederick F. Siegel, *The Roots of Southern Distinctiveness: Tobacco and Society in Danville, Virginia, 1780–1865* (Chapel Hill, N.C., 1987); Richard C. Wade, *Slavery in the Cities: The South, 1820–1860* (New York, 1964); Claudia Dale Goldin, *Urban Slavery in the American South, 1820–1860* (Chicago, 1976); David R. Goldfield, *Urban Growth in the Age of Sectionalism: Virginia, 1847–1861* (Baton Rouge, La., 1977); and Barbara Jeanne Fields, *Slavery and Freedom on the Middle Ground: Maryland During the Nineteenth Century* (New Haven, Conn., 1985).

Historians have also differed sharply over slavery's impact on white Southern social structure, ideology, family behavior, women, law, and politics. For the once prevalent view that the antebellum South was an "economic democracy" dominated by yeoman farmers, see Frank L. Owsley and Harriet C. Owsley, "The Economic Basis of Society in the Late Ante-Bellum South," *Journal of Southern History*, VI (February 1940), 20–45. Most (but not all) more recent analysts have reached very different conclusions; see Fabian Linden, "Economic Democracy in the Slave South: An Appraisal of Some Recent Views," *Journal of Negro History*, XXXI (April 1946), 140–89; Gavin Wright, " 'Economic Democracy' and the Concentration of Agricultural Wealth in the Cotton South, 1850–1860," *Agricultural History*, XLIV (January 1970), 63–93; Randolph B. Campbell and Richard G. Lowe, *Wealth and Power in Antebellum Texas* (College Station, Tex., 1977); J. William Harris, *Plain Folk and Gentry in a Slave Society: White Liberty and Black Slavery in Augusta's Hinterlands* (Middletown, Conn., 1985); Bruce Collins, *White Society in the Antebellum South* (New York, 1985); and Donald L. Winters, " 'Plain Folk' of the Old South Reexamined: Economic Democracy in Tennessee," *Journal of Southern History*, LIII (November 1987), 565–86.

For some differing interpretations of slavery's impact on the southern white "mind," see William S. Jenkins, *Pro-Slavery Thought in the Old South* (Chapel Hill, N.C., 1935); John Hope Franklin, *The Militant South: 1800–1860* (Cambridge, Mass., 1956); William R. Taylor, *Cavalier and Yankee: The Old South and American National Character* (New York, 1957); William Stanton, *The Leopard's Spots: Scientific Attitudes Toward Race in America, 1815–59* (Chicago, 1960); Clement Eaton, *The Freedom of Thought Struggle in the Old South* (New York, 1964); George M. Fredrickson, *The Black Image in the White Mind: The Debate on Afro-American Character and Destiny, 1817–1914*

(New York, 1971); Ronald T. Takaki, *A Pro-Slavery Crusade: The Agitation to Reopen the African Slave Trade* (New York, 1971); Robert E. Shalhope, "Race, Class, Slavery and the Antebellum Southern Mind," *Journal of Southern History,* XXXVII (November 1971), 557–74; Jon L. Wakelyn, *The Politics of a Literary Man: William Gilmore Simms* (Westport, Conn., 1973); Drew Gilpin Faust, *A Sacred Circle: The Dilemma of the Intellectual in the Old South, 1840–1860* (Baltimore, 1977); Thomas Virgil Peterson, *Ham and Japheth: The Mythic World of Whites in the Antebellum South* (Metuchen, N.J., 1978); Robert J. Brugger, *Beverly Tucker: Heart Over Head in the Old South* (Baltimore, 1978); John McCardell, *The Idea of a Southern Nation: Southern Nationalists and Southern Nationalism, 1830–1860* (New York, 1979); Dickson D. Bruce, Jr., *Violence and Culture in the Antebellum South* (Austin, Tex., 1979); Bertram Wyatt-Brown, *Southern Honor: Ethics and Behavior in the Old South* (New York, 1982); David Bailey, *Shadow on the Church: Southwestern Evangelical Religion and the Issue of Slavery, 1783–1860* (Ithaca, N.Y., 1985); and David F. Allmendinger, *Ruffin: Family and Reform in the Old South* (New York, 1990).

Important work on white women and families includes Anne Firor Scott, *The Southern Lady: From Pedestal to Politics, 1830–1930* (Chicago, 1970); Jane Turner Censer, *North Carolina Planters and their Children, 1800–1860* (Baton Rouge, La., 1984); Steven M. Stowe, *Intimacy and Power in the Old South: Rituals in the Lives of the Planters* (Baltimore, 1987); Catherine Clinton, *The Plantation Mistress: Woman's World in the Old South* (New York, 1982); George C. Rable, *Civil Wars: Women in the Crisis of Southern Nationalism* (Urbana, Ill., 1989); Joan E. Cashin, *A Family Venture: Men and Women on the Southern Frontier* (New York, 1991); and Sally G. McMillan, *Southern Women: Black and White in the Old South* (Arlington Heights, Ill., 1992).

On law, trials, and slavery, see Daniel J. Flanigan, "Criminal Procedure in Slave Trials in the Antebellum South," *Journal of Southern History,* XL (November 1974), 537–64; Michael Stephen Hindus, *Prison and Plantation: Crime, Justice, and Authority in Massachusetts and South Carolina, 1767–1878* (Chapel Hill, N.C., 1980); Mark V. Tushnet, *The American Law of Slavery, 1810–1860: Considerations of Humanity and Interest* (Princeton, N.J., 1981); Edward L. Ayers, *Vengeance and Justice: Crime and Punishment in the 19th-Century American South* (New York, 1984); Philip J. Schwarz, *Twice Condemned: Slaves and the Criminal Laws of Virginia, 1705–1865* (Baton Rouge, La., 1988); Alan Watson, *Slave Law in the Americas* (Athens,

Ga., 1989); Kermit L. Hall, ed., *The Law of American Slavery: Major Interpretations* (New York, 1987); and Donald G. Nieman, *Promises to Keep: African-Americans and the Constitutional Order, 1776–1989* (New York, 1990).

Among the large number of works dealing with the influence of slavery on Southern politics and government, some of the most useful include William W. Freehling, *Prelude to Civil War: The Nullification Controversy in South Carolina, 1816–1836* (New York, 1965); Ralph A. Wooster, *The People in Power: Courthouse and Statehouse in the Lower South* (Knoxville, Tenn., 1969); Wooster, *Planters and Plain Folks: Courthouse and Statehouse in the Upper South, 1850–1860* (Knoxville, Tenn., 1975); William J. Cooper, Jr., *The South and the Politics of Slavery, 1828–1856* (Baton Rouge, La., 1978); J. Mills Thornton III, *Politics and Power in a Slave Society: Alabama, 1800–1860* (Baton Rouge, La., 1978); Alison Goodyear Freehling, *Drift Toward Dissolution: The Virginia Slavery Debate of 1831–1832* (Baton Rouge, La., 1982); Kenneth S. Greenberg, *Masters and Statesmen: The Political Culture of American Slavery* (Baltimore, 1985); Lacy K. Ford, Jr., *Origins of Southern Radicalism: The South Carolina Upcountry, 1800–1860* (New York, 1988); and William W. Freehling, *The Road to Disunion: Secessionists at Bay, 1776–1854* (New York, 1990).

A number of local, state, and regional studies deserve mention. These include Theodore Rosengarten, *Tombee: Portrait of a Cotton Planter* (New York, 1986); Malcolm Bell, Jr., *Major Butler's Legacy: Five Generations of a Slaveholding Family* (Athens, Ga., 1987); Elinor Miller and Eugene D. Genovese, eds., *Plantation, Town, and Country: Essays on the Local History of American Slave Society* (Urbana, Ill., 1974); Orville Vernon Burton and Robert C. McMath, Jr., eds., *Class, Conflict, and Consensus: Antebellum Southern Community Studies* (Westport, Conn., 1982); Orville Vernon Burton, *In My Father's House Are Many Mansions: Family and Community in Edgefield, South Carolina* (Chapel Hill, N.C., 1985); Peter A. Coclanis, *The Shadow of a Dream: Economic Life and Death in the South Carolina Low Country, 1670–1920* (New York, 1989); John C. Inscoe, *Mountain Masters, Slavery, and the Sectional Crisis in Western North Carolina* (Knoxville, Tenn., 1989); Julia Floyd Smith, *Slavery and Plantation Growth in Antebellum Florida, 1821–1860* (Gainesville, Fla., 1973); Randolph B. Campbell, *An Empire for Slavery: The Peculiar Institution in Texas, 1821–1865* (Baton Rouge, La., 1989); and John Hebron Moore, *The*

Emergence of the Cotton Kingdom in the Old Southwest: Mississippi, 1770–1860 (Baton Rouge, La., 1989).

For the complex relationship between Indians and blacks, see Kenneth Wiggins Porter, *The Negro on the American Frontier* (New York, 1971); R. Halliburton, Jr., *Red over Black: Black Slavery among the Cherokee* (Westport, Conn., 1977); Daniel F. Littlefield, Jr., *Africans and Seminoles: From Removal to Emancipation* (Westport, Conn., 1977); Littlefield, *Africans and Creeks: From the Colonial Period to the Civil War* (Westport, Conn., 1979); and Theda Perdue, *Slavery and the Evolution of Cherokee Society, 1540–1866* (Knoxville, Tenn., 1979).

THE END OF SLAVERY (CHAPTER 7)

THE BEST and most recent overview of slavery's aftermath is Eric Foner, *Reconstruction: America's Unfinished Revolution, 1863–1877* (New York, 1988); an abridged version of this volume is available under the title *A Short History of Reconstruction, 1863–1877* (New York, 1990). Michael Perman, *Emancipation and Reconstruction, 1862–1879* (Arlington Heights, Ill., 1987); and Howard N. Rabinowitz, *The First New South, 1865–1920* (Arlington Heights, Ill., 1992) provide good brief syntheses of recent scholarship. For two very different earlier surveys, see William A. Dunning, *Reconstruction, Political and Economic: 1865–1877* (New York, 1907), a conservative work that inspired a host of "Dunning-school" studies typically far more crudely racist than their prototype; and W.E.B. Du Bois, *Black Reconstruction in America* (New York, 1935), a passionate work of radical scholarship that until recently was ignored by most historians. Two books that sensitively explore the wartime and postwar responses of black and white Southerners to radically changed conditions are Leon F. Litwack, *Been in the Storm So Long: The Aftermath of Slavery* (New York, 1979); and James L. Roark, *Masters Without Slaves: Southern Planters in the Civil War and Reconstruction* (New York, 1977). See also Robert Cruden, *The Negro in Reconstruction* (Englewood Cliffs, N.J., 1969).

For the evolution of federal wartime policy on slavery, emancipation, and the status of black Americans, see John Hope Franklin, *The Emancipation Proclamation* (New York, 1963); Herman Belz, *A*

*New Birth of Freedom: The Republican Party and Freedmen's Rights,
1861–1866* (Westport, Conn., 1976); LaWanda Cox, *Lincoln and
Black Freedom: A Study in Presidential Leadership* (Columbia, S.C.,
1981); Willie Lee Rose, *Rehearsal for Reconstruction: The Port Royal
Experiment* (New York, 1964); Louis S. Gerteis, *From Contraband to
Freedman: Federal Policy Toward Southern Blacks, 1861–1865* (Westport, Conn., 1973); and William F. Messner, *Freedmen and the Ideology of Free Labor: Louisiana, 1862–1865* (Lafayette, La., 1978).
Among the huge number of works exploring the formation of
congressional Reconstruction policy, the most useful general volumes are W. R. Brock, *An American Crisis: Congress and Reconstruction,
1865–1867* (New York, 1963); David Donald, *The Politics of Reconstruction, 1863–1867* (Baton Rouge, La., 1965); and Michael Les
Benedict, *A Compromise of Principle: Congressional Republicans and
Reconstruction, 1863–1869* (New York, 1974).

The black wartime experience and the disintegration of slavery
are covered in Benjamin Quarles, *The Negro and the Civil War* (Boston,
1953); Dudley Taylor Cornish, *The Sable Arm: Negro Troops in the
Union Army, 1861–1865* (New York, 1956); Joseph T. Glatthaar,
*Forged in Battle: The Civil War Alliance of Black Soldiers and White
Officers* (New York, 1990); James M. McPherson, *The Negro's Civil
War: How American Negroes Felt and Acted During the War for the Union*
(New York, 1965); Bell Irvin Wiley, *Southern Negroes, 1861–1865*
(New Haven, Conn., 1938); C. Peter Ripley, *Slaves and Freedmen
in Civil War Louisiana* (Baton Rouge, La., 1976); Victor B. Howard,
*Black Liberation in Kentucky: Emancipation and Freedom in Kentucky,
1862–1864* (Lexington, Ky., 1983); and Clarence L. Mohr, *On the
Threshold of Freedom: Masters and Slaves in Civil War Georgia* (Athens,
Ga., 1986). Drew Gilpin Faust, " 'Trying to Do a Man's Business':
Slavery, Violence and Gender in the American Civil War," *Gender
& History*, IV (Summer 1992), 197–214, provides an interesting case
study of how slaves took advantage of their male owner's absence
at war. For an outstanding overview of the wartime erosion of slavery, see the editors' introduction, "The Destruction of Slavery,
1861–1865," in Ira Berlin et al., eds., *Freedom: A Documentary History
of Emancipation, 1861–1867.* Series I, Volume I. *The Destruction of
Slavery* (Cambridge, England, 1985), 1–56.

For surveys of Southern politics in the Reconstruction era, see
two books by Michael Perman: *Reunion Without Compromise: The
South and Reconstruction, 1865–1868* (New York, 1973); and *The Road*

to Redemption: Southern Politics, 1869–1879 (Chapel Hill, N.C., 1984). On political struggle and violence, see Dan T. Carter, *When the War Was Over: The Failure of Self-Reconstruction in the South, 1865–1867* (Baton Rouge, La., 1985); Allen Trelease, *White Terror: The Ku Klux Klan Conspiracy and Southern Reconstruction* (New York, 1971); George C. Rable, *But There Was No Peace: The Role of Violence in the Politics of Reconstruction* (Athens, Ga., 1984); and Michael W. Fitzgerald, *The Union League Movement in the Deep South: Politics and Agricultural Change During Reconstruction* (Baton Rouge, La., 1989). The best book on the post-Reconstruction disfranchisement of Southern blacks is J. Morgan Kousser, *The Shaping of Southern Politics: Suffrage Restriction and the Establishment of the One-Party South, 1880–1910* (New Haven, Conn., 1974).

Much of the historical work on blacks in the Reconstruction South has focused on the state and local levels. Noteworthy studies include Vernon L. Wharton, *The Negro in Mississippi, 1865–1890* (Chapel Hill, N.C., 1947); Joel Williamson, *After Slavery: The Negro in South Carolina During Reconstruction, 1861–1877* (Chapel Hill, N.C., 1965); Carol R. Bleser, *The Promised Land: The History of the South Carolina Land Commission, 1869–1890* (Columbia, S.C., 1969); Peter Kolchin, *First Freedom: The Responses of Alabama's Blacks to Emancipation and Reconstruction* (Westport, Conn., 1972); John W. Blassingame, *Black New Orleans, 1860–1880* (Chicago, 1973); Robert F. Engs, *Freedom's First Generation: Black Hampton, Virginia, 1861–1890* (Philadelphia, 1979); Jacqueline Jones, *Soldiers of Light and Love: Northern Teachers and Georgia Blacks, 1865–1873* (Chapel Hill, N.C., 1980); Janet Sharp Hermann, *The Pursuit of a Dream* (New York, 1981), on Davis Bend, Mississippi; Armstead Robinson, "Plans Dat Comed from God: Institution Building and the Emergence of Black Leadership in Reconstruction Memphis," in Orville Vernon Burton and Robert C. McMath, Jr., *Toward a New South?: Studies in Post–Civil War Southern Communities* (Westport, Conn., 1982), 71–102; J. William Harris, "Plantations and Power: Emancipation on the David Barrow Plantations," ibid., 246–64; Peter J. Rachleff, *Black Labor in the South: Richmond, Virginia, 1865–1890* (Philadelphia, 1984); Roberta Sue Alexander, *North Carolina Faces the Freedmen: Race Relations During Presidential Reconstruction, 1865–67* (Durham, N.C., 1985); Paul A. Cimbala, "The Freedmen's Bureau, the Freedmen, and Sherman's Grant in Reconstruction Georgia, 1865–1867," *Journal of Southern History*, LV (November 1989), 597–632; and Barry A.

Crouch, *The Freedmen's Bureau and Black Texans* (Austin, Tex., 1992).

Local and state studies of blacks in Reconstruction politics include David C. Rankin, "The Origins of Black Leadership in New Orleans During Reconstruction," *Journal of Southern History*, XL (August 1974), 417–40; Charles Vincent, *Black Legislators in Louisiana During Reconstruction* (Baton Rouge, La., 1976); Thomas Holt, *Black over White: Negro Political Leadership in South Carolina During Reconstruction* (Urbana, Ill., 1977); Edmund L. Drago, *Black Politicians and Reconstruction in Georgia* (Baton Rouge, La., 1982); William C. Hine, "Black Politicians in Reconstruction Charleston, South Carolina: A Collective Study," *Journal of Southern History*, XLIX (November 1983), 555–84; Russell Duncan, *Freedom's Shore: Tunis Campbell and the Georgia Freedmen* (Athens, Ga., 1986); and the essays in Howard N. Rabinowitz, ed., *Southern Black Leaders of the Reconstruction Era* (Urbana, Ill., 1982).

Other works deal with specific subjects across the whole South (or large portions of it). On the Freedmen's Bureau, black rights, and the struggle for land, see George R. Bentley, *A History of the Freedmen's Bureau* (Philadelphia, 1955); William S. McFeely, *Yankee Stepfather: General O. O. Howard and the Freedmen* (New Haven, Conn., 1968); Christie Farnham Pope, "Southern Homesteads for Negroes," *Agricultural History*, XLIV (April 1970), 201–12; Edward Magdol, *A Right to the Land: Essays on the Freedmen's Community* (Westport, Conn., 1977); Carl R. Osthaus, *Freedmen, Philanthropy, and Fraud: A History of the Freedman's Savings Bank* (Urbana, Ill., 1976); Claude F. Oubre, *Forty Acres and a Mule: The Freedmen's Bureau and Black Landownership* (Baton Rouge, La., 1978); Donald G. Nieman, *To Set the Law in Motion: The Freedmen's Bureau and the Legal Rights of Blacks, 1865–1868* (Millwood, N.Y., 1979); and Michael L. Lanza, *Agrarianism and Reconstruction Politics: The Southern Homestead Act* (Baton Rouge, La., 1990).

Religious and educational developments are covered in Clarence G. Walker, *A Rock in a Weary Land: The African Methodist Episcopal Church During the Civil War and Reconstruction* (Baton Rouge, La., 1982); William E. Montgomery, *Under Their Own Vine and Fig Tree: The African-American Church in the South, 1865–1900* (Baton Rouge, La., 1993); Joe M. Richardson, *Christian Reconstruction: The American Missionary Association and Southern Blacks, 1861–1890* (Athens, Ga., 1986); William P. Vaughan, *Schools for All: The Blacks and Public Education in the South, 1865–1877* (Lexington, Ky., 1974); Ronald

E. Butchart, *Northern Schools, Southern Blacks, and Reconstruction: Freedmen's Education, 1862–1875* (Westport, Conn., 1980); Robert C. Morris, *Reading, 'Riting, and Reconstruction: The Education of Freedmen in the South, 1861–1870* (Chicago, 1981); and James D. Anderson, *The Education of Blacks in the South, 1860–1935* (Chapel Hill, N.C., 1988).

There has been a lively historical debate over postwar Southern race relations in general and the development of Southern segregation in particular. Begin with C. Vann Woodward's pioneering essay, *The Strange Career of Jim Crow* (New York, 1955 and subsequent editions); on this essay's history and influence, see Howard N. Rabinowitz, "More than the Woodward Thesis: Assessing *The Strange Career of Jim Crow*," *Journal of American History*, LXXV (December 1988), 842–56. For an important reformulation of the debate, see Howard N. Rabinowitz, "From Exclusion to Segregation: Southern Race Relations, 1865–1890," *Journal of American History*, LXIII (September 1976), 325–50; and Rabinowitz, *Race Relations in the Urban South, 1865–1890* (New York, 1978). See also, Roger A. Fischer, *The Segregation Struggle in Louisiana, 1862–1877* (Urbana, Ill., 1974); and—for a very different approach—Joel Williamson, *The Crucible of Race: Black–White Relations in the American South Since Emancipation* (New York, 1984), also available in abridged form as *A Rage for Order: Black–White Relations in the American South Since Emancipation* (New York, 1986).

Historians have devoted considerable attention to the character of the new social order that replaced slavery. They have differed sharply over the South's economic system, the amount of freedom that inhered in "free labor," the degree to which planters remained economically and politically dominant, and the extent to which the New South differed from the Old. For two historiographical essays that provide good introductions to this debate, see Harold D. Woodman, "Sequel to Slavery: The New History Views the Postbellum South," *Journal of Southern History*, XLIV (November 1977), 523–54; and Woodman, "Economic Reconstruction and the Rise of the New South, 1865–1900," in John B. Boles and Evelyn Nolen Thomas, eds., *Interpreting Southern History: Historiographical Essays in Honor of Sanford W. Higginbotham* (Baton Rouge, La., 1987), 254–307.

For examples of works that stress the competitive, democratic, and capitalist nature of the Southern economy, see Robert Higgs,

Competition and Coercion: Blacks in the American Economy, 1865–1914 (Cambridge, England, 1977); and Joseph D. Reid, "Sharecropping as an Understandable Market Response: The Post-Bellum South" *Journal of Economic History*, XXXIII (March 1973), 106–30. By contrast, coercion, class conflict, and continued planter hegemony are emphasized in Jonathan M. Wiener, *Social Origins of the New South: Alabama, 1860–1885* (Baton Rouge, La., 1978); Dwight B. Billings, Jr., *Planters and the Making of a New South: Class, Politics, and Development in North Carolina, 1865–1900* (Chapel Hill, N.C., 1979); and Jay R. Mandle, *Not Slave, Not Free: The African American Economic Experience since the Civil War* (Durham, N.C., 1992). Two important but divergent interpretations of the South's postwar political economy, both of which move beyond the "coercion vs. competition" dichotomy, are Roger L. Ransom and Richard Sutch, *One Kind of Freedom: The Economic Consequences of Emancipation* (New York, 1977); and Gavin Wright, *Old South, New South: Revolutions in the Southern Economy Since the Civil War* (New York, 1986).

For diverse interpretations of the conditions of free black agricultural labor, see Daniel A. Novack, *The Wheel of Servitude: Black Forced Labor after Slavery* (Lexington, Ky., 1978); Pete Daniel, "The Metamorphosis of Slavery, 1865–1900," *Journal of American History*, LXVI (June 1979), 88–99; Eric Foner, "Reconstruction and the Crisis of Free Labor," in Foner, *Politics and Ideology in the Age of the Civil War* (New York, 1980), 97–127; Ronald F. Davis, *Good and Faithful Labor: From Slavery to Sharecropping in the Natchez District, 1860–1890* (Westport, Conn., 1982); Michael Wayne, *The Reshaping of Plantation Society: The Natchez District, 1860–1880* (Baton Rouge, La., 1983); Ralph Shlomowitz, " 'Bound' or 'Free'? Black Labor in Cotton and Sugarcane Farming, 1865–1880," *Journal of Southern History*, L (November 1984), 569–96; Gerald D. Jaynes, *Branches Without Roots: Genesis of the Black Working Class in the American South, 1862–1882* (New York, 1986); and William Cohen, *At Freedom's Edge: Black Mobility and the Southern White Quest for Racial Control, 1861–1915* (Baton Rouge, La., 1991).

Other significant works that in varying ways deal with the nature of the South's post-emancipation social order include Kenneth S. Greenberg, "The Civil War and the Redistribution of Land: Adams County, Mississippi, 1860–1870," *Agricultural History*, LII (April 1978), 292–307; Lawrence N. Powell, *New Masters: Northern Planters During the Civil War and Reconstruction* (New Haven, Conn., 1980);

Crandall A. Shifflett, *Patronage and Poverty in the Tobacco South: Louisa County, Virginia, 1860–1900* (Knoxville, Tenn., 1982); Charles L. Flynn, Jr., *White Land, Black Labor: Caste and Class in Late Nineteenth-Century Georgia* (Baton Rouge, La., 1983); Steven Hahn, *The Roots of Southern Populism: Yeoman Farmers and the Transformation of the Georgia Upcountry, 1850–1890* (New York, 1983); Lacy K. Ford, "Rednecks and Merchants: Economic Developments and Social Tensions in the South Carolina Upcountry, 1865–1900," *Journal of American History*, LXXI (September 1984), 294–318; and the essays in Thavolia Glymph and John J. Kushma, eds., *Essays on the Postbellum Southern Economy* (College Station, Tex., 1985).

Index

abolitionism, ix, 3, 85, 187, 215; antebellum, 85–89, 94, 121, 128, 137, 169–99; Civil War, 201–9; Northern, 78–80, 81, 92, 93; postbellum, 215–16, 229–30; in Revolutionary era, 63–70, 76–85, 89

Adams, John, 70

Affleck, Thomas, 102

Africa, emigration to, 84–85, 185

African-American culture, xi, xiii; origins and growth of, 40–62, 147, 150

African churches, 84, 222

African slave trade, *see* slave trade, African

agriculture, 4–7; antebellum, 87, 94–97, 99–106, 171–76, 179, 180, 191; colonial, 5–7, 28–33, 49–54, 57; cotton, 94–96, 100–5, 169–76, 191; and origins of American slavery, 5–14, 23–27; postbellum, 212–21, 224, 227, 231, 233; in Revolutionary era, 68–76; sharecropping, 217–20, 226

Alabama: cotton, 96; Reconstruction, 219, 223, 234; slavery in, 96–98, 128–30, 160, 167, 184

Allen, Richard, 84

American Colonization Society, 185

American Missionary Association, 208

animal folktales, 154

antebellum era, 28, 32, 33, 47, 60, 61, 65, 81–82, 86–199, 241–42; agriculture, 87, 94–106, 171–76, 179, 180, 191; defense of slavery in, 181–99; diversity of conditions in, 99–111; economy, 87, 94–106, 109, 152, 153, 169–79, 182–83, 190, 191, 197; end of slavery, 200–37; free blacks in, 81–90, 99, 116–17, 127–28, 157–58, 165–66, 177–82, 185; historians on, 134–40; legislation, 127–32, 140; master–slave relations, 93–168, 169–99; Northern vs. Southern attitudes in, 169–99; organization of slavery in, 93–132; punishment of slaves, 120–22, 130–31, 142, 159–64, 167–68; religion, 86–87, 107, 112–20, 138, 142–48, 150, 151; slave-holdings, 99–105, 109, 112, 123, 155; slave life in, 113–18, 133–68; slave migrations, 96–98; slave occupations and status, 99,

293